W9-BXU-094

UNIVERSITY OF MAINE
AT AUGUSTA

WITHDRAWN
from
Katz Library

AUGUSTA CAMPUS LIBRARY

QUALITY PRINCIPLES AND PRACTICES IN HIGHER EDUCATION

QUALITY PRINCIPLES AND PRACTICES IN HIGHER EDUCATION

Different Questions for Different Times

by
Jann E. Freed
and
Marie R. Klugman

AMERICAN COUNCIL ON EDUCATION ★
ORYX PRESS ★
Series on Higher Education
1997

The rare Arabian oryx is believed to have inspired the myth of the unicorn. This desert antelope became virtually extinct in the early 1960s. At that time several groups of international conservationists arranged to have 9 animals sent to the Phoenix Zoo to be the nucleus of a captive breeding herd. Today the oryx population is over 1,000, and over 500 have been returned to the Middle East.

© 1997 by American Council on Education and The Oryx Press
Published by The Oryx Press
4041 North Central at Indian School Road
Phoenix, Arizona 85012-3397

All rights reserved. No part of this publication may be reproduced or transmitted in any form or by any means, electronic or mechanical, including photocopying, recording, or by any information storage and retrieval system, without permission in writing from The Oryx Press.

Published simultaneously in Canada
Printed and bound in the United States of America

∞ The paper used in this publication meets the minimum requirements of the American National Standard for Information Sciences—Permanence of Paper for Printed Library Materials, ANSI Z39.48-1984.

Library of Congress Cataloging-in-Publication Data

Freed, Jann E.
    Quality principles and practices in higher education : different questions for different times / by Jann E. Freed and Marie R. Klugman.
        p. cm.
    Includes bibliographical references and index.
    ISBN 1-57356-052-9 (alk. paper)
    1. Education, Higher—United States—Administration. 2. Total quality management—United States. I. Klugman, Marie R.
II. American Council on Education. III. Title.
LB2341.F689 1997
378.1'01'0973—dc21   97-33706
                                                        CIP

Dedicated to my sons, MacLean, Austin, and Marshall,
and particularly to my husband, John Fisher.

Jann E. Freed

Dedicated to my husband, Stuart, and my sons, David and Philip.

Marie R. Klugman

CONTENTS

PREFACE

Learning begins with questions we cannot answer; it ends with questions we can.

(Acknoff, 1993, p. ii)

This book arose out of our desire to discover how institutions that claim to be involved in continuous improvement efforts are actually implementing new principles and practices. We were particularly interested in what was working, what wasn't, and why. Before detailing our methodology, it is worth taking a brief look at the history of the quality movement and how it came to be associated with higher education.

WHAT ARE THE ORIGINS OF CONTINUOUS QUALITY IMPROVEMENT IDEAS?

After World War II, United States business and industry had the largest market, the best technology, the most highly skilled workers, the most wealth, and the best managers of the industrialized countries (Dertouzos, Lester, and Solow, 1989). With all of these advantages, it was easy for American business and industry to succeed without giving much thought to continuous improvement of products and services. At the same time, Japan was intent on improving its economy through manufacturing and trade; Japan's products, however, were inferior to American products. In an effort to improve their status in the world marketplace, Japanese companies worked together to acquire information on foreign companies. They also invited W. Edwards Deming and Joseph M. Juran, two of the pioneers in the continuous improvement movement, to conduct training courses on statistics and management for quality improvement (Juran, 1995). Japanese companies embraced Deming's and Juran's theories, and added their own ideas to continuous quality improvement. The culture that evolved from using quality principles and practices propelled Japan into the position of a world marketplace leader by the late 1970s.

By the 1980s, U.S. companies awoke to find they could not survive unless they changed their ways of conducting business. Products made in the U.S. were falling behind others in quality, especially those made in Japan. The Japanese products were less costly to manufacture, were produced much faster, and were sold at lower prices than U.S. products. The demand for U.S. products fell, and U.S. manufacturers found themselves playing catch-up to foreign manufacturers. To add to these problems, customers' expectations were constantly rising, and customers were demanding ever higher quality products.

To save their companies, several American businesses also turned to quality improvement specialists. The three best experts known, W. Edwards Deming, Joseph M. Juran, and Philip B. Crosby, each contributed significantly to the ideas of continuous improvement. The Deming philosophy is based on an all-embracing concept of quality improvement and an understanding of variation, combined in an environment in which teamwork rather than competition prevails (Deming, 1986; Neave, 1990; Walton, 1986). His belief is that if you improve the quality of your goods and services you will increase productivity, because there is less scrap and less rework. According to Juran's philosophy, employees must be involved in teams, managers must listen to employees and help them rank processes and systems that need to be improved, and managers must provide recognition to the entire team when a project is completed (Juran, 1988; 1989; 1995). The Crosby philosophy is based on the idea that zero defects is the only acceptable performance standard. He argues that companies must do things right the first time and not depend upon inspection to find problems (Crosby, 1979; 1992).

Seeing the resurgence American companies were enjoying with continuous improvement principles, a few pioneers began to advocate their use in higher education. Such a move is not that unusual, as higher education practices tend to reflect those in business and industry; for example, many higher education institutions experimented with long-range planning in the 1970s and with strategic planning in the 1980s, echoing similar trends in the business world.

Despite the precedent set by higher education institutions borrowing from business and industry, the question of why the institutions chose continuous quality improvement ideas remains. The best answer is that these institutions were, and still are, facing the same problems that business and industry had experienced. As competition from foreign products and a desire for better quality products gave American businesses the impetus to become involved in quality improvement, competition for students from other institutions and the resulting desire to enhance the institution provided the impetus for American colleges and universities to investigate quality principles.

At the end of the 1980s and the beginning of the 1990s, very few higher education institutions were implementing quality principles. In fact, most institutions questioned whether continuous quality improvement was appropriate for education. The first three institutions that became actively involved in continuous improvement were Northwest Missouri State University, Fox Valley Technical College, and Oregon State University (Freed, Klugman, and Fife, 1997). These institutions all had presidents with long-term commitments to apply quality improvement ideas. With the success of these early pioneers, more institutions became interested in the application of quality principles in higher education. The early followers were a mix of community colleges, four-year independent colleges and universities, and four-year public institutions. These institutions, although distinctly different from each other, found that continuous quality improvement was appropriate to their situations.

Interest in continuous improvement exploded in 1991 and 1992 (Freed, Klugman, Fife, 1994). At that time administrators no longer asked whether quality principles were appropriate for their institutions, but rather they asked how to make them relevant (American Association for Higher Education, 1994). Since 1991, the journal *Quality Progress* has surveyed higher education institutions to determine if they offer courses in continuous improvement and whether continuous quality improvement is applied in the management of their institutions. The number of institutions responding positively to these queries has steadily risen from 1991 through 1996. As the problems facing higher education have grown, more institutions have adopted quality principles and practices, and we predict that this trend will continue.

WHAT ARE QUALITY PRINCIPLES?

Before we examine the continuous quality improvement movement and its application in higher education in more detail, we need to define exactly what is meant by "quality principles." "Quality principles are a personal philosophy and an organizational culture that use scientific measurement of outcomes, systematic management techniques, and collaboration to achieve the institution's mission" (Freed, Klugman, and Fife, 1997, p. 44). Institutions practicing quality principles are continuously improving. Decisions are not made by managers, nor based on intuition, but rather they are made by those actually responsible for the processes. Not only are the rank and file workers empowered, but their decisions are based on data specifically gathered to analyze and improve a particular process. We discovered that the institutions practicing quality principles are *asking different questions for different times.*

In order for quality principles to work, however, they must become a fundamental and philosophical culture value. Institutions that treat quality principles as an incremental management approach used sporadically rather than as an organizational culture value are less able to incorporate them into the fabric of the institution. One of the ways that an institution can internalize the lessons of the continuous improvement approach is to become a learning organization.

Learning organizations are those institutions that develop enhanced learning capabilities through systems thinking, improving mental models, fostering dialogue, nurturing personal vision, and building shared visions (Senge, 1996). These characteristics translate into an institutional culture based on genuine trust and shared responsibility, a culture that unleashes the imagination, creativity, and passions of members and enhances their ability to form shared visions. Because of this shift in culture, the quality of thinking is changed and so is the ability of members to understand interdependency. The members realize they are part of interrelated systems working together to satisfy stakeholders. In learning organizations, people on the front lines are as important as people in senior leadership positions to the success of continuous improvement efforts because their intelligence, experience, and skills are used to address external environmental challenges. If this sort of trust and interrelationship is not present in a higher education institution, all the lofty quality language in the world won't change a thing.

DO QUALITY PRACTICES REFLECT QUALITY PRINCIPLES?

Because implementing quality principles is such a major cultural change for an institution, we conducted a two-part national study to find out if quality concepts are really being practiced by institutions that claim to have adopted principles of continuous improvement. Since the basic quality principles are widely known and published (Freed, Klugman, and Fife, 1997), our research centered on actual institutional practices. We wanted to discover what quality ideas are most commonly adhered to by institutions. In addition, we wanted to know whether the quality improvement practices of institutions actually reflect quality principles, and more importantly, whether quality principles are an effective approach for addressing challenges facing higher education institutions.

In exploring these issues, we wanted to develop a cross-institutional understanding of experiences of higher education institutions that are using quality principles to *ask the difficult questions*, looking for both commonalities and differences. In doing so, we wanted to focus on institutions' experiences, notable successes, and disappointing setbacks. We were interested in how these institutions learn and how they are building learning organizations. The answers we found can help higher education administrators and their institutions respond to the new questions in *these different times*.

Data were collected in two stages. In the first stage, a questionnaire was constructed to gather information from a large number of institutions that have implemented continuous improvement. These data were collected over a six-month period from February through July 1994. Data collection was followed by in-depth site visits to ten institutions that had been working on the implementation for at least three years. The site visits took place over a seven-month period, from the middle of July 1994 through the middle of February 1995. A summary of the methodologies employed for the questionnaire and the site visits as well as a discussion of the main topics included in these two stages of data collection are presented here.

Data Collection Stage 1—The Questionnaire

The questions that formed the basis of our first survey originally appeared in *TQM on Campus* (Freed, Klugman, and Fife, 1994) and were based on information reported in the literature on higher education institutions with active continuous quality improvement efforts (Chaffee and Sherr, 1992; Marchese, 1991; Sherr and Teeter, 1991; Seymour, 1992 and 1993; Seymour and Collett, 1991). The questionnaire (appendix A) was pretested on individuals associated with the American Association for Higher Education (AAHE) CQI Project and was modified based on their feedback.

The questionnaire was sent to 408 institutions in February 1994. Institutions that were selected either were members of AAHE's Academic Quality Consortium, were identified in an ERIC publication as practicing continuous quality improvement, or were listed in the annual "Quality in Education" survey printed by *Quality Progress*. The surveys were sent to contact persons who held direct leadership roles in the quality process as reported in these lists. The original mailing and follow-up postcard yielded a response rate of 28 percent. A second copy of the questionnaire was mailed to the noninterviewees, which raised the response rate to 52 percent. Response to a much-abbreviated postcard questionnaire brought the final response rate to 67 percent. The results of this survey are referenced throughout this text, but the full results can be seen in appendix B, page 219.

Data Collection Stage 2—Site Visits

The survey gave us baseline information on many institutions that are implementing continuous quality improvement concepts. The results from the survey reinforced those of others (Chaffee and Sherr, 1992; Marchese, 1991; Sherr and Teeter, 1991; Seymour, 1992 and 1993; Seymour and Collett, 1991). From the beginning, however, the goal of this research was to go beyond our initial survey and the studies that others had done, and to get much more detailed information. We wanted to determine the specific practices of institutions that are implementing continuous improvement principles and how these practices are allowing them to meet the challenges in higher education.

We visited institutions that have implemented continuous quality improvement and interviewed a wide cross-section of individuals at each institution. We chose the following ten institutions: Richland College, Rio Salado Community College, Belmont University, St. John Fisher College, Samford University, Winona State University, University of Minnesota—Duluth, University of Wisconsin—Madison, University of Michigan—Ann Arbor, and University of Chicago Graduate School of Business. These institutions are not a random sample of institutions, but rather were carefully selected so that they cover a wide variety of institutions which have had some degree of success with the implementation of quality principles based upon information from the literature and from individuals associated with the AAHE CQI Project. The institutions are a mix of four-year public, four-year independent, and two-year community colleges. They also are a mixture of research- and teaching-focused institutions, are a combination of sizes, and are located across the United States. Profiles of the ten institutions are included in appendix C.

We interviewed more than 20 individuals at each institution but one; at the University of Chicago we were able to contact four key individuals in the business school who are involved in quality improvement efforts. At each of the other institutions we requested interviews with the following people: the president, the coordinator of the quality project on campus, the chief academic officer, and the deans and some faculty of the business and engineering schools (if these schools existed at the particular institution). The reason for singling out business and engineering schools is that these are fields in which quality principles frequently are taught, and therefore those schools may be implementing quality practices before other academic areas. In addition, we asked to conduct three focus groups: one of faculty, a second of administrators, and a third consisting of staff.

Further, we requested that the focus groups be made up of a mixture of quality champions, team leaders or facilitators, known critics of the quality initiative, people involved with the implementation who were not the leaders, and any other people who would contribute to the discussion. To obtain a more balanced picture of the success of each institution's program, we were especially interested in speaking with people who resisted the implementation.

Meetings with the coordinator of the continuous improvement efforts and with the focus groups were scheduled for one and one-half hours. All other meetings were scheduled for one hour. We sent the questions to the contact persons in advance so that the individuals who would be meeting with us could examine the questions prior to our visit. Participants in these sessions were assured of the confidentiality of their responses.

The questions for the site visits were derived from information reported in the literature and from our initial questionnaire. They were pretested on individuals associated with the AAHE CQI Project and were modified based on their feedback. Some individuals at our institutions were not asked all of the questions based on time constraints and the relevance of the questions given a person's position in the institution. These site visit questions are listed in appendix D, but an outline of the types of questions appears in the following paragraphs.

The questions asked of individuals can be divided into several sections. The questions in the first section asked for an overview of the quality efforts—basic information on where, when, and why implementation began on campus and who is involved in the implementation. The next section was designed to obtain an overview of the institution's philosophy of quality improvement; this section included questions about how the senior leadership learn about continuous improvement, whose philosophy is being followed, and what the institution's statement on quality is. A section on the mission of the institution followed with questions about how well-known the mission is within the institution and what changes have been made to the mission since the implementation of quality principles and practices. In the next section, questions about leadership and management style addressed the leader's commitment, empowerment, and incentives, and how the institution's culture had changed since implementation. Education, teams, and tools were covered in another section with questions on who receives education on continuous improvement concepts and tools and how this education is accomplished; on choice of projects, teams, and tools; on benchmarking; and on the language of quality improvement. A section on successes, obstacles, and results followed, which included questions on how success is measured and on how things could have been handled differently. Additional questions dealt with future plans for institutional continuous improvement.

Questions were included on how quality principles and practices are being used on the academic side. We were curious about whether faculty members were being incorporated in quality improvement efforts, whether they participated in learning about quality improvement, and whether they supported implementation. As faculty members ourselves, we were especially interested in the extent to which continuous improvement concepts were being used to improve learning and teaching, what areas were incorporating the ideas in the classroom, some examples of successful teaching improvement, and what support was being given for faculty implementation by the administration.

Questions for the focus groups asked what worked and what didn't work in implementation, where the greatest impact has been felt, from where most of the resistance has come, what the hopes were and what the reality of continuous improvement efforts had been, and why the institution was implementing continuous improvement principles. The open-ended questions allowed the focus groups to spend larger amounts of time on issues that were of particular interest to their institution.

During the summer of 1995, follow-up interviews were conducted with the quality coordinators of each institution to determine what further developments had taken place since the site visit. Some of these interviews were conducted in person, some over the phone, and others by mail and e-mail. The questions on the changes that occurred since the site visits concentrated on leadership; training, teams, and tools; culture; successes, obstacles, and results; and from where any new resistance came.

Data Analysis

All interviews conducted as part of the site visits were taped and transcribed. In addition to the tapes, the interviewers took detailed notes during the interview sessions. The tapes were transcribed by a third party who had knowledge of quality principles and practices. The information collected on our site visits was analyzed using the constant comparative method for discovering theory from data (Glaser & Strauss, 1967). This method consists of the following: first, the data are unitized (the smallest pieces of information that can be understood in the context of the study are identified); then the units are then categorized; and finally the patterns present in the categories are determined (Lincoln & Guba, 1985). Details of this procedure can be found in appendix E.

Using this process, we developed a model of quality practices in institutions of higher education that is illustrated in figure 1. This model has five components: Drivers of the Quality Effort, Development and Implementation of Systems, Barriers and Overcoming Barriers to Systems, Outcomes of the Quality Effort, and Lessons Learned. These five components of the model are explained briefly below and provide the framework for this book.

HOW IS THIS BOOK ORGANIZED?

As mentioned in the previous paragraph, the organization of this book is derived from the five components of the model of quality practices in institutions of higher education. In chapter 1, we summarize the nine principles that are generally held to be the foundation to quality improvement and restate these principles in terms of *different questions* that need to be asked of institutions in these *different times*.

In chapter 2, we identify several drivers of an institution's quality improvement efforts and categorize them as external or internal. Major external drivers include shrinking resources, enrollment fluctuations, increasingly competitive marketplace, business and industry demands, suggestions from insti-

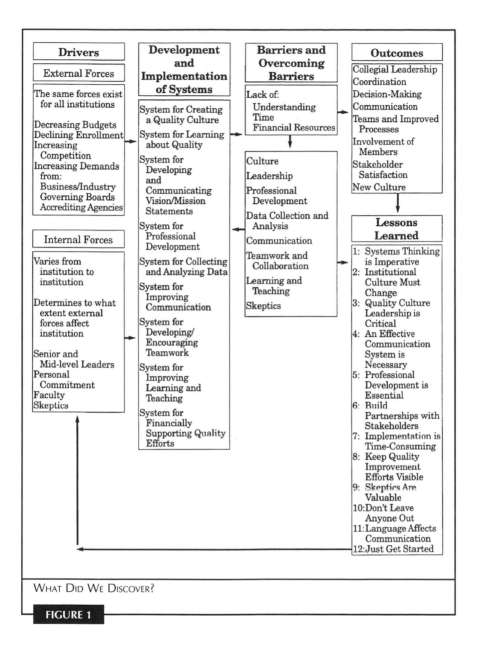

FIGURE 1

tutional boards, and pressure for outcomes assessment from accrediting agencies. The major internal drivers are dedicated leaders at all levels of the institution, members of the institution who have a personal willingness to improve, faculty members who want to improve their students' learning and their teaching, and skeptics.

Chapter 3 addresses the nine primary systems we found institutions using to implement quality principles. These systems allow the institution to create a quality culture, to learn about quality improvement, to develop vision and mission statements that are outcome driven and communicate these statements across the institution, to professionally develop individuals within the institution, to collect and analyze data for making decisions, to improve communication within the institution, to develop and encourage teamwork, to improve learning and teaching, and to financially support the quality efforts.

In chapter 4, we identify factors that act as barriers and explain how to overcome the barriers so that continuous improvement ideas can be used to improve processes and systems within higher education institutions. Many barriers to the continuous improvement efforts emerged from our interviews. We grouped these barriers under the following eight major categories: institutional culture, leadership, professional development, data collection and analysis, communication, teamwork and collaboration, learning and teaching, and skeptics.

Outcomes are measures of the progress of the continuous improvement process and include positive change in leadership style, improved coordination among members, data-driven decision making, improved communication, improved processes due to teamwork, more members involved in making decisions, greater stakeholder satisfaction, and positive culture change. These outcomes are covered in detail in chapter 5.

Chapter 6 addresses lessons learned by the institutions, both positive and negative. The 12 lessons that emerged from our interviews follow:

- Lesson 1: Systems Thinking Is Imperative
- Lesson 2: Institutional Culture Must Change
- Lesson 3: Quality Culture Leadership Is Critical
- Lesson 4: An Effective Communication System Is Necessary
- Lesson 5: Professional Development Is Essential
- Lesson 6: Build Partnerships with Stakeholders
- Lesson 7: Implementation Is Time-Consuming
- Lesson 8: Keep Quality Improvement Efforts Visible
- Lesson 9: Skeptics Are Valuable
- Lesson 10: Don't Leave Anyone Out
- Lesson 11: Language Affects Communication
- Lesson 12: Just Get Started

These lessons have been used by the institutions we studied as they continuously improve. The lessons have become internal drivers for these institutions, thereby completing the system. The fact that these institutions are continually learning from their experiences provides evidence that they are building learning organizations. As learning organizations, they are also interested in contributing to the success of others and are eager to have others learn from their experiences. Across institutions, a pattern emerged among interviewees indicating that they believe their experiences will benefit others. In turn, they also were anxious to learn from the other institutions we visited.

By understanding the model depicted in figure 1, members of institutions can learn from the experiences of others. They can learn about what drives the momentum of continuous improvement in institutions, about systems that have been developed that help institutions improve, about obstacles that arise and how to overcome them, about outcomes that continuous quality improvement institutions have experienced, and about mistakes to avoid.

WHO SHOULD READ THIS BOOK?

The context for this book is higher education, but quality principles and practices apply in any environment where the goal is to create a meaningful culture for continuous quality improvement. Because continuous quality improvement empowers members at all levels of an institution, this book is of interest to members ranging from the lowest level of staff member to the highest level administrators. To determine if this book is relevant to you, ask yourself if you desire to change the culture of your organization to one in which:

- people make maximum use of their talents?
- ordinary people do extraordinary things?
- people understand how their work relates to the vision and mission of the organization?
- people seek feedback rather than being threatened by it?
- people view each other as partners and team members, not just co-workers?
- people are willing to take risks to improve the organization?
- people seek input rather than approval from others?
- people are willing to make traditionally private information public?
- leaders cultivate leaders?
- leaders have faith and confidence in team decisions?
- leaders are responsive to suggestions and feedback?
- leaders admit their own weaknesses?
- leaders recognize that there is strength in weakness?
- leaders build trust through self-disclosure and shared pain?
- leaders go out of their way to include those who are skeptical or critical of them?

If you answered "Yes" to even one of these questions, you will benefit from reading this book.

IS TOTAL QUALITY MANAGEMENT THE SAME AS CONTINUOUS QUALITY IMPROVEMENT?

Language emerged as one of the main barriers to continuous improvement efforts. Many institutional members, particularly faculty members, were, and are, troubled by the business-oriented language associated with quality efforts, especially efforts associated with total quality management (TQM). Because this language has proven to be troublesome, we consciously have avoided using the term "TQM" in this book. Instead, we prefer to use terms such as "quality principles," "continuous quality improvement (CQI)," "quality initiatives," and "quality improvement efforts." Even though the terms can often be used synonymously, we neither want language to be a barrier, nor do we want to advocate any particular label. Rather, we want to communicate that when implemented holistically, principles of continuous improvement are a culture change. They are a way of acting and believing, not a technique, program, or vocabulary. In retrospect, institutions realized that it is easy to spend too much time discussing what to call the efforts, time that could have been spent on improving the processes and systems that really matter.

Institutions that have progressed the furthest on the quality improvement journey are those that have been able to clear the hurdle of language. Although a common language is helpful in developing a common understanding among institutions members, the best way of keeping the focus on continuous improvement without talking about it is by *asking questions*. This theme was best summed up by one response, "Quality means getting everybody to ask questions about how we do things, why we do things, and whether we should be doing different things."

We discovered that the institutions we studied have been able to change behaviors and to shift the thinking in members without using specific quality language but by *asking different questions*. In fact, one president told us that he does not even use the word "quality," but rather leads continuous improvement efforts through his actions. Added another administrator, "I am not calling it anything. I think quality improvement is a way of thinking."

ACKNOWLEDGMENTS

We are grateful to those we interviewed and to the people who helped make the interviews possible. Without the opportunities to hear their stories and experiences, we could not have determined the effectiveness of practicing quality principles in higher education. Thank you for being generous so that others may learn from your experiences. We concluded that people practicing quality principles are quality people.

Steve Brigham helped us select the most appropriate institutions. Daniel Seymour edited an early draft that reframed the book. He coached us through the project with his honest feedback. Without his support and encouragement throughout the entire process, this book would not be a reality. Yvonna Lincoln answered key questions at the most critical times of the data analysis. Jim Ratcliff helped us "learn the ropes" as our project turned into this book. Our thanks to you all.

We appreciate the time given so kindly by every person interviewed, whether individually or as members of a focus group. In addition, we thank all of the quality coordinators who established our interview schedules. The spirit of cooperation and the information sharing was overwhelming. Our interviewees truly wanted us to learn from their experiences, and they wanted to learn from the results of our study.

As we think about the people who helped make this project happen, many names and faces come to mind: Bill Troutt, Susan Hillenmeyer, Linda Thor, Carol Scarafiotti, Sharon Koberna, Bill Pickett, Dennis Crowley, Maury Cotter, Bob Holmes, Harry Roberts, George Bateman, Darrell Krueger, Bruce Gildseth, John Harris, and Burt Peachy. Since it is not possible to name every person who contributed to the successful completion of this book, please know that we are grateful.

Susan Slesinger and Sean Tape at The Oryx Press are excellent advisors. Susan made the process easy, and Sean's feedback improved the project. Thanks for believing in this book and supporting us.

Jann Freed and Marie Klugman

I am indebted to Central College for granting me a sabbatical leave to conduct my research and for the research grants to pursue this project.

When I think of an effective leader, I think of Bill Troutt of Belmont University. He "walks the talk" and surrounds himself with leaders such as Susan Hillenmeyer, Jerry Warren, Richard Smith, Kathy Baugher, Butch Eley, Morris Early, Martha Kelley, Mike Awalt, and Eleanor Dunn.

I thank Marie, who agreed to be a partner in an earlier project that continued to grow. We complemented one another and our synergy kept both of us going. She is also a quality person; someone who lives up to commitments and who can be trusted to give honest feedback. This project was fun because of the team effort. Thanks for hanging in there.

Finally, I thank my family. John put some of his goals on hold so that I could devote significant blocks of time to this book. I know he is proud of my accomplishments and that understanding has kept me focused. For the boys, I will remember how they always asked me if I was "going to be working on the computer." Well, all of the effort has paid off and I am done working on the computer. Click.

Jann Freed

I thank my colleagues who attend the annual Making Statistics More Effective in Schools of Business conferences. It was through them that I was introduced to the ideas of continuous quality improvement in teaching.

Writing this book has been a sometimes-great-sometimes-not-so-great experience. Throughout the entire process, however, Jann has been upbeat and encouraging, and has challenged me to do my best. Without her, I would not have completed the research, much less finished writing about it. Thank you, Jann.

I thank Drake University for funding this research through its Faculty Research Grant program and for granting me a sabbatical leave when I needed the time to write.

Above all, I thank my family. My husband, Stuart, was also writing a book during this same period, and therefore may have been more understanding about the time and effort that goes into such an endeavor than most spouses might be. Through it all, he was extremely supportive of my efforts. When I struggled, he was able to build my confidence so that I didn't give up. When things were going well, he always was quick to praise. Our sons, David and Philip, were very understanding even when finishing the book became more important to me than doing activities with them. In addition, I am sure that everyone in my family is happy now that the makings of this book are no longer scattered all over the dining room table.

Marie Klugman

QUALITY PRINCIPLES AND PRACTICES IN HIGHER EDUCATION

CHAPTER 1

How Did the Quality Improvement Journey in Higher Education Begin?

He who asks questions cannot avoid the answers.

—Cameroon proverb

WHY IS THE QUALITY IMPROVEMENT JOURNEY NECESSARY?

Financial issues dominate most higher education institutions today. Across the country both public universities and independent colleges are being forced to cut their budgets at a time when their customers—students, parents, and employers—are being more selective and demanding better results. According to Levine (1992), "all of our publics are asking *hard questions* about the cost, pricing, productivity, access, outcomes, and effectiveness of college. . . . Higher education needs to begin addressing those *hard questions* in a serious manner—campus by campus, system by system, state by state" (p. 4).When business and industry were faced with similar difficulties, many organizations responded by improving quality and service through total quality management (TQM) or continuous quality improvement (CQI). There is a growing trend in higher education to implement these same quality principles to address challenging issues that threaten the health of higher education.

In case these threats seem overstated, read the following facts that underscore some of the problems facing higher education (Morganthau and Nayyar, 1996; Siebert, 1996; and U.S. Department of Education, 1995):

- The percent of students who drop out between their freshman and sophomore years at independent schools has risen from approximately 23 percent in 1983 to approximately 26 percent in 1996. The dropout rates for public schools have fluctuated between approximately 28 and 30 percent for the same time period.

- Graduation rates, the percent of students earning a degree in five years, has dropped from 52.2 percent to 44.6 percent for public schools during the period 1983-96. For independent schools, the five-year graduation rate has fallen from 59.5 percent to 57.1 percent.
- The total cost of attending independent colleges and universities has grown 95 percent between 1984 and 1994; the total cost for attending public institutions has risen 82 percent. During this same time period, median income has increased only 47 percent.
- The actual days spent in school have decreased from an average of 191 days in 1964-65 to 157 days in 1993-94, while average annual tuition has increased from $5,415 to $15,978.
- Today only 20 percent of U.S. colleges and universities are healthy financially, 60 percent are struggling to adjust, and the remaining 20 percent are in trouble.
- Federal and state governments began curtailing funding from an annual 15 percent increase in the early 1970s to a more modest 4 percent increase in the 1990s.
- To save money, maintenance on institutional buildings has been deferred. It is estimated that the cost of this maintenance is now about $60 billion.
- The average annual salary of professors has risen while their teaching load has been reduced.
- To cut costs, class sections, courses, and some programs have been canceled. In some cases, the number of credit hours needed for graduation has also been reduced.
- The average Graduate Record Exam verbal score has not recovered from the decline experienced during the 1960s, 1970s, and 1980s; in 1993 the average score was 49 points lower than the average score in 1965.

Given these facts, is it any wonder that parents and students are *asking different questions* and demanding more from higher education institutions in these *different times*? Can institutions continue to survive as they have in the past? If not, what must they do differently?

We found people in higher education are using principles of continuous improvement to *ask the hard questions*. In fact, these institutions report that because of quality improvement they are *asking different questions*. The power in asking questions is that questions direct our focus; they influence how we feel and how we act. Our core beliefs affect the questions that we ask (Robbins, 1991). Therefore, it follows that by *asking different questions*, people practicing quality principles have actually changed their core beliefs.

In our nationwide study of 10 institutions that have embraced continuous quality improvement, interviewees reported improvements in systems, communication, morale, job satisfaction, and teaching. These institutions are learning how to cut costs while improving the efficiency of the institutional system. When systems are improved, the quality of the institution is improved. Ultimately, quality of the end product, students, is measured by outside sources such as employers and graduate schools, and we found that the reputations of several institutions were enhanced because of their quality improvement efforts.

As a result of their enhanced reputations, these institutions are able to attract more and better students while satisfying employees and other custom-ers of the institutions as well. These institutions are becoming better stewards of public and private funds, and they are enabling students to achieve at a level closer to their intellectual potential. They operate according to the following tenet: *when there is a choice to do something well or not well, they choose to do it well.*

Institutions that use quality improvement efforts to cut costs and to im-prove under crisis conditions are positioned to be more competitive in the future. They critically examine their current processes and systems with the intention of reducing and improving them so that the organization functions more efficiently. They collect information from their stakeholders to help them improve customer satisfaction. They are not afraid to ask for new ideas and feedback from all members of the organization. The quality improvement mind-set that helps institutions survive through the lean times will also allow the institutions to take advantage of times of growth. The strongest testimony to the benefit of engaging in continuous improvement was a statement made by a staff member we interviewed, "Quality management saved this institu-tion."

HOW HAS THE QUALITY IMPROVEMENT MOVEMENT IN HIGHER EDUCATION EVOLVED?

American higher education has responded to serious challenges in demo-graphics, economics, and social values since the middle of the twentieth century. For several decades after the end of World War II, enrollments rose dramatically and revenues increased. The large influx of students caused overcrowding and greater demands were placed on faculty, staff, and facilities. New programs were created, buildings were built, and more faculty and staff were hired. During these times, outside competition from corporate training and degree programs was limited, and federal funds were readily available to help offset rising institutional costs. Institutions followed the resource model for defining excellence in education (Seymour, 1993). This model states that if a college or university is able to attract more resources, perceived quality increases, which leads to greater public trust and therefore, increased resources. Under this model, measurement of the quality of an institution is based on its reputation, which is often a reflection of admission test scores, size of endowment, library holdings, and the percentage of Ph.D.s on the faculty.

In the 1980s and continuing in the 1990s, federal funds were drastically cut, leading institutions to raise tuition faster than the inflation rate. Competition also increased during these years from other institutions and from corporations that began offering courses and degrees. This new competition appeared at a time when enrollments dropped because of the declining number of traditional college-aged students. In addition, there was increased public demand for accountability and productivity from the institutions. Unfortunately, many educational institutions were locked into the resource model mind-set and evaluated their own performances accordingly.

Many institutions are just now realizing that the foundation upon which excellence in education is measured needs to shift from a resource model to a performance model. This second model states that as performance increases relative to resources, the perceived value of the institution increases and public trust increases (Seymour, 1993). The goal of the performance model is an institution that delivers a "quality" education. A quality education is achieved by relying more on performance and less on resources. This contrasts with the resource model which is driven by reputation, not by educational excellence. Seymour (1993) states that "the key to enhancing performance is to continuously improve the efficiency and effectiveness of operational processes . . . through the application of quality management principles" (p. 14). To facilitate this much-needed shift from a resource model to a performance model, new questions must be asked, new data must be collected. We must again ask *different questions for different times*. The differences between the philosophies are reflected in the questions asked under the two models. (See table 1.)

TABLE 1	
HOW HAVE THE QUESTIONS CHANGED?	
Old Questions	New Questions
How many volumes are in your library?	What is your aim?
What is the average admission test score?	How do the parts fit together?
What is the size of your endowment?	Who leads the creation of a new culture?
What percent of alumni support you?	How do you update your knowledge?
What percent of your faculty are Ph.D.s?	How do you make decisions?
What is your average salary for faculty?	Who makes decisions?
What is your grant income per year?	How do you improve?
What is your student-to-faculty ratio?	How do you prepare for the future?
What is your average class size?	How is the change supported?

External forces that continue to influence institutions today affect all institutions; yet the responses to those forces vary from institution to institution. Some institutions have reputations or large endowments that help to offset the effects of those forces. Other institutions, however, do not have the luxury of relying on such flexibility. Regardless of an institution's situation, external forces such as shrinking resources, declining enrollments, and competition from other institutions and from business and industry programs need to be addressed; institutional cultures need to change.

Continuous improvement in higher education is one way to create a new institutional culture focused on a quality education. Performance is enhanced by continuously improving the efficiency and effectiveness of operational processes. Commonly reported outcomes at institutions that have adopted quality principles and practices include time savings, increased efficiency, reduced costs, higher morale, more involvement of employees, improved communication, greater customer satisfaction, less rework, and changed culture (Freed, Klugman, and Fife, 1997). Outcomes such as these indicate that institutions implementing continuous quality improvement will be able to address the *different questions* that are being asked in these *different times*.

WHAT ARE QUALITY PRINCIPLES AND PRACTICES?

Quality principles and practices are generally known and accepted; they are being used in business, health-related areas, and education. They are philosophical, logical, sound, easy to buy into, and hard to dispute. They prescribe a personal philosophy and organizational culture that utilizes scientific outcomes measurement, systematic management techniques, and teamwork to achieve the mission of the organization (Freed, Klugman, Fife, 1997). Continuous quality improvement involves using quality principles and practices to improve processes and systems. As stated by one of our interviewees, "Every day in every way we are trying to continuously improve."

Principles are guidelines for human behavior, and they facilitate the change process for individuals and organizations. There are nine principles that are most often mentioned by quality authorities (Chaffee and Sherr, 1992; Cornesky, et al., 1991; Crosby, 1979; Deming, 1986; Juran, 1989). (For a detailed explanation of these principles, see Freed, Klugman, and Fife, 1997.) The nine principles are restated below in terms of *different questions* that need to be asked of institutions in these *different times*.

What Is Your Aim?

An institution needs a clearly defined vision and mission; these, along with measurable outcomes, give an organization a clear sense of direction and focus. The outcomes, such as improved student learning, lower costs, and superior services, must be defined by the expectations of stakeholders and must be in harmony with the mission and values of the institution. Stakeholders for a higher education institution include students, parents, employers, funding agencies, faculty, and society in general. Since quality is based on the perception of those served by the institution, the expectations of stakeholders must be taken into account when the mission and outcomes of the institution are defined.

How Do the Parts Fit Together?

All actions, processes, and procedures are part of interactive and interdependent systems; a change in one part of the institution affects other parts of the institution. In a continuous improvement environment, most of the problems within an organization are associated with the system, not with the people who work in the system.

Who Leads the Creation of a New Culture?

It is important that the leadership of the organization guide the implementation of quality principles and practices. For most organizations, the adoption of continuous improvement requires a radical change of institutional culture. For such a change to occur, leaders must bring together all groups of the institution and must encourage all members to align their efforts with the mission of the institution. Leaders must demonstrate their quality beliefs through their actions.

How Do You Update Your Knowledge?

Organizations constantly undergo changes; therefore, it is necessary that the knowledge and skills of the members be continuously maintained and updated to meet the demands of the changes. The members must be involved in continuous professional development through education. Professional development is the responsibility of the organization.

How Do You Make Decisions?

There must be systematic gathering of data within an organization before a decision is made. What kinds of data need to be gathered to make a rational decision? Data are needed to measure the desired outcomes, to measure the processes, and to develop a contextual understanding of a particular problem or issue.

Who Makes Decisions?

Individuals within the organization must understand how their positions and actions relate to the mission of the institution. People have to learn that they are individually responsible for the achievement of the mission. The closer a person is to the actual issue, the more involved that person should be in the decision-making process.

How Do You Improve?

Individuals working together to improve a process or to finish a project produce better results than people working alone. Teams should include as many people as possible who directly and indirectly influence a process so that there is a greater chance of understanding all the facts about the process. If a decision is made this way, there is a greater feeling of ownership for the success of that decision.

How Do You Prepare for the Future?

The mission of an organization is based on the expectation of the stakeholders. Since these expectations change over time, the mission will also evolve. Organizations must embrace change as being positive and must make planning for change a high priority.

How Are the Changes Supported?

The leadership of the organization not only must guide the implementation of quality principles and practices, it also must see to it that the change is sustained. Therefore, there has to be constant support from those who can influence the culture. This leadership must be willing to reinforce the changes through a positive reward system.

The principles in these nine quality questions represent a culture change for higher education. Such a major shift is necessary if institutions are to achieve academic excellence in the future. In building a quality institution, leaders need to share information with individuals and teams to build a shared vision for the institution. An institution must view itself as systems of interdependent parts that contribute to achieving the institutional mission. Practices in higher education must be assessed, and the outcomes of processes must be measured. All employees need to be educated in new methods and practices. Institutions must learn to focus on the expectations of stakeholders and must collect data to help make decisions. Feedback must also be collected to drive continuous improvement efforts as institutions continue to learn from their experiences.

WHY ARE QUALITY PRINCIPLES A CULTURE SHIFT?

At first glance, the use of continuous quality practices seems a natural fit for colleges and universities. Quality principles and practices are logical; people often describe them as common sense. A clearly defined vision and mission based upon stakeholder expectations gives many individuals a feeling of involvement in the institution. Strong leadership to lead continuous improvement within institutions is practical. Developing members of the institution and helping them grow professionally is a good philosophical goal. Basing decisions on fact rather than intuition, whims, or complaints is important economically. Allowing people who are close to a problem to participate in decision-making processes is reasonable. People working together in teams is a logical way to make decisions. But as logical as these principles and practices may seem, higher education has not been eager to implement them. The question is why.

Historically, colleges and universities have taken pride in operating as a collection of isolated, individual parts. Faculty members tend to work independently of one another and do not readily exchange information, and departments often fight with each other over scarce resources. The success of the college or university has not been judged by the outcomes—student success—but by inputs—number of Ph.D.s on the faculty, number of volumes in the library, and achievement scores of incoming students. Instead of rewarding faculty for improving how they teach, faculty have been rewarded for receiving research grants and on the number of their publications.

The quality model in higher education is a paradigm shift, a complete culture change. Quality principles and practices that lead to continuous improvement require a change from the organizational philosophy of "if it ain't broke, don't fix it" to the quality ideal of "nothing stays perfect, therefore we must continuously work to do things better." In organizations that have moved to the quality paradigm, there are new rules, new boundaries, and new ways of behaving, in short, a new culture.

In such a culture, the expectations of stakeholders are constantly monitored and systems are developed to integrate stakeholder feedback into the decision-making process. Interdisciplinary and cross-functional efforts develop and support the institutional mission. Incentives encourage members of the institution to align their efforts with the mission. Reward systems are redesigned so that members strive to accomplish the primary institutional mission. Institutions recognize improvements in the quality of teaching and reward those improvements appropriately. Development of all members of the institution is a continuous process. Innovation and creativity are encouraged by providing faculty members the freedom to take risks and to make changes. In addition, the staff is given the opportunity to attend classes and workshops and is allowed to participate in decision making, conveying the idea that they are also valued members of the institution. In the new paradigm, members understand that the institution operates as a system with measurable outcomes instead of as a collection of isolated parts.

WHAT MUST BE DONE TO ENSURE CONTINUOUS IMPROVEMENT?

Institutions must be proactive in responding to the challenges facing higher education. They need to change their management practices and the way work is done. New standards, new systems, and new responsibilities must be developed. A culture of quality improvement encourages members to have ownership in the institution and to take responsibility for managing themselves. The shift to this new quality culture is accomplished when quality efforts become an internalized standard of excellence for members within the institution rather than a way of doing business imposed by upper-level management.

One way to encourage such a culture change is to operate an institution on the principles of the "learning organization." In *The Fifth Discipline*, Peter Senge (1990) coined the phrase "learning organizations" and described how they could be used to shift the ways people think and interact. Learning organizations create structures and systems in which people continually expand their capacity to create results they truly desire, develop patterns of new thinking, and continually learn how to learn. A learning organization is one in which processes maintain or improve performance based on experience (Nevis, DiBella, and Gould, 1996).

Flexibility and quick response to change are two strengths of a learning organization. Learning organizations are able to weave a continuous and enhanced ability to learn, adapt, and change into their culture. The values, policies, practices, systems, and structures of a learning organization encourage, support, and accelerate learning for all employees (Bennett and O'Brien, 1994). According to Wishart, Elam, and Robey (1996), the ability to continue learning is ensured through the institutionalization of structures and processes designed to promote learning. Structures and mechanisms do not guarantee learning will take place; however, the important criterion is whether the structures and mechanisms support the process of learning. If they do, then any organization has the potential to be a learning organization.

"The whole process of learning to learn hinges on an ability to remain open to changes occurring in the environment, and on an ability to challenge operating assumptions in a most fundamental way"(Morgan, 1986, p. 91). This learning process can be developed in four basic ways. First, openness should be encouraged and valued. Members should reflect on errors, recognizing that organizations are complex and environments are changing. Second, different viewpoints should be encouraged. Problems and challenges should be approached in open-ended ways, taking various perspectives into consideration. Third, avoid top-down planning that imposes goals, objectives, and targets. A bottom-up or participatory approach to planning keeps all members of an organization abreast of changing environments and lets those members "own" the new environments. Finally, institutions need to create organizational structures and processes to implement the above principles. Organizations become learning organizations when they have systems in place to question whether the operating norms, policies, and operating procedures are appropriate in regard to changes in their environment (Morgan, 1986).

In describing a quality culture, Senge (1990) states that people should shift their old ways of thinking (mental models), learn to be open with others (personal mastery), understand how their company or institution really works (systems thinking), form a plan that everyone can agree upon (shared vision), and work together to achieve that vision (team learning). The focus is on organizations and individuals alike becoming continuous learners.

DO QUALITY PRACTICES REFLECT QUALITY PRINCIPLES?

As noted previously and throughout the literature, many institutions of higher education across our nation are responding to internal and external pressures by employing principles of continuous quality improvement developed for business and industry. The use of quality principles represents a culture shift for higher education institutions, changing the paradigm of education from a resource model to a performance model. Now that institutions have had a chance to implement quality practices, the time is right to ask whether quality practices in higher education reflect quality principles.

We conducted a national study to explore if quality improvement concepts are being practiced by institutions that claim to have adopted principles of continuous improvement. (See the preface, p. xiii, and appendixes A–E for a complete description of our studies.) Since the basic principles of continuous improvement are widely known and published (Freed, Klugman, and Fife, 1997), our research centered on institutional practices. We wanted to discover what quality improvement ideas are most commonly adhered to by institutions. In addition, we wanted to know whether the practices of institutions that are implementing the ideas of quality improvement reflect quality principles, and whether quality principles are an effective approach for addressing challenges facing higher education institutions.

The following chapters present the results of our surveys as well as emerging themes from the people directly involved in the quality initiatives at their respective institutions. Chapter 2 outlines what interviewees saw as the drivers of the quality movement at their institutions, and chapter 3 examines the systems that institutions have implemented as a result of the continuous quality movement. Some of the barriers to continuous quality improvement and how to overcome these barriers, as seen by interviewees, are discussed in chapter 4. The results or outcomes of adopting quality principles are analyzed in chapter 5, and chapter 6 reviews the lessons learned by those institutions involved in implementing quality principles. This feedback from the lessons learned becomes part of the infrastructure for learning and serves to drive improvement efforts in the institution.

CHAPTER 2

What Are the Drivers of the Quality Movement?

A s the twenty-first century approaches, higher education is in a time of stress and transition. Higher education institutions are experiencing pressure from state agencies for accountability, from accreditation bodies and government units for their increasing requirements, and from shrinking resources and demographic downturns. Many higher education institutions are feeling a sense of powerlessness. This study investigated the degree to which continuous quality improvement may address these pressures. We were particularly interested in identifying patterns and themes across institutions that have been making conscious efforts to implement quality principles and practices.

Our study revealed that the forces driving the quality improvement movement on campuses were a combination of external and internal forces. The forces, once identified, became red flags that attracted the attention of leaders. Once the leaders were acutely aware of these forces, they initiated continuous improvement efforts on campus. After quality initiatives were started, the internal forces that quality processes tend to uncover drove the movement.

WHAT ARE THE EXTERNAL FORCES?

The external forces mentioned most by administrators, faculty, and staff were decreasing budgets, declining enrollments, increasing competition, and increasing demands from business and industry, board members, and accreditation organizations. Our interviewees also reported that employers, governing boards, and state legislators were *asking difficult questions* about productivity and faculty workload, which drove them to seek help from quality principles since continuous improvement is recognized in business and industry as a cost-effective approach.

Decreasing Budgets

One common theme among faculty, administrators, and staff was "having to do more with less." As budgets are held stable, or even decreased, institutional members are having to do more work with fewer resources. Administrators consistently mentioned that tight budgets motivated them to find ways to improve while decreasing costs. Retrenchment, reallocation of resources, salary freezes, and high levels of debt were commonly mentioned as reasons for their interest in quality improvement. We were told that the level of engagement in quality improvement efforts increases when a crisis is sensed and that a financial crisis or the perception of one is a strong driver. The idea that crisis changed attitudes was expressed by an administrator in this quotation:

> Even though quality improvement is mostly common sense, we went through the motions because we thought it was obligatory. Department chairs got involved just because we were asked to do it, and we did not take the quality principles very seriously. When it was time to budget we were told about the external forces. This got our attention so we began to take quality improvement seriously. As a new administrator, I wanted us to make continuous improvement our own. We are now doing just that.

Another administrator elaborated on this point:

> The carrot that got us into the quality movement was the budget, but in the end we can't see that any budget accommodations were made as a result of quality. It doesn't mean that they're not made, but we can't see them. Our quality efforts have given us some ideas about how to solve problems without extra money. It has encouraged us not to wait around for people to give us more money.

Most of the institutions in our study became involved in continuous improvement because they were seeking a framework to transform themselves to meet the forthcoming challenges resulting from tighter financial restraints. Because of their quality efforts, most interviewees felt that they had been better able to counteract the external pressures. They focused on how to improve systems and processes in ways that did not increase costs. One administrator articulated the driving force of quality improvement this way:

> The quality principles provide a framework for the leadership of the institution to think about and communicate the foundation for action so that we can move forward. It enables us to function and act as a whole system so that the things we do have more impact.

Continuous improvement can provide an overall framework for institutions to address problems such as decreasing budgets and declining enrollments. The institutions we studied understand that decreasing costs by improving processes and systems is one of the best strategies for maintaining the same quality of programs and services using the same amount of money or less.

Declining Enrollments

The second theme we discovered revolved around declining enrollments. Fluctuating enrollment is an emotional strain on all members of the institution, especially at tuition-dependent institutions. Today, parents and students are "shopping" for an institution that will most effectively meet their needs, often basing their decisions on perceptions and costs. They are in search of the best value for the dollars spent.

For many institutions, it has become more difficult to attract enough students to keep enrollments stable. Demographics have changed, particularly the number of traditional-age college students (18–22 years), to the point where there are not enough prospective students for all of the institutions. In essence, supply is greater than demand. Therefore, institutions must be concerned about providing value for tuition dollars in the competitive arena of higher education.

As parents and students become more consumer oriented, they are aware of the market value of a college degree from institutions perceived as being elite or of exceptional quality. Parents realize that a college degree is a minimum requirement for the workforce of the future, and they want to get their money's worth. In our study, administrators and faculty members told us that parents were *asking different questions* on campus visits. Because some parents work for companies that are downsizing, outsourcing, or stressing continuous improvement, they are asking what higher education institutions are doing to maintain or decrease costs without sacrificing quality. Parents are concerned about the ever-increasing costs of higher education. One administrator said it best:

> Quality improvement impresses parents. They see that their money is being used to benefit students and not solely for research which would benefit the faculty only.

Another college president echoed this theme:

> When I talk to parents, maybe a thousand of them, I ask how many of them are working for companies that are involved in the quality movement. At least 60 percent of the hands go up. It doesn't take long to figure out if you have that many and knowing how the expectations have changed, to know that they are interested.

In an intensely competitive market situation, we found quality improvement efforts being used as a recruitment tool for attracting parents and students. Prospective students have many available choices for higher education, and parents are particularly concerned about value gained for dollars spent. Institutions that strive to continually improve have an edge in recruitment over comparable institutions that have not implemented the ideas of quality improvement.

One growing market is part-time or returning students who tend to be adult learners. They work in corporations, and they are often already involved with continuous improvement efforts in their organizations. Our interviewees reported that these students return to school desiring more practical courses and more realism in classroom experiences. Their expectations are reflective of their work experiences.

While the admissions "game" continues to challenge many institutions, retention becomes an issue once students are on campus. Our interviewees noted that the perceived quality of the institution contributes to higher retention rates. One administrator said

> Our institution is driven by the desire to make the environment conducive to learning which will help with retention.

In institutions that have budgets primarily driven by the number of enrolled students, the institution's ability to attract and to retain students is critical. Designing systems that decrease costs while improving service and achieving the educational mission is critical to their success. Downturn in enrollment and tuition income are major forces motivating institutions to pursue quality initiatives.

Increasing Competition

The third external force reported by our interviewees is the competitive marketplace. Higher education institutions are not accustomed to responding to market conditions, but the time has come when marketing is no longer a choice. The competition for students in higher education institutions is as intense as it has ever been. Public universities, independent colleges, and community colleges are all competing for the same students at a time when the number of traditional-age college students (18–22 years of age) have decreased. Some colleges have targeted the returning adult learner as a new market in a strategy to counteract this external force, but this approach is not without risk. Higher education institutions are competing for the returning adult learner with corporate training programs and corporate universities such as Motorola University where continuous improvement is often the focus. Corporations believe that quality principles and practices are so important that they significantly invest financial resources to develop programs and institutes so that their employees have continually updated knowledge and skill development in this area.

We found that areas of institutions which are more closely related to business and industry (i.e., admissions, registrar, student life) are further along in the quality journey. One area where this was particularly true is in the health care field. The rapid changes in the health care industry have made medical schools more responsive than other parts of the university. In our interviews with universities that have medical schools, medical schools were frequently cited for their pursuit of quality improvement because they were often the first area within an institution that embraced quality principles and practices. Part of this responsiveness is a direct reflection of the pressure from accrediting and certifying agencies. It appears medical schools understand that health care is a business, and that they have to compete as a business in these times of health care crisis. Their involvement indicates they see the value in using continuous improvement practices to improve the quality of health care. One administrator reflected this sentiment by stating:

> The medical center is successful at embracing the quality principles because of the training and determination from top level administrators.

Throughout our study there was a pattern of adopting quality practices in areas of the institution where the competition is most intense. Common competitive areas included housing, where competition comes both from other housing in the community and from the desirability of housing at other colleges, and food service, since students often have the option of eating off campus. When people have alternatives, the areas most affected have the most imminent need to be competitive. The desire to improve the quality of programs and services is driven by the need to compete for students who use those programs and services.

Increasing Demands from Business and Industry

Demand from business and industry is the fourth driver. Business and industry are pressuring business and engineering schools to supply them with students who will be able to satisfy their skill and knowledge requirements. Several interviewees claimed that some employers have threatened to stop recruiting graduates from schools that are not teaching the philosophy, tools, and concepts of quality improvement. In other instances, it was reported that prospective employers expect institutions to be practicing quality principles.

A pattern emerged of institutions partnering with businesses to learn about continuous improvement and to pool resources. Partnering with businesses is facilitated when corporations in the area are actively engaged in continuous improvement efforts themselves. Several of our institutions are located in the same communities with their partners. In some of these cases, the partners have helped to financially support the efforts, particularly with respect to education and development.

Increasing Demands from Governing Boards

The fifth external driver is the pressure from governing boards. Several of the institutions reported that their board members are important drivers of the movement. Interviewees explained that board members see the results of using quality improvement concepts in their own firms and in the popular literature, which leads to a desire to see higher education institutions improve their practices as well. The institutions in our study have boards with members from Kodak, Xerox, IBM, and Procter and Gamble, to name a few, who have encouraged their institutions to become involved in continuously improving their processes and systems. As expressed by one administrator

> The trustees are excited about quality improvement because they see it in the business world. They know the big names are using quality, and when they hear about it from us they are impressed.

Board members not only initiate the quality improvement efforts on some campuses, but they also play an important role in helping institutions form partnerships within the community. They have seen the value continuous improvement has had in regaining competitive positions in business and industry, and they want to see their institutions benefit as well.

Increasing Demands from Accrediting Agencies

Accrediting agencies also emerged as drivers of quality improvement efforts because of their increasing focus on outcomes and values added. Assessment is being mandated more and more by accrediting agencies, and it is through the assessment movement that several of the institutions have evolved into a broader quality emphasis. Assessment requires analyzing critical processes, often accomplished by using cross-functional teams. As said to us by one administrator

> The accrediting agencies want to know how our students progress. They want us to talk to students to determine the level of student satisfaction. They also want to talk to employers in order to know employer satisfaction. Quality is all about being responsible to the people to whom you need to be responsible.

Even though assessment and quality closely dovetail, the assessment movement measures educational outcomes and often neglects identifying ways to improve. One president illustrated the relationship between assessment and quality improvement by saying:

> We had principles and practices and over 20 years of measurements that showed people who had followed the principles were the ones who had shown the gains. So when I came here, I thought we should focus on improving processes. I'm very interested in assessment and in quality but there is a big difference. Assessment focused on the instructional side. Then we started moving the nonacademic side more toward the formal quality practices.

Most administrators we interviewed realized that using assessment to measure outcomes was not enough, just like the old paradigm of measuring inputs was not enough. Assessment got them thinking about outcomes, but the desire for something more than assessment motivated them to learn more about continuous quality improvement. In general, assessment and quality improvement are complementary efforts, but continuous improvement is a more encompassing concept.

Summary of External Drivers

These external drivers are not unique to institutions, but rather they affect all institutions, regardless of whether the institution is involved in quality improvement. The difference lies in how the institutions are prepared to address these forces. For example, a healthy endowment can help an institution counter decreasing fiscal budgets and fluctuating enrollments. If an institution has established a reputation as a selective institution or carved out a particular market niche, it is easier for that institution to compete for students without extra efforts. In the long run, even in financially healthy institutions, continuous improvement efforts can help institutions to be better stewards of funds. By improving quality, by streamlining processess, and by deleting no-value-added steps, stakeholder satisfaction increases and funds can be invested for future growth.

For those institutions without the benefit of an endowment or similar funds, continuous improvement is one approach for helping them address these environmental forces. We found institutions driven to seek more effective and efficient ways to manage their resources because of increasing demands from business and industry. The external pressure by accrediting agencies for outcomes assessment has also been transferred into a pursuit of quality improvement by some institutions. As competition continues to increase, governing boards will become even more familiar with quality principles and will demand that scarce resources be used efficiently and effectively. They are having to take a more proactive approach to governing institutions and will be held accountable for overseeing institutional performance.

External pressures are not the only driving forces; a majority of the responding institutions cited a combination of external and internal sources as the driving forces for implementing quality improvement on campus. Often external threats to the institution are used as a means of initiating quality principles and practices, but engaging in the quality concepts uncovers internal forces that drive and sustain continuous improvement. Although the internal forces are more individualistic, we found several common internal forces across the institutions in our study.

WHAT ARE THE INTERNAL FORCES?

We identified four major internal forces that drive improvement efforts on the campuses we studied. The first internal force is the president and other top-level and mid-level leaders. The second driver is the personal commitment of people throughout the institution who are devoted to continuous improvement. Each individual devoted to practicing quality principles helps to sustain and drive quality efforts. The third force is the faculty. The last internal driver is people who oppose the movement, skeptics, who ironically help to drive the movement by constantly reminding the other three forces of the need to articulate the value of continuous improvement in higher education. These forces are interrelated; they are presented here in the order of strength, based on comments and interactions throughout our numerous interviews.

Senior and Mid-Level Leaders

The engagement of top-level leaders emerged as a primary driver of the pursuit of quality improvement. Usually, it is the president who has initial interest and who starts the discussions on continuous improvement or who decides to bring a quality improvement consultant to campus. The president plays a critical role in the movement at nearly every stage. Across the institutions in our study, presidents are almost always the people who spearhead the quality improvement initiative. At one institution, for example, quality efforts were essentially on hold until the arrival of a new president. At this institution, we were told that the continuation of their quality efforts depended on the interest in quality improvement of the new person hired.

At one institution, several interviewees remembered a speech by the president that they called "the train is going north" speech. The president asked members where they wanted to go and what their dreams for the institution were. Then the president said:

> This train is going north and I hope you see fit to stay on board, but if you
> do, I want a commitment.

According to one vice-president at this institution, the president was going to change the whole direction of the institution, the way business was done, the way they relate to each other, and the way they relate to students. He added, "It has been an exciting time."

Our interviewees felt that top-level engagement is necessary to make quality improvement an integral part of the culture. In contrast, the grassroots approach is usually perceived as too difficult. We were told that continuous improvement efforts are dependent on the commitment level of the leaders. This commitment level is usually measured in budget allocations and amount of time allowed for development and implementation.

Several of the presidents expressed that they are motivated to try quality principles by wanting to do a better job leading the institution. One president explained his motivation for pursuing a quality initiative despite the school's unusual upswing:

> Our initial efforts began when we were enjoying a positive upswing in enrollment, campus facility development, fundraising, faculty recruitment, operating budget increases; everything was positive. This trend has continued and our improvement efforts have continued to be internally driven. I simply wanted to find a better way to lead and manage, a different way than I had been taught and watched in others, a way that was more consistent with my own basic values. Several of us wanted to build a better academic workplace, where people could be excited about coming to work in the morning.

Another president commented that he is motivated to participate in the quality efforts out of respect for the employees. Investing in continuous improvement efforts is viewed as an investment in employees. For this particular institution, professional development in quality improvement is the largest single development effort the university has undertaken in its history. In this school, investing in the development of employees is viewed as evidence of the commitment of leaders to quality improvement.

One interesting theme that emerged is how the presidents have changed their perspectives on their role as president. They explained how they perceive their responsibilities changing and how they have become much more market-oriented. Since their institutions have started using quality principles and practices, they spend more time planning strategically and deciding how to control costs and how to generate external funds. In the past, some of the presidents we interviewed had been involved in a downward spiral in which they had to eliminate people. Because of that negative experience, they have been motivated to practice continuous quality improvement to avoid being in that situation again. For example, several presidents remarked on why they became interested in continuous improvement:

> I've focused on changing the way we're funded. I'm getting more money to fund quality through legislation. When I came here, I said that enrollment-driven formulas have undermined the quality of education in this country more than any other variable. What is measured is what is valued. What is valued is what is funded.

I saw quality as a way to bring about cultural change. The idea struck a lot of values that are spiritual or humanitarian that I hold dear. It allowed us to concentrate on the distinctiveness of our institution, and to differentiate our product in the marketplace.

When I read about Dr. Deming, I saw this type of servant leadership was consistent with my values as a Christian. I thought it would help me as a person and it would make the campus what it was intended to be. Servant leadership is congruent with a personal sense of mission at church-affiliated institutions.

One of the presidents came from California where shared governance is the law. Since shared governance is already this president's style, moving into continuous improvement is a natural progression. Empowering others by involving them in decision making is how this president wants to lead the institution. Administrators who work with her said that this president follows quality practices in her day-to-day operations. It is her style and her philosophy of leading. They described her as someone who leads by example and who works hard to make decisions by arriving at a consensus.

If a continuous improvement culture is to be created on campus, our research consistently revealed the significance of having leaders at all levels involved in the quality initiative. As administrators told us,

You have to get commitment from the top. They have to believe in it. There is always a line item in the dean's agenda to discuss quality. Half of the time we do not have anything to discuss, but he will not let quality issues dry up and blow away. As a former Baldrige examiner, he is definitely committed to quality.

What has made this work? Consistently strong leadership from the top has made this work, but it involved giving up some control.

It became clear to us that people expect leaders to change their own behaviors before leaders encourage others to change. Members at all levels want leaders to develop action plans and to have the courage to change the reward and recognition structures to positively influence the behaviors of members. Members need to know what changes will take place, and why, before they feel committed to follow. Our interviews revealed that members are continuously judging the actions and behaviors of leaders. One administrator described the influence of leaders:

I've talked to some schools who have said they tried quality but there was not really an involvement on the part of leadership; they were very spasmodic. Leaders have to demonstrate their commitment by being engaged. It takes a while for it to permeate the culture.

How top-level leaders demonstrate their support for quality initiatives varied across institutions. Examples of presidential and administrative affirmations ranged from one president who interviews everyone hired and leads many of the development workshops, to another president who has a steering committee on quality improvement that meets every Monday and an internal planning group that meets every Friday, both of which address quality issues on campus. Another administrator expressed commitment this way:

> I have a commitment to see this thing through for two years. After we were able to arrange a partnership with a Baldrige winner, I said that somebody needs to stick with this for a number of years. I am determined to stick with this. I am encouraged.

When the decisions, actions, and behaviors of top leaders are not consistent with the philosophy of quality improvement, members become ambiguous about quality improvement and progress slows down. Interviewees implied that they monitor and watch the behaviors, actions, and words of leaders, particularly presidents. Once leaders promise to practice quality principles, others constantly evaluate their actions and behaviors. Three quotations illustrate this ambiguity:

> I perceive continuous improvement as dumping more on nonfaculty and professional support staff. We have no guarantee of the support of middle- and top-level administrators.

> Our leaders are very committed, although they get accused of not doing things in the quality improvement way.

> We are committed to quality although the follow through is not as strong as it could be. We need more support from top management, even though the senior staff has been the driving force and now they do much of the training.

One faculty member stated the skepticism this way:

> It is not clear how well quality is understood on the part of the senior administration. They have negotiated a contract with Peat Marwick to help the institution implement the quality principles in a reengineering effort. I ran into the administrator who is the second in command and asked him about this. He was not even aware of what it was called. No matter what you call it, if you do not fully engage all senior lieutenants as well as others across campus by keeping them informed, you are very unlikely to be successful. My instinct is this will be downsizing and cost reduction rather than a focus on quality.

In many instances, members of the faculty and staff reported their ambiguity about the dedication of the top administrators by comments such as

> The chancellor said this is going to be our quality initiative breakthrough project for this year. This could be a really good outcome, and I would like to see this happen. I am a little worried about the commitment to it though.

> Evaluating their commitment is tricky. The provost has bought in. The deans used to meet on a regular basis to discuss quality issues, but as far as I know, those meetings have not occurred for months. The current dean of the business school supports it strongly and has encouraged quite a bit of activity in that school. The engineering school is undergoing a change of deans, and I am not sure where they are in the process or what has happened to their quality efforts in this interim period.

If presidents are going to create a culture supportive of quality principles and practices, it seems natural that the culture influence every institutional decision. Hiring employees is such a decision. Each new person hired influences the institution's culture. Because presidents who have adopted quality practices focus on creating a culture that supports quality, we asked if knowledge of quality improvement is a criterion in hiring new leaders. Although leaders believe this element is important, it is usually *not* a factor in the hiring process. Creating a quality culture should be a consideration in hiring at all levels. Yet, hiring decisions often send mixed messages:

> In searching for a new dean, they clearly should have been looking for someone who was an active manager, who was going to be a visionary leader, and who would focus on our constituencies or customers.

> Since we became committed to quality, we have a new provost who was an internal candidate who has been with the institution for over 20 years. He was already committed to quality.

> I think it depends on the composition of the selection committee. If there are people on the committee who are convinced that continuing quality improvement will be valuable, then they will look at the candidates and see whether or not they are receptive to pursuing quality.

One president made it very clear where he stands on this issue:

> We have hired and promoted six leaders with a passion for improvement. As Dr. Deming says, I only work with outstanding people.

Because presidents and provosts have the clout to make the significant changes in the institution, they need to demonstrate their dedication to continuous improvement efforts. Institutional members are constantly monitoring the behaviors of leaders, and leaders' behaviors need to be consistent with quality principles. Faculty and staff regularly commented that they are always monitoring whether leaders are simply paying lip service to continuous improvement or if the leaders "walk the talk." We learned the importance of having the presidents and the other top-level administrators understand the quality principles so that they could lead implementation. It is also important that they demonstrate their commitment through their actions and behaviors.

Mid-level leaders also drive the movement from within the institution. One department chair shared how he restructured the department based on quality improvement concepts. He became involved in the quality efforts because of his desire to improve processes and relationships within this large department. With the assistance of his institution's office of quality improvement, he realized engaging in principles and practices of continuous improvement might help him accomplish his goals. His story illustrates how he practices quality improvement:

> We were losing some of our best mid-career people because of the male-dominated closed society. They did not like the mentality where a couple of people had a lot of influence over many other people. I did not necessarily want to be chair but I wanted to reform the department. I created cross-functional councils: a faculty council, a graduate council, and an undergraduate council. The entire department focuses on issues rather than turf or intellectual alignments which tended to divide us. We had a year-long discussion about restructuring.
>
> I still feel like I do not have the faculty sufficiently engaged. I have restructured department meetings so that we debate strategic planning issues at meetings, and the rubber stamp issues are delegated to newly formed councils within the department. Whatever can be done at the council level is done there and announced at department meetings. Our meetings are limited to one hour and a major issue is included at every meeting. We talk about what needs to be changed and how we should change it.

An academic dean shared one of his small wins in the continuous improvement process:

> At the Dean's Council we have shared leadership. We rotate the leadership, and they decide where to hold the meeting, and they plan the agenda. This has had good ramifications.

Another administrator explained her strategy on leading people down the quality improvement path this way:

> The hard part was going out to departments and convincing them to change, and we decided that you just can't do that. You have to go to talk to them about their needs and continue to ask them why until it is a whole culture change.

One administrator has shifted his research and writing to focus on continuous improvement:

> I work hard to help my colleagues get what they need. I am writing about quality in higher education to explain things to people so they can understand. I am working hard to have them trust me.

Trust is an important part of a quality culture, and leaders at all levels set the tone for people to trust one another within the institution. We found that institutions are establishing systems to develop a culture of trust and empowerment. This system will be explained in detail in chapter 3, on the development and implementation of systems.

In our interviews with mid-level leaders, they said that facilitators are important in the quality improvement process. Mid-level leaders felt more comfortable in the new roles required in the quality efforts when facilitators assisted in meetings. Facilitator development is one of the areas in which people learn how to lead meetings effectively and how to build consensus among members. Since the concept of facilitation is contrary to *Robert's Rules of Order*, which are used by most institutions, interviewees told us that knowledge of facilitation is critical in shifting the paradigm and in changing behaviors. According to our interviewees,

> The role of facilitator is important because it results in better organization. It will make our jobs as middle managers easier. We should be one-minute managers.

> Although our dean is not a top-down driver, he is a facilitator and that pointed out to me that you don't always have to have a Bob Galvin [Motorola Corporation] leading the charge. There can be other models of leadership that obtain good results.

The role of mid-level leaders changes when institutions practice quality principles. The focus moves from managing to leading. Responsibilities change so that people are involved in different ways, particularly in meetings. People strive for consensus instead of voting on important issues.

Presidents, other senior leaders, and mid-level leaders are strong drivers of the quality efforts on campus, but the power of quality improvement is in individual improvement. Organizations improve when individuals improve. When people are individually committed to quality principles and practices, it is more likely that the changes will become integrated into the culture of the institution.

Personal Commitment

According to our analysis, the second strongest internal driver is the personal determination of individuals within institutions to improve. Regardless of the position of the person, interviewees continued to reaffirm that they are driven because of the intrinsic rewards of self-improvement. People who embrace change and perceive change as positive drive the quality movement on campus. "I started on my own because it made sense" was a statement made by a faculty member who has adopted quality principles and practices. People are motivated to improve because they want to solve problems and because they want to do good work. In one faculty focus group, one member said that in this particular institution it is "almost overkill in trying to improve things. I've never run into it anywhere else and I have been at six different institutions."

We concluded that once people understand quality principles and practices, they are personally committed to seeking out improvements to make. As people search for ways to solve problems, quality principles and practices provide a needed framework.

Many interviewees expressed concern about how to encourage people to embrace the quality concepts and continuous change. Even though some reward systems have been incorporated, the strongest incentive stated by our interviewees is self-interest. One administrator said it best:

> For me, the concept of quality is the change that takes place in the individual, not the change that takes place in the organization. I do not think the organization can change unless individuals change. Individuals change because you change incentives and attitudes, and attitudes change slowly.

Once people understand the basic philosophies of quality improvement, they are more likely to examine their own behaviors and actions, looking for ways to improve the work processes and systems in which they are involved. For continuous improvement to become woven into the institutional fabric, individuals have to want to practice quality principles. They need to perceive continuous change as positive and need to look for ways to continually improve.

Faculty

Faculty members who become involved in continuous improvement efforts are also internal drivers, though to a lesser degree. Although our research reinforced the quality improvement literature in higher education, which holds that quality initiatives almost always start on the administrative side of the institution (Seymour and Collett, 1991; Seymour, 1991), we did find a strong pattern of more faculty involvement as momentum for the quality journey grows and as people witness the improvements on the administrative side. Sometimes, all it took was bringing quality principles and practices to the attention of the faculty. One president shared this story:

> Myron Tribus visited in the spring of 1992 and spent the day on campus. When he met with the steering committee he asked us what we were doing in the classroom. He said, "I don't understand why you aren't putting all of your energy into continuous improvement in the classroom. After all, isn't that the business that you are in?" That is when we switched to more of an emphasis on the classroom activities. That may also have had an impact on the support staff because we shifted our attention away from the traditional kinds of teams that colleges have into those kinds of activities that are not as evident to the person who works in admissions.

We were not surprised to learn that faculty members say that their commitment is to teaching and conducting research, and that they often perceive quality improvement to be another managment approach. Many interviewees concluded that the way to appeal to faculty members is to stress how quality principles and practices can be used to improve learning, teaching, and conducting research. Since quality improvement should be vision, mission, and outcomes driven, we found that the interest in effective teaching drives faculty members to be more concerned about their primary mission—teaching. Faculty members accept the student-centered component of a vision and mission statement. The faculty members who we considered to be internal forces are driven by the need to improve their teaching so they can better satisfy student needs. They understand that they need to be responsive to the needs of stakeholders.

Experienced faculty members consistently remarked that they are *asking different questions* about the learning and teaching process. They stated that they focus more on the "big picture" since being involved in quality improvement efforts. We found faculty members questioning teaching practices of the past and replacing them with more valuable learning experiences.

For the faculty members incorporating the philosophy of continuous improvement in the classroom, their experiences are almost like an awakening. Once they understand quality concepts, they want to improve their performance and effectiveness in the classroom. Faculty members reminded us that implementing quality principles in the classroom initially takes time, but they believe they are more effective as a result of their quality efforts. They stated that they pay more attention to teaching processes up-front. As a result, they experience fewer complaints during the course and at the end of the course.

Many faculty members at our institutions expressed a renewed drive to improve the learning and teaching process, and they attributed this to quality improvement efforts. As one faculty member said, "We need to teach so that students are interested." Faculty members have been criticized for teaching as though "one size fits all," using the lecture method that is based on one-way communication with little opportunity for student input. The traditional paradigm where the professor is "sage" and knows all of the answers usually does not allow students the opportunity to provide feedback on the teaching process. In other words, the focus is usually on teaching rather than on learning.

In contrast, the institutions we studied asked the following common questions to drive the continuous improvement process: What do students need to know? How are they going to learn this information? Is there too much duplication in courses? Our research revealed that informal discussions among faculty members about "what they are doing and why they are doing it" are a growing trend. Even though these are basic questions, we found faculty members enlightened by the renewed focus on learning. At institutions where research is a priority, the faculty members interviewed indicated that the quality movement has caused them to be more in touch with teaching processes that are often lost in the pursuit of research and grants. One faculty member was even driven to develop a book on how to make the classroom more interactive. The book is becoming nationally recognized in chemistry, a discipline not typically perceived to be interactive or discussion oriented. Another faculty member stated

> There is interest in teaching. Even though we are a research faculty, we want to be good teachers. We are very competitive about it. We have published evaluations so we want to be good teachers.

When student expectations are clarified and become more realistic, students experience higher levels of satisfaction. Many faculty members agreed that students are more demanding than they used to be. This trend may be a reflection of an increasingly demanding consumer society, but nevertheless, students come to college with specific expectations. We also discovered a pattern that when the administrative side of the institution is practicing quality improvement, students often expect higher quality in the classroom. We were told that as students become cognizant of having their expectations met by administrators and staff members, they expect improved systems and processes in the classroom as well.

While the focus on improving teaching would seem to be a natural for college professors, past traditions and many current practices make this a hard sell. Typically, professors are not trained to be effective teachers and are not rewarded for effective teaching. The emphasis in their education was on mastering a discipline rather than on helping students learn a discipline. Unless the discipline is education, people teaching in higher education institutions usually have not taken any courses to prepare them to be effective teachers. In contrast, students desiring to teach at the elementary and secondary levels must student teach and become certified to teach at these levels. Ironically, this assessment step is not required of people teaching at the college level. Our interviews confirmed these findings:

> We never really address how we teach. We've always sort of assumed you bring people in and by osmosis they will learn how to teach. They will model what they received from graduate school or what they learn from being around. We don't do anything formal or informal.

> My wife is qualified to teach courses in our graduate school of business, but she cannot teach the third grade in this state and I am in a similar position. But in a place like ours, the faculty members do not see themselves as teachers. That is not what their career is. The first time Ph.D.s are exposed to teaching is in their first class. There have been lots of discussions on that and whether Ph.D.s should get more training in teaching, but it has not happened yet.

Anecdotally, the perception has always been that research and publications drive reward structures rather than effective teaching. People do not focus on establishing teaching credentials because they are not as transferable as research credentials. A recent study by the National Center on Postsecondary Teaching, Learning, and Assessment provided evidence that the rewards go to researchers. This study found that for full-time tenure-track faculty

- The more time spent on teaching and instruction, the lower the salary.
- The more time spent in the classroom, the lower the salary.
- The more time spent doing research, the higher the salary.
- The more publications one had, the higher the salary (Fairweather, 1993).

Despite this legacy, faculty members across institutions in this study indicated that there is a growing sub-community interested in improvement. They believe the approach should emphasize how to improve teaching rather than how to implement quality improvement concepts in the classroom. The former is disarming and nonthreatening to talk about, while discussing quality improvement implies that the teachers have been doing less than quality work or that education should be run as a business. As more faculty members learn about quality principles and practices, there is a spillover effect to the classrooms. Faculty members begin to question the teaching practices of the past. Because of education and development about quality principles, faculty members expressed that they are acknowledging the problems with the traditional higher education paradigm and that they are trying to make changes to improve learning and teaching.

Those faculty members with whom we spoke had, with few exceptions, changed their assignments to ones that require less memorization and that emphasize understanding. Even though the new assignments take more time to evaluate, the faculty members believed that the assignments are more appropriate for the skills needed beyond the classroom. They said applying quality practices in the classroom gives new life to disciplines, particularly to disciplines that do not change because the fundamental concepts are constant. Those faculty members who have adopted quality practices have changed how the fundamental concepts are presented, and they have become more interested in their professions. One faculty member attended a week-long quality improvement seminar at Procter and Gamble and returned with a whole new way of thinking about the profession he has been involved in for numerous years:

> The course content in introductory chemistry has not changed in the last 25 years. I am changing the teaching processes.

Because faculty members have not been educated in quality concepts to the extent of most administrators and staff, it is unrealistic to expect that they would be as dedicated to engaging in quality initiatives. As a result, they are not as strong in driving the quality improvement efforts as senior and mid-level leaders. If the faculty as a whole does not understand quality concepts, the emphasis placed on continuously improving varies. This finding shows the significance of developing people in continuous improvement at all levels of the institution from the start, so that there is a consistent knowledge base across the institution.

Skeptics

Strangely enough, we found that people who oppose quality improvement efforts often help to keep the movement visible and growing. Institutions utilizing training from the Covey Institute emphasize the importance of help-ing people understand the win/win attitude involved in practicing quality improvement concepts, but some people won't buy in no matter what. Yet, we were told that these skeptics actually help keep the momentum going:

> There are detractors. They are valuable. You would overlook issues that they cause you to examine. They are a genuine blessing. We do things better because of the skeptics. They force us to think harder, longer, and better about how we are going to get where we want to go. We have better processes and solutions because of the detractors.

While it is logical that not everyone will automatically become involved in the quality initiative, we were surprised to realize that some skeptics actually drive the movement. Their resistance and opposition constantly remind the leaders that they need to better articulate the benefits of quality improvement practices to overcome the objections. The skeptics act as devil's advocates, forcing leaders to continually explain the advantages of implementing quality principles and practices.

The threat presented by skeptics can be turned into an opportunity to keep the quality initiative alive and visible. Our interviewees said that some of the most vocal skeptics became zealous about continuous improvement once they understood the philosophy. We were told that these conversions, from skeptic to champion, helped to serve as testimonial of the value of implementation.

Summary of Internal Drivers

Presidents play a critical role in driving the quality movement on campus. Presidents and the other members of their leadership team are usually the first people who learn how valuable quality improvement can be to their institu-tions. A strong pattern that emerged across all types of institutions in this study is that leaders set the tone for how successful improvement efforts will be. Staff, faculty, and students pay close attention to how leaders set their priorities, how they spend their time, and how they allocate the budget. It is important that leaders "walk the talk."

Mid-level leaders also play an important role because of their ability to facilitate improvement efforts. If these leaders are educated in quality principles and understand the quality improvement philosophy, they are not threatened by involving people who report to them in making decisions. It is vital for leaders at all levels to adopt quality principles and practices.

The bottom line is that people have to be personally engaged in the quality initiative in order for the institution to be engaged. As Deming (1986) says, nothing happens without "personal transformation" and the only safe place for this transformation to occur is in a learning organization (Kofman and Senge, 1993). Our interviews reinforced the idea that people need to positively embrace change and to learn from their experiences. The institutional culture influences whether people are able to do this. Some of the strongest drivers on campus are individuals personally determined to improve the processes and systems in which they are involved. As one respondent remarked, "I'm not the same person after engaging in quality improvement that I was before I became involved."

Faculty members who are involved in continuous improvement efforts are also drivers. Because quality improvement is being adopted more slowly on the academic side, faculty members are often perceived as skeptics rather than drivers. Our findings indicated that faculty members who understand the quality philosophy are becoming more concerned about the relationship between student learning and effective teaching. Continuous improvement is of interest to teachers when they understand how quality principles and practices can help them improve what they do on a daily basis, whether that is teaching, conducting research, or advising students.

Skeptics, people who oppose the quality initiative, also drive the movement. Because they continue to raise objections and doubt the benefits of quality improvement efforts, skeptics force leaders to continually articulate the benefits and advantages of continuous improvement. To overcome the opposition, leaders have to demonstrate their dedication by changing their behaviors, attitudes, and beliefs. Skeptics who became champions of quality improvement after engagement are perceived as strong drivers because of their attitude and behavioral change.

The external and internal drivers discussed in this chapter led institutions to engage in quality improvement efforts and helped to sustain the momentum once the movement started. Our next question focused on how institutions implement quality practices. What we discovered is that across institutions systems have been developed to implement quality improvement concepts. The next section explains these systems that make quality improvement an integral part of the institutional culture.

CHAPTER 3

What Are the Systems That Institutions Have Developed and Implemented?

C ontinuous improvement is based on continuously making changes. One of the key principles of quality improvement is thinking of the institution as a system. Systems thinking takes place when all actions are considered to be part of interactive and interdependent systems. This means that a change in one part of the institution has an impact on the other parts. In analyzing the interview data, we discovered systems that emerged as a result of using continuous improvement. Therefore, we are using the concept of systems as an organizational scheme.

We identified nine significant systems across our institutions to implement quality principles and practices. The first one identified is a system for creating a culture of quality improvement. The second system helps people learn about quality principles and practices in order to start continuous improvement on campus. This initial learning is usually followed by a third system to develop and communicate the vision and mission statements. The fourth system facilitates and encourages professional development and growth in the area of continuous quality improvement. The fifth system is a method of collecting and analyzing data for decision making. The sixth is a system to develop improved methods of communicating among institutional members. The seventh system establishes ways to encourage and develop teamwork and collaboration. Because the behaviors, actions, and decisions that are made in the classroom are critical to the accomplishment of the educational mission of institutions, the eighth system focuses on how faculty members are improving the learning and teaching process. The final system revolves around how institutions are financially supporting their quality improvement efforts.

SYSTEMS THINKING

Before each of the nine systems is described, the significance of systems in general should be explained. A system is a whole that cannot be divided into independent parts. Each part of a system affects behaviors and properties of the whole system (Ackoff, 1995). According to Senge (1990), "Systems thinking is a conceptual framework for seeing interrelationships rather than things: for seeing patterns of change rather than static 'snapshots'" (p. 68). The outcome of a system is based on how each part is interacting with the rest of the parts, not on how each part is doing (Kofman and Senge, 1993). Likewise, for quality principles and practices to have the greatest impact, all of the principles need to be practiced simultaneously and systematically. Each principle affects the entire institutional system and is not as effective as an independent principle.

"Systems thinking is the cornerstone of how learning organizations think about their world." (Senge, 1990, p. 69). Senge (1990) believes that the need for understanding how organizations learn and accelerate that learning is essential in the increasingly dynamic, interdependent, and unpredictable environment. This is particularly true for higher education institutions. Learning organizations emphasize adapting to change by shifting the thinking from reacting to the present to creating the future.

The institutions in our study understand the concept of systems thinking and are working hard to shift the paradigm from acting and operating independently to thinking and working dependently. Most interviewees said that they try to promote this type of thinking so that decisions are consistently made with an understanding of how the outcome will influence other parts of the institution. One quality coordinator described their quality efforts this way:

> Our goal is to learn from each other. We are creating a system and technological network to help us learn. We are also training a pool of facilitators who are available to help wherever needed within the system.

One faculty member expressed it as follows:

> Because of continuous improvement efforts, I understand more about how interdependent we all are than in my first 25 years in the district. I work with people across this campus. Now I understand how the success of my class is directly related to so many different people on this campus. It is not just me on the center of that stage.

Through our interviews we were able to ascertain that the key principle in continuous improvement is an understanding of the interrelationships among the numerous parts of the system. Systems thinking, however, has not been the norm in higher education. For example, we heard:

> Systems thinking is difficult for faculty because they often have little connection with the larger picture. They are more like independent entrepreneurs who are accustomed to working alone.

One president said that developing a systems perspective is the most challenging part for him:

> One of the most difficult personal changes that I am making is the interdependent point, the respect for diversity and differences, and honoring persons at all levels of the organization. It is so easy to bring out a competitive sense with which we have been ingrained. I have tried to resist this and to work for the greater good of the interdependent reality that we are trying to build.

One administrator elaborated on the shift in mind-set that is required:

> The planning and budgeting processes that we used in our institutions in the past had been set up in a paradigm of competition and what we are working toward is an alignment to see how one area supports the other. We are working on a way of sharing and understanding how the resources need to be deployed systematically.
>
> There are inputs that come into the system in terms of planning; you have to talk about what the budget does to support your mission and your vision and what indicators are being worked on. Then when there has been an initial pass on how the budget is going to be distributed, this information goes back to the workforce before decisions are reached with instructions.

Another administrator warned against using quality tools without systems thinking:

> Process management and process data collection is the only way you are going to get to true systems analysis, and that requires significant quality efforts. But the context for me is much larger than just that. This does not mean that quality is not programmatic, but that it is an integral process. Thinking systematically is central to the whole process. Without being able to use that in the service of looking at a broader context of systems is missing the point. It is easy to get focused on the tools and process management and not be able to see where all that is going in terms of a larger picture. It is important to understand the interdependence of the processes within the system.

Even though systems thinking has not been the thinking of the past, we were told by several interviewees that the future of their institutions depends on the ability of administrators, faculty, and staff to develop a systems perspective and to make decisions that benefit the entire system.

Because a systems orientation is thinking "outside the box" for many in higher education, we realized that it requires *asking different questions* from those asked in the past. Decisions based upon tradition or history are not adequate anymore. A president provided us with an anecdote to illustrate this point:

> Why do we need to have deadlines with graduation? Why should we make someone who finishes in February wait until May to get the degree? These questions were raised by a graduate student who made us think about our system. We decided to change the system. Since we are not a traditional college, we decided that we did not need to follow the traditional model. This has been a great service to students. We continue to question the status quo.

Systems thinking views students as stakeholders and perceives every interaction as an opportunity to satisfy them. Engaging in systems thinking for faculty members means that they understand that what they teach is related to what their fellow faculty members teach.

In our interviews, we heard about departments asking how they can better serve other departments when teaching support courses. The following story best illustrates how faculty members are beginning to think about the interrelationships of what they do:

> I taught the first-level theory course, and I was asked to teach the second level. Since I did not know what the third level required, I enrolled in the third-level course so that I would know how to teach the second level. I wanted to be a good supplier for the third-level instructor.

The following account is along this same line:

> The program of which I am most proud is a program evaluation system. This uses CQI and the learning systems approach. We have had four departments go through that with some outstanding results. The breakthrough is in faculty understanding how interconnected they are and how they need to work together as a group.

Retention of students and developing relationships with alumni are important areas for institutions to address. Before the quality initiative, faculty members indicated that they did not think about students as potential alumni. Even though it seems logical, many faculty members remarked that looking at students in terms of long-term relationships with the institution is new to them. When enrollments were consistently growing, faculty members did not worry about having enough students to fill their classes. One faculty member remarked, "In fact, sometimes there were too many students." Because of the intense competition for students, public and independent institutions are now more concerned about retention:

> We have a student refund process that would have been easy to fix as an administrative process, but we included faculty and students. The process went from over four months to get a student refund to where the student can receive the refund in 72 hours. But inside the process we have an

ombudsperson who works for the students to try and save the transaction and to get the student back into a class before the institution has to refund the money. This process agrees with our mission of student learning.

Another example of systems thinking is the pattern we found of some faculty members treating each other as stakeholders with needs. Some members are also beginning to change how they think about students both in and out of the classroom. As a result of this thinking, institutions have developed systems to better satisfy and retain students.

Another important member of the system is employers of college graduates. Higher education institutions need to be concerned about how potential employers are evaluating the quality of their graduates. In the institutions in our study, we sensed a heightened awareness about the competency of graduates and their ability to satisfy the needs of employers. One administrator stated it this way:

In our field, the human service professions are decidedly the future employers of our students. Not only do I have to graduate a "product" that is acceptable to them, but it is odd for faculty members to think of students as the product. If we graduate ill-trained social workers, ill-trained counselors or teachers, we would be negatively influencing our reputation in the community.

Another aspect of systems thinking is including the board as an important component of the system. Since governing boards often serve to drive quality initiatives, it is important to understand that they are also part of the system to improve processes and systems. As part of the system, boards are spending time on systemic and quality improvement issues. At one institution, the board initiated a teaching center:

The chair of the trustees long-range planning committee got the idea of a planning commission that would involve trustees, faculty, and administrators. The commission was divided into subgroups, one of which was charged with long-range planning for learning and teaching. That group recommended a teaching improvement center. Foundation support was received through grants written by several members, one of whom was the president.

According to one president,

Our board meets quarterly, and we try to educate our board at every meeting. We try to showcase improvement such as having a team come in to present improvements made or it might be the provost reporting on some innovation.

It was common to hear faculty members, administrators, and staff members use system terms when they described their quality efforts. They indicated that they are aware of the interconnections of what they do. Below are some administrators' comments that illustrate systems thinking:

> We are working to develop better systems that provide excellent customer service.

> We are taking a systemic view so that we can measure and improve the system. We are identifying the major systems that operate in the university and developing measures so that improvements can be made.

> We need to open our doors and understand the relationships and connectedness between people. We need to get outside our own space.

These comments emphasize concepts that are not typical in most higher education institutions: interconnectedness, systems, measurements, and improvements. They imply that people are thinking differently about the work they do. We found a pattern of people *asking different questions* about interdependence and relationships. In other words, across institutions people are cognizant of the systems in which they operate and the interconnectedness of the systems.

It was fairly easy for the people we interviewed to provide examples of systems. One administrator described the changes in how goals are being established. Because of the university's quality efforts, all departments have goals and objectives. Many of the goals are related to the budget process, and the departments continuously evaluate their progress so that improvements are made. Goals are established by taking into consideration the interrelationships among the departments.

In another example, an administrator explained how systems thinking is used to apply for the Malcolm Baldrige National Quality Award:

> The committee started to work early in the spring on adapting the Baldrige criteria to the university. We used those criteria for the self-study such as customer feedback, benchmarking, and plans for improvement. All of the budget units will use these methods in writing up the Baldrige assessment. We will apply for the Baldrige, but what is really important to us is that we have a valuable tool with which to look at ourselves. We took the criteria and made someone in charge of each one. Each one of these processes is being studied by a group. They are mapping out each of the processes. For example, the bookstore will study the process used to order textbooks. They will flowchart that process in order to improve it.

When the institutions in our study are striving to improve processes, the parts (department, divisions, programs, majors) are not as significant to them as the interrelationships of the parts. This shift in thinking is a prerequisite for understanding how to implement quality principles and practices. Systems thinking is a new way of operating that involves *asking different questions* than in the past.

If an institution is systems oriented, processes are continually being ana-lyzed to determine if improvements can be made. Regardless if the goal is to reduce costs or to improve service, processes are studied with a systems perspective. Institutions discovered that some of the most dramatic improve-ments are made by improving the relationships among people within processes and between processes. By analyzing the whole process as a system, people begin to understand the significance of streamlining processes to save time and to improve services.

Continuously improving processes involves making changes that benefit the entire institution. Even though departments traditionally act as indepen-dent units, many of the processes are the same across departments. Many of the tasks requested of faculty members regarding students and courses are standard processes. It makes sense then that if the process is improved, multiple departments benefit from the improvements.

Interviewees consistently expressed that as a result of the quality efforts they are more aware of processes and the interrelationships of the processes. People stated that they have to think about what they will do next, the next steps in the process. As one described,

> We have more of a focus on the customer, which is a major change in thinking. We used to think we knew what students needed and wanted. We used to do what was best for us, not them. Now we consider employees to be customers, and we respect students and employees. We focus on processes and systems. We examine how things are done where before processes were haphazard. We ask ourselves what will the students think about this and we get their input.

Once people become aware of the process, they have to think about how to continuously improve it. Systems thinking is a continual cycle: focus on the process, practice the process, and improve the process.

Most institutions begin making changes by examining processes. The following quotes are representative of how institutions are systematically reviewing processes:

> When I came here, we went through every process from top to bottom. We put together a master schedule of all of the processes.

> We identified the processes that needed immediate attention. Then we created teams for groupings of processes.

> We used quality principles to get ready for reaccreditation. In the self-study, we identified the processes that needed to be improved.

When we asked how to start improving processes, interviewees commonly advised us to start by finding an existing process or system that needs to be improved, a process that many people have to use with some regularity. This strategy engendered the least resistance because people can see tangible results from work put forth by improving an existing system. Examples of processes that were addressed include:

> Career placement services are using the quality principles. They had been on different calendars, different accounting systems, it was very confusing. They formed a senior experience group and started examining the place-ment statistics. They reorganized the process. That would not have happened without a commitment to quality.

> In one office, they kept track of students in card files. They had two card files of several hundred cards because there were two different offices that used the information and each wanted the cards organized differently. They were maintaining double records on cards because they did not believe the process could be computerized because it was too personal. This process is now computerized and drastically improved.

> A common problem for community colleges is how to promote the degree-planning process. In studying the process, we discovered there were so many things we were not doing; we were impeding the process by not making it real and important to them. This is important in retaining students. We now have a degree-planning process driven by faculty.

Institutions are using quality principles and practices that have been incorporated into their own systems in order to continuously improve. Our analysis revealed several systems that support the never-ending drive for improvement. These systems enable the institution to create a culture of quality; to learn about quality; to develop and communicate vision and mission statements that are outcomes driven; to develop employees in quality improvement concepts; to make decisions based on data; to effectively com-municate within the institution; to involve and empower employees toward teamwork and collaboration; to improve learning and teaching processes; and to financially support the quality efforts. The remainder of this chapter describes the various systems that our institutions have established to help them sustain quality initiatives on campus. While reading about these systems, keep in mind that each system is dependent upon the other systems for meaningful change and improvements to occur.

SYSTEM 1: CREATING A QUALITY CULTURE

Institutional culture is the "invisible tapestry" that weaves together all parts and members of the institution (Kuh and Whitt, 1988). It influences how people feel, think, and act. More specifically, culture in higher education is the collection of norms, values, practices, beliefs, and assumptions that guide behaviors of individuals and groups in institutions. To successfully implement quality principles, institutional cultures must change. As one administrator stated, "That is what this whole quality thing is about. It is about culture change."

The institutions in our study developed an awareness and a clearer understanding of the significance of institutional culture because of the need to change it. People practicing quality principles are needed to create a quality culture. Getting people to practice quality principles can happen in different ways: people change their attitudes and behaviors, people are hired who believe in quality improvement, or people who do not believe in quality improvement tend to leave. Because an institution is a collection of individuals, culture is a reflection of these individuals, and any change must start at the individual level.

Through professional development, people learn that quality improvement is a part of every position and that improving systems and processes is not the responsibility of another department or someone else's job. Rather than viewing principles of quality improvement as more work, people who have been educated in quality principles are beginning to understand that continuous improvement is how work should be done, that quality improvement is not an add-on. We were told that the most productive people seem to be open to new ideas and want to become better at whatever they are doing.

There are numerous ways to make continuous improvement part of the institutional culture. An important step is to establish an infrastructure that supports taking risks, learning from experiences and from each other, and incorporating feedback. In addition, several institutions are cross-training people so that they do not have to replace every person who leaves the institution. Involving people in decision making at all levels is another way to create a culture in which people feel valued and believe that their ideas are heard. Institutions are more likely to retain members when employees are satisfied with their positions. Increased participation usually leads to higher levels of loyalty, which, in turn, contributes to retaining employees. Designing reward structures and incentives to encourage people to think, feel, and act in ways that are consistent with continuous improvement also helps to create an environment that supports quality initiatives.

To understand how to create a culture that supports continuous improvement and continuous learning, we asked our interviewees to state their core principles. The main ideas that emerged focus on striving to satisfy stakeholders, involving others in improving processes and solving problems, thinking differently about their work, and driving fear out of the organization.

A general belief across institutions was that members have become more stakeholder focused as a result of implementing quality principles. "Satisfying those we serve" was explained as an institutional transformation. A college president expressed the importance of serving others:

Our core principles include helping people reflect on the aim of their work, which is clarity of mission. We have people reflect on their work by using cross-functional teams and gathering data. We particularly emphasize reflecting on the people served such as student needs, related customer preferences. We focus on finding out the real needs of the people we serve.

Getting an institution to this point is not an easy task. Before any progress can be made, individuals must change their behaviors.

Changing Behaviors

Changing a culture requires individuals to change. One college president shared this sentiment about culture:

A quality culture is about aligning to a shared mission and vision. Once this takes place, the styles, skills, systems, and the strategies used are synchronized to help move the institution in a common direction. This is the culture you are trying to develop. The important point is that it is a process that is inside out. It involves a personal transformation. At our institution, we allow members to bring their significant other with them to development sessions. We have educated whole families as a result of the quality movement. People are personally affected by this.

Changing the culture also involves changing management practices and systems. It includes creating an environment in which people can learn and grow on their own. Interviewees at three institutions shared examples of how the culture in the physical plant of the institution was changing as a result of implementing quality principles:

We have had major changes in the physical plant. We did away with punch in and punch out time cards. The supervisors were threatened, but they were the problem. One supervisor would not change from the command and control type leadership, and he was removed.

We are working with the plant department, ingrained union guys. I found it was good to agree with them at first, acknowledging this is the way it is and we want to improve. So much of building commitment is hanging in there and going slowly.

The physical plant had a bad situation with leadership. The quality culture got in up there because people wanted to get outside a dictatorial style of leadership. It brought us to a crisis. Now the leadership has changed to be more personal. They have become more customer-focused, asking how things could have been improved. They have streamlined processes and improved customer relations.

It was interesting that administrators and staff members selected examples dealing with the physical plant of the institution. Employees in the physical plant work behind the scenes and are not necessarily considered to be front-line service people. In reality, these workers have a major impact on how the facilities operate and how the operations are perceived. They play a key role in student and employee satisfaction. Getting people in the physical plant interested in quality improvement efforts makes great strides in changing the institutional culture.

To understand quality improvement, our interviewees had to shift their mind-set from one of competition and independence to one of collaboration and interdependence. One respondent elaborated,

> There are many misconceptions about quality. It is really an attitude. People think it is about following manuals and using tools. Instead, it is an attitude of collegiality and continuous improvement.

Changing a culture also requires an environment that encourages members to continue learning. The role of management becomes one of establishing this learning environment for members. In the institutions we studied, people reported feeling comfortable in taking risks in order to learn from their mistakes. Problems are viewed as opportunities to focus on *what* was wrong, not *who* was wrong. With this perspective, continuous learning results in continuous improvement. As one respondent noted,

> An indicator of our commitment to quality may be our ability to admit our mistakes and to correct the mistakes for customers.

As organizations learn to adjust to the societal and economic challenges, quality improvement becomes an asset. One staff member related how quality practices have created a more accepting culture of diversity. She observed that the quality practices are in harmony with the practices advocated for valuing diversity:

> As a black American in a predominately white institution, the respect for people concept of the quality movement is very important. We have rules of conduct posted at meetings such as no person is more important than any other and everybody has something to offer. We generate the rules at the meeting.

Changing individual behaviors is the start to creating such a culture of diversity, trust, and understanding, but institutions must take steps to ensure that these behaviors are encouraged and rewarded.

Creating a Culture of Quality Improvement

Before analyzing ways to change the culture, it is important to keep in mind that creating a culture that supports quality principles and practices does not mean disregarding the existing culture. People continue to value the historical culture, particularly the aspects that have been successful for the institution and for the members. Interviewees stated that they want the institutional culture to be respected even as attempts are made to change the culture. "Preserve the Best and Improve the Rest" is a motto that reflects what we heard throughout our interviews. One of the presidents said that even as the leaders are trying to open up communication channels, utilize teams, involve others, and improve systems, it is important to work within the culture in which the leaders find themselves. Respecting the past while improving the future requires an awareness and level of sensitivity that is easy to overlook as leaders pursue continuous improvement.

Because of this difficulty of balancing a respect for the old culture with the desire to create a new culture, we were especially interested in specific examples of how the quality culture is being created. Several examples were shared with us. Some of the actions taken are major changes from how business was conducted in the past; other examples seem rather small and trivial. What we discovered, though, is that smaller actions can make as significant an impact as major changes.

All of the examples cited here are methods used to create a different tone and atmosphere in the workplace. The goals are to open up communication channels, to recognize the efforts of others, and to involve people in decision making. Even though this transformation is a long-term process, the ultimate goal is to drive out fear so that people feel comfortable in making improvements and focus on learning from their experiences. The following are experiences of people who are taking steps to create a culture of quality improvement:

> We conducted an employee survey and there were serious issues of communication and trust on campus. So the president held open forums with everyone. Several teams spun off from that, but one team was charged with making this a more joyful workplace. They conducted focus groups to determine what kind of events to host. They requested a dress-down day on Fridays. We have had parades and Halloween costumes. We hosted a laugh therapist. Everyone gets to go to the events if possible. We give a lighten up award to the department, individual, or work area that has demonstrated the lightest, most fun attitude at the institution. It has enabled us to not be so serious about everything.

> We embrace new ideas and philosophies and we have garnered unusual benefits because of this attitude. We have wonderful visionaries in the community surrounding the institution who are supportive. The visionaries helped to create an Institute for Effective Teaching, which helps teachers at all levels address the dramatically changing environment. They have unlocked the doors to progress.

> We started to have afternoon teas composed of a mix of 20 faculty and staff each time. Two administrators attended each tea. Each group receives a formal invitation. The governing ideas are to say thank you for

their efforts; to define reality such as what are our mission, vision, and values; and to discuss another pressing question at the time. The question for the last tea concerned how to pay people better. We wanted to talk about questions in the compensation system.

We want people to understand the system. We spend 60 percent of the budget on salaries. When we hire people, we dilute the pool of money for salaries. People need to work smarter and understand the system of improvement. Everyone was given a lapel pin and shook hands with the president. Before people came to the tea, they had to complete a card with two basic questions: How does my job impact retention? What are the best things going at this institution? Plus we had great desserts!

These examples reveal that quality practices have been implemented at these institutions. People at all levels of the institutions are being involved and empowered to make decisions. They understand the value of creating a culture where people want to work and where they strive to improve, which is the very essence of the quality movement. The remaining subtopics of this system describe ways institutions can ensure that this culture change takes place, on both the individual and institutional level.

Hiring and Retaining the Best People

When members view the institution as a system of interrelated parts, they understand the significance of hiring a new person into the system. Institutions have improved their hiring systems to help them hire the best person for the system by making the interview process more rigorous and data driven. The following examples illustrate some of the changes that have been made in the hiring process:

We are careful in the hiring process. We go through a script about the vision, our two focuses of academic excellence and continuous quality improvement. I try to impress on these people what we are trying to accomplish with quality.

We are working on a synopsis of what we mean by quality so that all candidates can read it over before they come for interviews. In the interviews they can react to it and tell us to what extent they are concerned about customer satisfaction. We ask to what degree they are interested in cross-functional relationships.

When hiring people, we look for people who are open to new ideas, are willing to go through quality training, believe in assessment, and are enthusiastic about change. We highly encourage faculty to attend workshops on various teaching topics.

Every person hired by the institution has a chance to influence its culture, so every position takes on greater significance in the hiring process. As one administrator said,

> We try to view all positions as professional positions. Instead of perceiving positions as clerical, we view people in student services as professionals. Our goal is to hire the best people for all positions.

One institution in our study continues to stress that quality principles, particularly servant leadership, are congruent with the mission of an institution with a religious affiliation. At this institution, all full-time employees are required to indicate on the application that they are practicing Christians. (The institution is allowed to do this because it is an independent institution with a church affiliation.) This policy has aligned people to the institutional mission because they share common values and acknowledge that fact.

Another institution hires people for only one year to see if they fit into the culture. This policy is another way to apply the Plan-Do-Check-Act (PDCA) cycle, collecting data before making long-term decisions.

Many interviewees told us that some people do not want to change, do not believe in the quality efforts, and do not fit into the quality culture. It is thought that many of these people leave because they do not feel comfortable in the new culture being created:

> At the library we had a staff person quit because we had empowered her to make decisions and she was not comfortable with that. She was doing her job well, but she wanted a structured environment. When we hire people now, we tell them that we expect them to be team members and to be willing to change things.

> One faculty member retired because he could not stand the word "customer."

> If people do not have the incentive to be a part of the quality movement, that is not the problem. The problem is we have the wrong people.

Because quality improvement is based on individuals improving, each person in the institution either helps or harms the culture. One president shared the following story:

> At one institution with a quality culture, a new president came in who did not appreciate the culture. The president did not survive in the culture. Now another leader has emerged who seems to be able to support and enhance the culture, and I predict the new leader will survive.

A staff member made this comment:

> Sometimes the personnel changes have not been made that are really needed. We are told it is the process not the person, but sometimes it really is the person.

The people we interviewed said that members are extremely aware of decisions that are made, particularly hiring decisions. Administrators are making a conscious effort to hire people who believe in the mission of the institution and in continuous improvement.

Involving and Empowering Members

Once institutions hire the best people, they want to keep them. We were told that retention is improved by empowering members. Empowering others entails involving them in decision-making processes. Our research revealed that for the most part members feel more involved in decision making after quality initiatives were begun than before. The new systems have changed how people think about their work and how they interact with one another. They are taking more ownership, and because they are being included in the decision-making processes, they are coming up with new ideas. As a result, institutional members have more input and believe more in the system.

Our interviewees emphasized that responsibility accompanies empowerment. It is difficult to involve and empower members if they are not prepared to accept the responsibility. Perhaps the best working definition of empowerment was expressed by one administrator:

> Empowerment means giving the people with the knowledge, skills, and abilities to affect the system the power to change the system. The infrastructure has to give people the knowledge, skills, and abilities in the first place.

She continued,

> Empowerment is not giving a six-year-old a gun. Empowerment has responsibility to go with it. People cannot change their work unless they know their work.

One administrator added,

> People have not been punished for making mistakes as we would have expected in the past. There is an appreciation for solving the problem. Our provost said that one person used to be leading a meeting. Now it is better because people are not so passive, they participate because they feel empowered.

Another elaborated,

> In an empowering culture, the role is to lead and not to manage. People need to carve time out to be leaders. People will find the time to do the things that are important because these things are job enhancing. The difference is that someone is not telling you to do it, but rather it becomes your responsibility.

Interviewees made it clear that they believe good leaders create other leaders. Effective leaders develop others by placing them in positions and liberating them to do their work. In the institutions we studied, leaders at all levels have significant roles in driving quality improvement. We found that creating more leaders adds momentum. According to one administrator,

Empowering others begins with listening to people on the fringes of the existing paradigms. These people start challenging the status quo, challenging the mind-sets. One of the things the leaders can do is help promote that. Leaders need to encourage people to discuss the undiscussables. If leaders foster creativity and dialogue, leadership will emerge, and it will sustain itself in that organization over time.

A president expressed a similar view:

Leaders are people you follow to places where you would not go yourself. I think you have to create a lot of leaders and in the process hopefully destroy some of the old images of control. When you begin to move from controlling to trying to influence the organization, you make it possible for many people to take on leadership roles.

When we asked for examples of how employees are being involved and empowered, interviewees responded by saying things such as there is more participation in decision making, more people are willing to delegate to others, and there is a conscious attempt to listen to everyone. People reported that new committees have been formed that would never have existed before the emphasis on quality improvement. For example, one institution formed a Human Resource Advisory Board that has collegewide representation, including staff. This board advises the human resource department on personnel issues concerning faculty, administrators, and staff. Since the success of continuous improvement efforts is based on all members working together, it is important to address the concerns of everyone, which this board does.

Another example of involvement focused on empowering a team. At one institution, a cross-functional team from six offices came together to solve a problem that emerged in a student survey. Students perceived that they were getting the "runaround" from various offices on campus, and this perception led to student dissatisfaction. A team of front-line people, no deans and no vice-presidents, was given the opportunity to study and to make recommendations to improve the situation. Based on the team's recommendation, they were able to create a one-stop shopping experience for all students without adding personnel. As the president of this institution reported:

We were able to create leadership capacity in the people who work in the various offices and to promote them. This experience gave them a chance to grow and to learn. That is what needs to be done throughout the institution in order to build the capacity for leadership.

At another instutution, a staff member said that his president encourages employees to go to conferences to spread their quality improvement story and to help other institutions. At this institution, front-line people organized a quality conference for the state that 200 people attended. This is what the quality movement is all about—the people doing the work are given the authority and freedom to make changes.

Recognizing and Rewarding Members

Because continuous quality improvement is based on changing behaviors and attitudes, a system of recognizing and rewarding members facilitates and even accelerates these changes. This is a critical system in developing a new culture. Yet, interviewees across institutions informed us that they are most ambivalent about the progress and effectiveness of this reward system. When we asked what incentives have been used to encourage people to learn and to apply the concepts of continuous improvement, a general consensus emerged that ways to recognize and reward employees is the area in which most institutions are struggling. Making it even more challenging is the reality that most institutions are operating their quality efforts on an extremely limited budget, if any budget at all. As one quality coordinator stated,

> We select outstanding teams at our comprehensive quality event where all teams display their projects, and then we do not know how to reward or recognize them. Since the institution has a tight budget, we do not feel like it is appropriate to spend money on quality awards.

From another perspective, a president said that at his institution they continue to have a philosophical debate on this topic. The president continued by saying

> We try to remove the barriers that keep people from doing good work. How do you reinforce the culture you are trying to create? This is a question we continue to discuss.

Many interviewees concluded that the methods to recognize and reward people at their institutions are ineffective. The most common reason given was that rewards are not a norm in the culture of higher education institutions, and therefore, institutions are inexperienced in this area. Administrators understand that rewarded behaviors tend to be repeated. As a result, they are in the process of developing different ways to recognize and reward members. They realize that recognition is a powerful motivator, but on limited budgets institutions are finding this system to be a challenge. One respondent explained the dilemma by saying

> We have floundered with rewards and recognition. We have had a difficult time finding ways to recognize people. Employees feel they are not recognized, yet it is hard to individualize rewards so that people are satisfied.

To determine what rewards are appropriate and what members value, some institutions conduct focus groups and/or design surveys to collect data from employees rather than relying on assumptions. At one institution, the findings of the focus groups were communicated by e-mail for reactions from the rest of the workforce. In another institution, a staff member told us that everyone on the payroll was surveyed to determine what efforts should be rewarded and how these efforts should be rewarded. Their findings revealed that people want to be recognized for attendance at work and for not fully utilizing their sick time. The most popular response as an incentive was not monetary, but for a supervisor "to come to us and say thank you."

Echoing this pattern, another president said that her institution also uses surveys and focus groups to find out what people value. Employees are asked questions such as the following: What do you want to be recognized for? Who should recognize you? How should you be recognized? The results revealed that the majority of employees want to be recognized for customer service, commitment to quality improvement, money savings, innovations, and team-work. They want to be recognized by their immediate supervisor and the college president. They want a letter to go in their personnel file and a certificate or plaque to place on the wall.

Rewards play a powerful role in creating a quality improvement culture, yet rewards are often used ineffectively. According to Kerr (1995), numerous examples of reward systems exist that recognize behaviors that the rewarder is trying to discourage, while the desired behavior is not being recognized at all. Some examples from Kerr (1995, p. 15) include

We hope for . . .	But we reward . . .
Teamwork and collaboration	The best members
Innovative thinking and risk taking	Not making mistakes
Development of people skills	Technical achievements
Employee involvement and empowerment	Tight control over operations and resources
High achievement	Another year's effort and work

The interviewees commonly admitted that it is difficult to break out of old ways of thinking about rewards. Institutions often lack a holistic, systematic view of performance factors and results. Although they realize that rewards should be based on the performance of the whole system and not subunits or departments within, traditional habits, policies, and procedures are hard to change. The focus should be long-range, not on short-term results.

Giving Rewards

Despite the problems with giving rewards, we discovered that institutions are trying a combination of tangible and intangible rewards. Because quality improvement requires that individuals improve, many members reported that they are most satisfied and motivated by intangible or intrinsic rewards. At one institution, cross-functional teams make presentations to senior leadership and to the governing board. Interviewees related that they value the respect and consideration given to their work. The fact that they are interacting with senior leaders and trustees is interpreted as special recognition for work well done. At other institutions, teams gain recognition during a special event on campus. During these events, teams from all over campus have the chance to display their process improvement projects to the rest of the college community. Our research revealed that people perceive these events as rewarding and as a source of motivation to continue with their quality efforts.

In the institutions studied, many of the most powerful incentives and rewards are often simple, such as institutional staff being rewarded with additional education. Other small incentives are acknowledgments from a supervisor for a job well done, which are often considered enough of a reward for members of the institution. A thank you note from the president is considered to be a special reward at one institution. Another president awards presidential mugs for special recognition, and people indicated the mugs are appreciated. A team photo acknowledging services rendered displayed on a prominent wall and a tree planted in honor of a dedicated worker are two more examples of rewards.

Along this same line, one institution conducts a survey of graduating seniors. Included on the survey is a question that asks the students to name the person(s) who has had the most positive effect on their college experience. A letter is sent to the individuals stating how many students mentioned them (e.g., 13 people listed you as having the most positive effect). This institution also asks a question about one positive experience that will be remembered after leaving the university. Each person who is mentioned is notified via e-mail and is congratulated in a hand-written note from a senior administrator. Sometimes an entire department is recognized. If this is the case, an e-mail message is sent to all members of the department. We were told that members find this feedback to be very positive.

Several administrators mentioned a suggestion system as another example of an incentive system. In the campus buildings, there are suggestion boxes with forms to be completed by anyone walking in the buildings. They tried to develop a process by which a certain number of suggestions submitted earn individuals coffee mugs or other small gifts, but the interviewees reported that they were not interested in these items. The administrators realized that the tangible gifts are not the driving force behind the suggestions, and instead they found that people are intrinsically motivated by the fact that action is being taken based on their suggestions. They concluded that when people who submitted suggestions saw action being taken, they felt rewarded. Once they realized how powerful an action-oriented suggestion system could be, the administrators at this particular institution became even more determined to listen to the suggestions being offered.

It was interesting that people perceived working for a charismatic, well-liked, and respected president as intrinsically rewarding. They reported that notes of appreciation from the president are valued and that working with an individual who is inspiring increases the level of motivation. One president said that handwritten notes of thanks and appreciation are sent regularly. Even though this method of recognition may appear small and common, the difference is that a sincere effort is made to make it a systematic process that happens continually and not sporadically. It was stressed that if sending a note of appreciation is going to be a regular occurrence, effort needs to be made so that the note is regarded as sincere and not perceived as an impersonal form letter. This is where creativity and innovation become important. These actions and gestures are perceived to be rewarding and motivating only if members believe the incentives are sincerely given by credible people and only when they are continually given. In other words, rewards must be systematically distributed in a culture of trust.

Although tangible gifts are usually thought to be less motivating, they are helpful in keeping quality initiatives visible. The institutions we studied are continuing to develop reward systems. One institution developed a system in which any member could nominate another member at any time for a quality award. In this system, there are no losers. Anyone who is nominated receives an award in the form of a plaque and icon at the department level. The department determines whether the name of the nominee will be forwarded to the president for college-level recognition. If the department recommends the nominee, the award is given. It is also possible for someone from outside the department to make recommendations to the president, and those nominations are considered for awards as well. All award winners for the month participate in a drawing for a $50 gift certificate. Presidential coffee mugs are given by the president to people who have an outstanding accomplishment that is outside the standard criteria. Although the system is being continually improved, we learned through our interviews that members are beginning to feel a sense of accomplishment and recognition for their continuous improvement efforts.

Many of the people involved in continuous improvement do not expect rewards for what they do. In fact, a faculty member commented about our visit, "The fact that we are here talking today with you and communicating about our efforts, that's rewarding enough." But the truth is that rewards and recognition can help to create a culture that reinforces making changes and challenging the status quo. Rewards let members know that new behaviors are expected and encouraged.

Rewards for faculty teaching already exist in many institutions whose primary mission is teaching, but research-oriented institutions have also started to look at effective teaching and service as being important components in a faculty member and are trying to decide how these activities should be rewarded. One administrator of a research university commented

This is a new attitude in a research institution. You were rewarded on your research and the dollars you brought in. Teaching improvement is not financially rewarded yet, but at least people can talk about it. We have never addressed teaching before. Teaching used to be irrelevant. It was not a respected way to spend your time. The recognition for effective teaching has grown. The culture has changed. There has been a shift from perceiving teaching as irrelevant to perceiving it as a worthwhile endeavor.

Even though there are apparent problems with recognizing and rewarding members, we were still impressed with the time, thought, and energy of a few institutions. One institution, in particular, demonstrated creativity in how it funds its quality improvement budget. Because this institution is nationally recognized for its continuous improvement efforts, administrators are often featured speakers at conferences where honoraria are presented, and money received is donated by everyone to the quality improvement budget to help fund awards.

We were told that money is a prime motivator. There are different ways to distribute monetary awards so that more than one individual benefits:

In the hospital, we said that if we make the budget this year, we will share half of everything we make above the budget with the employees. The first year we wrote some $2,000 checks. We did not increase the base for anyone because it is a lump sum incentive. But we demonstrated that if employees help us save money through continuous improvement, employees will share in the savings.

We believe that quality has to be tied to compensation in order for people to make it a priority. We used to award people with plaques. Now we have a $5,000 stipend, $2,500 for the faculty member to use in making quality improvements, and $2,500 to help fund the department's quality efforts. It has been a tremendous motivator.

Systems to recognize and reward people are important because they encourage members to embrace change. Even actions that can be perceived as insignificant to people outside the institution are perceived by members within to be important steps in driving out fear and in creating an environment that supports continuous improvement.

Creating a Culture of Quality—Summary

Quality principles and practices require a shift in thinking to a systematic perspective and a long-term focus to create a culture of quality. Our interviewees were very conscious of their actions and behaviors and how what they do influences other members in the institution. We were told that this new awareness is a result of individuals changing their attitudes and behaviors. A change in personnel can also contribute to changing the culture. It became clear through our interviews that with each person hired the institutional culture is ultimately influenced. Involving and empowering members help them embrace the changes necessary for creating a quality culture. Methods to recognize and reward people can serve as incentives for members to engage in improvement efforts, although this area is one that interviewees felt needed the most work. Despite this problem, institutions are trying a combination of tangible and intangible rewards with varying degrees of success.

Although people in higher education are not accustomed to receiving rewards, it was insightful to learn that institutional leaders are collecting data to determine what people value. They are *asking different questions* of members so that they can make decisions based on facts rather than on tradition, intuition, or assumption. Only when behaviors change; when the best people are hired, involved, and empowered; and when they are recognized and rewarded appropriately are most institutions able to change the culture to one that supports continuous improvement on campus. Creating a quality culture is essential because as we were told

> Senior leaders come and go, unless you get continuous improvement into your culture, it will blow away.

We discovered that the institutional culture is the fabric that weaves quality principles and practices together. When people are trusting and able to openly communicate with one another, they are able to continuously improve. As one administrator stated, "We have to make quality a part of the culture." We found that people who are loyal to quality practices do not see any other options. As one administrator said, "I don't think we ever do NOT want to be a quality institution."

Creating a culture of quality begins with learning about how to implement quality principles and practices on campus. The next section, system 2, explains how leaders have established systems for learning about quality improvement.

SYSTEM 2: LEARNING ABOUT QUALITY PRINCIPLES

One of the first things that struck us as we conducted our interviews was that people at all levels are particularly concerned about learning and growing. Those with whom we spoke demonstrated, with few exceptions, a strong desire to learn from their mistakes and to improve situations within their institutions. These organizations are beginning to develop learning organizations "where people are continually expanding their capabilities to shape their future—that is, leaders are responsible for learning" (Senge, 1990, p. 9). This section describes specific ways leaders are learning about quality improvement and how they are creating learning organizations.

Starting to Learn about Quality Improvement

Typically, administrative leaders emerge through their specific disciplines, and they do not have backgrounds in management or leadership. This pattern was true in the institutions we studied as well. If leaders are going to drive the movement on campus, it is imperative that they learn about quality principles so that they can integrate quality practices. Therefore, how leaders are learning about continuous improvement is of primary interest since this learning is where most institutions need to start.

In the institutions in our study, presidents and other members of the senior leadership devote significant amounts of time to learning about quality principles. Most of the initial learning is done through reading. This reading is usually followed by leaders attending various seminars on quality improvement from which they develop a network of contacts and resource materials. A president expressed the system of learning this way:

> Top leadership has taken the lead in learning. We've gotten in there and learned ourselves not just by being the first people in classes but by doing a number of leadership activities ourselves. The most important part of that learning is that we have created some honest conversations about our own assumptions, our own ignorance, and our own shortcomings. I think it has been very important for people to see us reflecting candidly about our own practice.
>
> It is hard to overdo the top leaders having to learn. I think we should spend more time at the senior level developing an in-depth understanding about what we are trying to learn. I do not believe there are enough leaders out there who are willing to sit down and learn, who have the patience over the long haul to learn what needs to be learned and to do the quality of self-reflection that is part of that learning.

Another president added

> The first thing that I did was to read common literature with the leadership of the institution. We read and discussed the quality literature, and then a number of them started to attend conferences.

One president had a sabbatical to study leadership and continuous improvement by reading the literature and by visiting organizations in business and industry identified as making a commitment to quality improvement. He specifically interviewed the senior leaders about creating a continuous improvement culture. The goal was to study and benchmark leaders in businesses who had been identified as champions of quality improvement so that he could expedite his learning process. One of the best ways to learn is to teach. This president teaches a leadership course for first-year students every fall which includes quality principles and practices.

Usually leaders begin by reading the works of the U.S. quality "gurus," Deming, Juran, and Crosby. Several of the presidents began by attending a

Deming seminar; often they were accompanied by several senior officers, or they sent their senior staff to later seminars. One institution actually adapted Deming's 14 Principles (Deming, 1986) by rewriting them specifically for that institution. At this early point in their quality journeys, most of the institutions have not attempted to follow any one philosophy but are selecting the best from the literature and developing their own quality philosophy. In addition to the quality literature, some of the other books and reports mentioned by the presidents include *The Reflective Practitioner, Nation at Risk, Involvement in Learning, Servant Leadership, The Human Touch, The 7 Habits of Highly Effective People, The Deming Managment Method*, and "Seven Principles of Good Undergraduate Practice in Education."

Since the quality movement in higher education has gained momentum, there is a substantial literature base about continuous quality improvement in higher education. Authors such as Daniel Seymour, Dean Hubbard, Ted Marchese, Robert Cornesky, Ellen Chaffee, Lawrence Sherr, Brent Rubin, Trudy Banta, John Harris, and Steve Brigham, to name a few, have provided a wealth of background information for learning about the tools, techniques, and philosophies of continuous improvement in the context of higher education.

Once leaders have assimilated this new knowledge and feel comfortable with the concepts of quality improvement, the overall trend is to create learning organizations that educate members in quality principles and that support continuous learning.

Creating Learning Organizations

Learning organizations create structures and systems in which "people continually expand their capacity to create the results they truly desire, where new and expansive patterns of thinking are nurtured, where collective aspiration is set free, and where people are continually learning how to learn together" (Senge, 1990, p. 3). Learning organizations are able to weave a continuous and enhanced ability to learn, adapt, and change into their culture. The organizational values, policies, practices, systems, and structures encourage, support, and accelerate learning for all employees (Bennett and O'Brien, 1994). Wishart, Elam, and Robey (1996) believe the ability to continue learning is ensured through the institutionalization of structures and processes designed to promote learning. Structures and mechanisms do not guarantee learning will take place; however, the important criterion is whether the structures and mechanisms support the process of learning. If they do, then any organization has the potential to become a learning organization.

There were numerous examples of institutions working to become learning organizations in our study. For example, to facilitate a dialogue about the literature they read, several of the presidents have formed a leadership or quality council on their respective campuses to initiate and encourage the learning of others. The councils become the building blocks of learning organizations by selecting topics to discuss such as new paradigms, systems thinking, reengineering, and learning organizations. An administrator shared this story about how his institution continues to learn:

> We have what is called the uncommittee. This group is a reading group, like a literary circle. It started many years ago; it's supported by the foundation and this was an indication of the president's support for learning on the campus. There is a group that picks 10 books a year. It is a cross section of the faculty that selects books that are on the cutting edge for society and that may have some effect on higher education. People subscribe for $25 to help support it and once a month we have a discussion group. There are over 300 people on the campus involved in the uncommittee. It becomes a way of exchanging ideas. That told me a lot about the learning paradigm at this institution. All those things are really related to community building. The president feels that is the purpose.

A pattern also emerged of institutions creating links with their greater communities so that everyone can learn together. Particularly for financial reasons, the institutions in our study benefited from teaming up with business and industry. Several institutions are developing their people in quality principles for lower costs or for no costs because of their relationships with businesses in the area. We were told that staff, administrators, and people from the community enroll with college students in classes on quality management.

Personal transformation as a prerequisite for understanding quality improvement is a theme that was reinforced throughout our interviews. Since quality principles and practices emphasize that individuals must change for organizations to change, Stephen Covey's *The 7 Habits of Highly Effective People* is one source that is being used as a starting point for educating people about the quality movement at several of the institutions in our study. The habits in Covey's book are said to help people personally relate to the concepts of continuous improvement. As stated by one president,

> I am an advocate of Stephen Covey's principles because they link personal behavior with the organization. As far as I know, there is no other theorist who does this as clearly as Covey. The fundamental principle at the personal level is trustworthiness. I thought it was only character and then I found out that it is confidence as well. I thought that empowerment was given. It's not; it comes from within. If you have the right kind of environment, you will have empowerment. Then you have the concept of alignment. I carry a compass with me to remind me of my moral compass. I don't govern my life by a calendar or a watch, but by my moral compass.

Once the learning system is in place, it appears to take on a life of its own. The more people learn about quality improvement, the more they seek out additional information. For example, it was common for a group of people within an institution to attend a workshop through a connection with industry and to bring the information from that workshop back to campus. The size of the group varied, but interviewees consistently indicated that the people who attended the seminars returned with a new philosophy on how work should be conducted and for whom they are working. Using one top administrator's description as an example, the story line went like this:

> I have a friend who was vice president for health care for a large private hospital. He kept updating me on what he was learning about the quality movement. He was a member of the quality board of the hospital, and his peers on the board were quality people from Xerox, 3M, IBM, and Millikan, to name a few. That is how I got the initial exposure to quality. I brought that information back to the institution. Then I was introduced to a quality champion at another institution and I invited him to campus for a visit. He recommended I call another quality champion, which I did, and he came for a one-day visit. He told us about a consultant who helped them get their movement off the ground. She came for a three-day orientation to the senior leadership team. After three days, the Chancellor said, "I am interested enough. We should have a steering committee." So that is how we got started.

We found that once institutions have an introduction to quality principles and practices, many of them rely on outside consultants to spearhead the movement on campus. Interviewees said that consultants bring expertise from other institutions, which helps to jump start quality improvement efforts. Many of the same consultants were mentioned across institutions as people who have helped them pursue their quality journey.

The leaders we interviewed have learned new behaviors to enable them to drive the quality improvement efforts and to transform their institutions into learning organizations. They stressed that they have to listen to members at all levels, demonstrate their commitment to quality improvement by their changed actions, cultivate trust between all constituencies and themselves, and involve others in making decisions. When leaders communicate effectively, they realize that people notice. The following statements reflect these important leadership characteristics:

> We have an enrollment problem. We have never had layoffs and the fact that we are considering them can be a time for panic. Ideally under a quality improvement philosophy, this is a time for brainstorming, for creativity, for looking for different ways of doing things. For thinking outside the box . . . . Our administrators are doing that.

> Our president uses silence as a tool. He knows when to be quiet and listen. There is clearly a difference in the administrators' daily routines and in their management styles. It is much more orderly and positive.

It is vital that leaders use their new quality knowledge to create learning organizations that constantly look for ways to improve—the essence of the quality movement.

Learning about Quality Principles—Summary

We discovered a clear pattern related to the level of knowledge and understanding of the quality movement: the deeper the understanding, the stronger the dedication and drive. The natural place to begin is by reading the literature. Since continuous improvement in higher education is a growing field, articles and books are readily available. Oftentimes senior leaders begin by attending several quality seminars to become familiar with quality principles and practices, and after this initial stage, they use consultants to initiate efforts on campus.

It is not enough to read the literature and to hire a consultant to start continuous improvement on campus. The essential ingredient is to create a culture where people are encouraged to learn and where they are not reprimanded for taking calculated risks, a learning organization. The best way to start building a learning organization is for the leaders to change their behaviors. In this way, they lead by example by demonstrating their commitment. Members are much more likely to want to learn new behaviors when they witness different actions on the part of leaders.

In an environment of continuous improvement, people need to be rewarded for asking pertinent questions in order to improve. We were told that members throughout the institution need to feel comfortable questioning existing processes and systems. Even though the institutions we studied are working on creating a culture that supports quality improvement, they understand that this new culture supports a new way of thinking and feeling. The leaders with whom we spoke are prepared to make the necessary changes so that members at all levels can make continuous improvements.

Once leaders have learned about quality improvement and are prepared to be primary drivers of quality improvement on campus, writing or rewriting the vision and mission statements becomes their first priority. Their second priority is to properly communicate these statements to institutional members. The next section explains how institutions are using quality principles and practices to develop and communicate the vision and mission statements of the institution—system 3.

SYSTEM 3: DEVELOPING AND COMMUNICATING VISION/ MISSION STATEMENTS

We consistently found that institutions start the implementation process by developing or reexamining their vision and mission statements and then follow that up by continually articulating these statements to the various constituents. A vision statement is a philosophy about values; it is futuristic and optimistic. In contrast, a mission statement is more specifically focused; it outlines the institution's purpose and differentiates the institution from other institutions. A vision statement answers the question: Where do we want to be in five to 10 years and what do we want to be doing? On the other hand, a mission statement answers the question: What is our purpose?

Most of the institutions in our study did not have a vision statement before they became engaged in improvement efforts. Several have developed vision statements since starting the quality journey, but mission statements are more common. In the absence of a vision statement, the mission statement drives the quality initiative on campus. Most interviewees are much more familiar with their mission statement and the role it plays in continuous improvement efforts than they are with their vision statement, if one exists at all.

Institutions develop these statements in several ways. First, they gather input from a variety of constituencies. Although it might be common practice to involve the faculty and administration, the institutions in our study typically include representatives from several of the following groups: students, alumni, business and industry, board members, past faculty, and past deans. Second, quality principles and practices and systems thinking are used in developing the statements. Creating a mission or vision statement that an institution can get behind and claim as its own takes some time and effort, but the rewards of this work are well worth that effort.

Many interviewees made it clear that they understand the value of a shared vision and that this process is critical in aligning people in the institution to these statements. They strongly stressed that it is important for all members of the institution to think about the mission daily, regardless of their positions. As one president stated, "Everyone needs to have the mission in mind everyday whether you cut grass or cut checks." Another president said that they are linking all of their improvement efforts and changes to a shared vision:

> We have spent three years trying to get a vision of what we want to become. We have tried to create an alignment with that vision, helping people to truly connect their work with that larger sense of mission.

Using quality tools to develop the vision and mission statements is crucial. One interviewee described the importance of understanding the relationships among quality concepts this way:

> You get excited about the vision, but you don't know how to do it. And when you start to adopt the quality principles, you can't get it done because you do not know how to work together.

By using quality tools to collect data from a variety of perspectives, institutions have been able to more narrowly define their missions. Two stories that illustrate the development of the vision and mission process follow:

> We arrived at the vision and mission statements using quality tools. We had a steering team made up of representatives of all of the constituents, approximately 26 members. We did an affinity diagram about the vision. The driving question was: How would we like people to describe the institution in the year 2000? Everyone started putting up their Post-it notes. There was a moment that everyone realized that their positions within the institution were irrelevant. People from all levels were putting up the same kind of things, the same values and hopes. The ideas were grouped and an assigned small group drafted the vision and mission statements.
>
> Three people took the statements out to each work unit and asked each what was missing. The driving question at this point was: How do you see what you do every day in this mission statement? We also utilized e-mail for reactions from everyone. We lived with the statements for a year and then we revisited them and made changes. We keep updating the statements. The key was having people own and understand the statements while understanding the processes.
>
> We had a series of meetings with 45–50 people. We had a sampling from administrators, faculty, students, staff, alumni, and trustees. We had an outside public relations firm facilitate the meeting. Finally, we came out with vision and mission statements, and there was a very bad reaction to them. So we threw them out and started all over. This time we did some surveys of focus groups. . . . We reached a consensus on these three concepts and then drafted the language. The Quality Steering Group went on a retreat to wordsmith. They then had a series of meetings in groups of 15–20 led by senior leadership to talk about it. A consensus was reached. Even though it was a long (two and a half years) and sometimes painful process, it was one of the best projects we have undertaken.

A pattern across the institutions in our study was that mission and vision statements are developed by using quality improvement tools to build a consensus. Even though it is a time-consuming process, interviewees repeatedly stated that building a consensus helps to create a shared vision. When people are involved in the development of the mission statement, they recognize its value and are dedicated to fulfilling it.

Since the vision and mission statements play a significant role in guiding the institution internally and externally, it is important to align institutional members' attitudes and values to the ideas expressed in those statements. To do this, the institutions we studied established a system to continually inform people of the mission and to keep the mission alive. These institutions designed some creative approaches to communicate these statements.

We saw, for example, copies of the mission and vision statements posted around one campus, in some cases even above the water fountains and in the restrooms. At another campus, the three major points of their mission and vision statements appear on numerous doors: teaching, learning, and community building. At other institutions, we noticed inspirational posters that focused on some aspect of quality hanging in various buildings. Statements reflecting quality principles appear in college catalogs and, in one case, on employee paycheck envelopes.

In addition to making the mission visible, most institutions in our study spend time educating new faculty members about the mission during orientation meetings. Continuous updates on improvement efforts is another way to keep the mission at the forefront of members' minds rather than just a statement in the university catalog. One institution has a vision- and mission-oriented convocation at the beginning of each academic year at which a status report is given and video clips are shown so that progress toward fulfilling these statements is visible to all members.

At another institution, departments write commitment statements that relate to the mission statements. These are posted around campus. We were told that these actions help people visualize how they are a part of the system and help align them to the mission. Departments shared their commitment statements with pride, and they communicated an understanding of how their departments fit into the overall system.

As with any formal document in academe, there is a tendency for mission statements to become too elaborate, integrating unnecessary verbiage that detracts from the message. But at the institutions in this study the mission statements are revised frequently enough to keep them up to date and meaningful. At one institution the mission statement is condensed into eight words so that everyone can remember it. According to the president of this institution,

> We have tried to shorten the actual mission statement so that it was more "graspable" by the person operating the mower who may not be that interested in esoteric matters. The one thing that is getting out there is "nurture." We want to nurture the new member and the 40-year employee. We had the eight-word mission statement stapled to every pay envelope: "We nurture persons—for God, for learning, forever." We want the mission to stay in front of us.

Once these statements are developed, they become an important part of the communication system. We consistently heard people say that when they have to make decisions, they use the mission and vision statements to *ask different questions*. They ask questions such as the following: How does this decision fit in? Do we want to do this? Does it add value? Administrators ask people if their decisions are congruent with the mission of the institution.

Presidents warned us that they are very careful about what goes into writing and that the word "quality" is *not* always incorporated into the mission statement. In fact, some institutions have a separate statement on quality. According to the presidents, quality improvement is successful when it resides in the hearts of the people, not in the language of the mission and/or vision statement. Because the quality language was reported as intimidating to many, one administrator uses questions:

> I wanted to get my colleagues to think in more strategic ways so I put aside quality language and focused on strategic planning instead. What is our mission and how are we going to accomplish it? What do we want to do? I do not even talk mission. How do we place ourselves? Where can we selectively compete? They can listen to this language. I keep banging away at this.

According to the interviewees, developing the vision and mission statements is important, but communicating them is more significant. These statements are meaningful and are used in making decisions; they are "living" documents not just empty statements posted on walls at these institutions.

Because the institutions in our study understand the value of mission statements, they are much more aware of stakeholders. They have shifted in their thinking about whom they serve. They understand the interrelationships of positions within institutions and how these positions contribute to serving customers. As one person said: "We are each other's customers. We need to talk to each other." People within these institutions are striving to be even more customer oriented and this emphasis has changed conversations, which ultimately changes the culture.

When we asked interviewees to identify the core quality principles for their institution, the number one response centered around the concept of customer and the value of customer service. It was common to hear comments such as

> When people ask you why they can't do something a particular way, you think about that more carefully now. You think about ways to decrease that customer's frustrations. You did not think that way before.

> We are now looking for ways to measure customer satisfaction. It is part of our normal conversation. We are customer driven.

> Often good customer service is not noticed. You can't make students stay with good customer service, but poor service can make them go away.

One institution has three overall values that help to build teaching and learning communities. These values are communicated throughout the institution. Everywhere, everyone, every day will (1) promote student learning, (2) promote customer satisfaction, and (3) improve community and student contacts with institutional programs and services. When members understand these values and incorporate them into their daily work, a major step has been taken toward creating a new quality culture.

In general, we found that mission statements are important in aligning members within the institution and in helping them become aware of various stakeholders. Once a vision or mission statement has been developed, it is vital that the statement is communicated to all members of the institution and that members understand the statement and refer to it in their day-to-day work. But if continuous improvement is going to become ingrained in the culture, members need to increase their knowledge about quality principles and practices. In the next section, system 4, we outline what institutions have done to professionally develop members so that they can actively participate in quality improvement efforts.

SYSTEM 4: PROFESSIONALLY DEVELOPING MEMBERS

Knowledge development and education are important for all institutional members. A commonality across institutions in our study is that members who have been professionally developed in quality principles, tools, and techniques have a deeper understanding of quality improvement. This understanding almost always results in higher levels of commitment and determination to continue improving processes and systems.

System 4 consists of the methods used to develop senior leaders and all other members. Special attention is given to the professional development of faculty since this group is often the most resistant. We also outline how some of the institutions are developing students in quality principles and practices.

When we asked what areas receive professional development, we repeatedly heard that people in administrative areas—registrar, admissions, administrative affairs, housing, and physical plant—were educated about quality principles rather than employees in academic areas. This was true in our national survey as well. It is common for administrators and staff to have at least 20 hours of professional development, even though they are not required to participate. When knowledge levels vary, unnecessary divisions are created which hamper quality initiatives. Professional development for all members is essential if people are going to think seriously about becoming involved in continuous improvement efforts. All members need to have a similar background in order to build a common language base from which to communicate.

Developing Administrators and Staff Members

A pattern emerged that senior administrative leaders are the first to learn about quality principles, either through consultants or through business relationships in the community. In our national survey, support staff and members of the administration were reported being educated in quality principles and practices at about the same rate. The senior leaders we interviewed are knowledgeable in many aspects of the continuous improvement movement, such as its philosophy, tools, and techniques, which enables them to drive the process.

Once senior administrators are developed, it was common in our institutions for them to determine how other administrators and staff members would be educated. Consultants were often brought in early in the process and then were followed by in-house personnel.

Devoting the time to learn is critical because it provides a common language and knowledge base across the institution. The current push is to educate all institutional members—administrators, staff, *and* faculty. A few of our institutions are currently at this level, and the others recognize the necessity of and value in investing time and money in continuing education. One administrator had this advice:

> Get everyone educated as soon as possible. Developing one group at a time can create a two-class society—those trained and those not trained.

We found people at all levels perceive professional development as an investment in their personal development. Before the quality initiative began on campus, many of the interviewees had not been specifically educated in any particular skills. In our interviews, staff members typically stated that professional development has created a more level playing field. They feel more respected in their institutions, and therefore, they take their positions more seriously. It may be that development seminars have helped them to understand their place in the system and the interrelationships within the system.

We realized that members welcome the educational opportunities and enjoy the chance to interact with others. Sometimes development was even mentioned as a reward. One staff member reflected

> It meant a lot to me that the college was investing in my education, so I found the time to add it to my schedule.

Interviewees reported that investing in people's development helps to build relationships with people in various parts of the institution because diverse groups of people are brought together in seminars. Many of the members admitted that they do not know what others do at different levels in the institution. Because of cross-functional continuous education, members have been integrated across the institution, and they appreciate the inclusiveness of the education. The development seminars were described as safe environments where people feel the hierarchy is nonexistent. One staff member said it this way, "After our seminars, we were fired up. It was the greatest experience after eating chocolate!"

Developing Faculty Members

"Why don't they start with educating the faculty if the mission is to educate?" This question was posed to us by one administrator. The results of our interviews reflect that faculty members are usually developed after administrators and staff or that they have not been developed as part of the quality initiative at all. Again, this reinforced the findings from our national survey. (Refer to table 5 in appendix B.) As a result, the faculty tend to be the most resistant to continuous improvement. As one faculty member said

> We have to find a way to force them to be developed without letting them know they are being forced.

There seems to be a constant conflict between administrators and staff members who are frustrated because of their perception that faculty members will not participate in the development processes and faculty members who are feeling "left out," operating with a lesser knowledge base about continuous quality improvement. Faculty members who are not fully educated in the quality philosophy, tools, data collection, and customer service are not as comfortable using them and therefore are not as committed to participating. When we interviewed faculty members who had gone through a full week of continuing education in quality principles and practices, we discovered they are as willing to practice continuous improvement as the administrators and staff we interviewed. This result is indicative of the power of developing people so that everyone has the same knowledge base and can act accordingly.

Faculty members who teach in the business and engineering schools are often the first instructors to become aware of and learn about quality principles and practices. This awareness is often the result of the growing number of partnerships being formed between business and industry and higher education institutions. Since quality courses are becoming part of the curriculum in business and engineering colleges, faculty members in these disciplines usually have the knowledge base. As one faculty member in business stated, "I want to teach quality principles because I want the school administrators to use them." Faculty members involved in the assessment movement also tend to accept quality principles and practices. For these faculty members, continuous improvement in the classroom is a natural progression and often leads to improved learning.

There was strong agreement across institutions and interviewees that faculty members need to understand quality principles and practices. The interviewees believed that faculty members who resist the quality initiative do not understand it. Another common theme which emerged is that development for faculty members needs to be voluntary. As valuable as the professional development is, we were warned not to force it upon faculty members because of their nature to be autonomous and independent thinkers. We received this advice:

> Even though we need to educate our colleagues about the value of process improvement, do not mandate development on the faculty. The workshops for faculty should be voluntary.

The following are the three most important lessons learned in designing development systems for faculty: (1) faculty members teaching faculty members is an effective approach; (2) the way to engage faculty members is to begin the learning process by *asking questions* that faculty members find interesting; and (3) quality improvement education should be incorporated into faculty orientation programs.

We were told repeatedly that using faculty members to teach other faculty members is most influential. Several institutions utilized consultants or in-house educators first, but then realized that this method was doomed to failure. The following stories express this realization:

> With teaching faculty about continuous improvement, we had administrators teaching faculty, and the initial response was not good. We turned the teaching over to the faculty, and they had a team who wrote out what was important to faculty about quality. They created their own development program, and it was much more effective and accepted.

> We have a separate quality course for faculty, taught by faculty. All new faculty take it, and most of the more experienced faculty take it also. More than half of the faculty took the 20-hour course.

> We had an emeritus faculty member write an elegant paper that incorporates 30–40 years of research from the social sciences and behavioral sciences. His paper on quality seemed to reach the faculty. He talked to the faculty senate and told them not to get hung up on the word "customer," but to focus on the interdependence within our institution, that all of us need to work together to do the best we can for whoever we are serving. The tough faculty audience became more accepting.

The second lesson is to *ask questions* that interest faculty members to drive faculty development. How can student learning be improved? How can student participation be increased? How can we better balance teaching with research? Many repeatedly expressed that for faculty members to participate they need to understand how this new knowledge will improve the processes to which they are most devoted—teaching and research. Because faculty members like to engage in dialogue and debate, interviewees said that the best way to begin learning is to start a dialogue about quality improvement so they can debate the value of quality principles and practices as they look for applications in their own responsibilities.

The third lesson is to change faculty orientation programs to incorporate development on quality improvement. Typically the orientation programs are for new members of the faculty, but we found that some of our institutions have all faculty members participate in quality orientation programs. The following examples illustrate how institutions are developing systems to educate the faculty about quality principles and practices:

> For our new faculty orientation, we spend eight hours of a two-day orientation on quality. The orientation process was redesigned by faculty who teach a course on introduction to quality.

> We have a faculty institute for a full semester, one entire week is devoted to continuous improvement.

> We have a system of forums and workshops. The forums are geared toward an academic audience where the faculty talk to us about how processes work. It is more of a dialogue. The two-hour workshops are more hands-on training. The focus is on having them describe what they do and why they do it. Then we talk about how to improve the process to make it better for everyone. Both methods have been received with open arms. Participants tell us that no one has ever asked their opinions before. They say that no one has asked them what worked or did not work.

These comments reflect the importance of integrating quality improvement concepts when new faculty members enter the institutional community. By helping these faculty members learn the value of continuous improvement as they begin their relationship with the institution, it is more likely that they will be open to the inherent changes. The goal is to have them adopt quality practices from the start. Interviewees reported that the efforts with new hires are effective in maintaining the momentum for quality improvement.

Developing Students

Another group that should be developed is students. Including students in development seminars is a natural spillover effect as the level of institutional engagement increases. Some institutions incorporate quality concepts into the leadership development for student campus leaders. In addition, a few institutions are establishing student teams to improve processes on campus. Some are teaching quality concepts in the new student orientation week so that when students walk into a classroom they have a general understanding of how continuous improvement concepts can be applied.

Ironically, graduate teaching assistants typically are not educated in effective teaching techniques. This glaring weakness is changing in several of the institutions we studied. As faculty members begin to understand how quality principles and practices improve learning and teaching, they care more about how the teaching assistants are teaching their classes. One faculty member in a graduate school shared this revelation:

> After attending a quality conference at Procter and Gamble, I became very interested in student involvement. In order to improve the teaching and learning process, we institutionalized requiring teaching assistants to attend training programs every semester. The development is led by TAs, but we integrate teaching experts from within and outside the college. The TAs in the engineering school and the business school have teamed up and are educated together to ensure some consistency in teaching methods and expectations. The partnership is exciting. Procter and Gamble emphasized how we need to work with people outside of our own college, and this idea was born.

Choosing Methods of Professional Development

One of our conclusions is that the quality journey is a journey of learning. Ideally then, development is a never-ending process. Unfortunately, funding and supporting development force institutions to choose less ambitious methods than never-ending development. Common questions emerged that appear to drive which methods to use: (1) Who should be developed? (2) When should they be developed? (3) Who should conduct the training and development? and (4) What knowledge and skills should be taught? The following answers emerged: (1) develop all members; (2) develop members in the skills they need when they need them; (3) use consultants early on to educate members, but integrate development internally later; and (4) start the learning process by having people complete an introductory session on quality improvement that typically focuses on awareness and understanding followed by sessions on tools and data collection, facilitator development, team leader development, customer service, and transformational leadership. The reality is that learning about quality improvement takes a great deal of time.

Three different methods of educating members are explained in the following statement by an administrator:

> One model is to educate everybody at once so that everyone is speaking the same language before you think about implementation. It is more economical because you do not have to pay continuing consulting fees. Another model is just-in-time training where the team leader teaches people. Yet another model is to educate an area or department. Then when that area is complete, they start to implement. We developed by departments, and the admissions office was educated first, followed by the registrar's office. Now every department except housing and the cafeteria have learned about quality, but they are outside businesses.

Since developing members takes time and costs money, institutions struggle with the best method to use:

Maybe we should have tried to do a basic, hands-on training for everybody at the beginning. There were two reasons why we didn't. If people did not have a leader who was ready to do it and they received the training, they became frustrated. Secondly, I believe that the ideas should percolate down through the organization through the line leaders. I spent my time trying to increase the knowledge of the people who lead the university hoping that they would begin to share it systematically with the people down the ranks. That has had a negative and a positive effect. The negative is that we have sometimes drifted pretty far into the abstract and theoretical about continuous improvement. On the other hand, the president, the provost, and others have begun to own this.

The trend in the institutions in our study appears to be toward employing just-in-time development in which people are taught concepts at a time when it is most appropriate. Institutions are finding that this method is more cost-effective and less frustrating than educating everyone at one time or educating an area or department. We interviewed people who attended team-building sessions, but were never assigned to a team. If they are placed on a team at a later date, they have to be reeducated because they will have forgotten what they have learned. In essence, if you don't use it, you lose it.

Along with the timing of development, we learned that it is equally important to start people working on manageable projects upon the completion of development. They need some small wins early so that they realize the benefits of development. One respondent said it best:

We make sure that people either have a project when they come into development or as soon as they are done. Then we facilitate getting them onto a project team so they can apply some of the things they have learned as early as possible.

Development seminars are the most common way to educate members. The most frequently included topics are an introduction to the philosophy of quality improvement, facilitator development, team leader development, and customer service training. These seminars are usually followed by less formal meetings to discuss quality topics, view videos, and engage in dialogue with members across the institution.

Brown-bag lunches are a popular method of continuing the learning efforts. Several institutions bring nationally recognized speakers to campus to lead important workshops on a quality-related topic. Interviewees commonly told us of ongoing seminars on campus for people who have already completed the initial training. We concluded that the professional development effort can always be increased. The people we interviewed feel their institutions are making progress, but educating and developing members is an area that needs to continue to be improved.

Consultants are consistently used to initiate the learning of senior leaders and/or internal people responsible for educating others. Consultants are used to "jump start" the learning process. They also tend to be integrated on a just-in-time basis when needed. Using outside consultants helps to train on-campus facilitators so that the quality movement can build momentum on campus without external help or expense. We were told when hiring consultants, it is important to find someone who "clicks" with members of the institution, someone who has the personality to work well with people within the institution. Interviewees believe that while consultants lead the change efforts, it is critical that consultants understand and respect the existing culture of the institution.

Interviewees across institutions identified several advantages and disadvantages of using consultants to implement quality improvement. The advantages include having people with the expertise when needed. Interviewees reported that people from the outside often have their ideas more easily accepted, and therefore, they are able to make some of the fundamental changes more easily than someone within the institution. Since they are not on the payroll, they are perceived to be a cost-effective way to obtain specialized skills. On the downside, interviewees warned us that the momentum sometimes leaves when the consultant leaves. The concern is that the consultant is not an internal employee who demonstrates on a daily basis what needs to be done. In general, consultants are helpful in setting the initial framework for quality improvement, but they need to be followed by senior leaders who incorporate quality principles and practices in daily work and who have a long-term perspective to implementation within the institution.

One advantage of having internal personnel responsible for development is that they can demonstrate loyalty to quality initiatives. They are also available on an ongoing basis, which ensures that continuous improvement remains continuous. The institutions we studied have found ways to educate and develop members using full-time employees. One institution obtained a grant to establish a development center. The center develops institutional members, but it also generates revenue by conducting training seminars for other organizations within the business community. We were told that having a continual source of funding from sources external to the institution has reduced resistance to continuous improvement efforts because members do not feel that funds are spent at the expense of other institutional projects and academic programs.

We discovered that who conducts the professional development seminars is often dependent on how the development takes place. As institutions partner with businesses in the community, some reported that they took advantage of the professional development opportunities available at those businesses. Those institutions without partners developed the educational programs as needed. Several institutions developed their own training videos, particularly in the customer service area, to educate people about providing quality service to internal and external customers. If they have not developed their own videos, they locate high quality videos to educate members about quality principles and practices.

One of our institutions is using Stephen Covey's *The 7 Habits of Highly Effective People* as the foundation of their education because it stresses continuous improvement as a personal transformation process. The principles identified by Covey emphasize characteristics such as trustworthiness, personal integrity, and stewardship. These timeless, yet powerful, characteristics help members understand the value of personally shifting their thinking. According to this president, "Development training has changed family lives and relationships within the institution."

The institutions in our national survey followed a similar pattern of development. The most common response to who was providing the development was a combination of staff, faculty, and consultants. (Refer to table 6 in appendix B.) We interpreted this to mean that consultants are used to initiate efforts, but that internal members of the staff and/or faculty are utilized to continue development efforts after the consultant leaves.

Professionally Developing Members—Summary

It was clear to us that members feel that learning about quality improvement has made a difference in their lives. Development has even had a contagious effect in our institutions. One administrator put it this way:

> Out in the system, people see others working with the information they gained in development, and they become interested. People who have quality knowledge have an advantage; it is stated in some job descriptions so people are expecting new hires to have the information and skills. Promotions are sometimes based on having continuous improvement knowledge and skills.

Throughout this study, we were impressed at the consensus regarding the value of professional development. There is no doubt that members appreciate having the time to learn and that they consider education to be an institutional investment in their personal development and growth. Even though it is time consuming, people feel that time spent learning about continuous improvement is time well spent. One staff member expressed the effect development has had on her by saying

> I got so turned on by the sessions on how to be a team leader that I took on an internship in the development area. It was the best year. I am going to change my career because of the continuing education I received.

The institutions we studied demonstrated that they are *asking different questions* about the skills and knowledge that members need to function now and in the future. They provided numerous examples of innovations in finding time, money, and energy to educate members about continuous quality improvement.

Professional development is a pivotal quality principle because it influences the degree to which people understand the value of continuous improvement. The trend in the institutions we studied is to begin educating people on the administrative side of the institution before the academic side, but institutions have recognized that this situation is not necessarily the ideal. Although engaging the faculty is a challenge, these institutions are rethinking how they develop faculty members. Commenting on this situation, a president remarked

> We might have engaged the faculty by educating them differently, by giving them information to read because they are great readers. Then we could have asked them to write their impressions and ask that they present that to their peers.

We were advised to educate all members as soon as possible in the philosophy of quality improvement and to professionally develop people when they need it most, just-in-time.

We found several trends in the methods of professional development. Consultants are often used to initiate the learning process, followed by internal staff members who take over the professional development. On the academic side, it is effective to have faculty members teach faculty members. Training sessions, videos, newsletters, readings, and discussion groups are used by institutions to continually educate people in quality principles and practices. So far, professional development efforts focus on helping members understand quality initiatives and on teaching them how to work effectively in teams and in meetings.

Although many interviewees said that professional development efforts could be increased, we noticed that there is a dedication to learning and an attitude that professional development efforts have made a difference in their lives, both professionally and personally. Because the knowledge and skill development of members are so vital, we found that interviewees are searching for ways to improve upon methods, techniques, and the timing at which people are developed. This system, as with the other systems, continues to evolve as institutions learn from their experiences and make improvements.

One of the areas in which people need to acquire skills and knowledge is in data collection and analysis. In system 5, we describe how and why data are collected. Included are the specific tools and techniques used by the institutions we studied.

SYSTEM 5: COLLECTING AND ANALYZING DATA

Across the institutions in our study, data are collected systematically for decision making. The people we interviewed understand the value of data; it was common for them to tell us that "data drive the decisions made." System 5 is described in this section, beginning with several examples of how data are being collected to improve decision making. These examples are followed by an explanation of how the most commonly used quality tools improve effectiveness and efficiency. How the institutions in the study benchmark other institutions and businesses to improve their data-gathering processes and systems is analyzed next. Also included is how some of our institutions have developed partnerships with businesses to facilitate learning about continuous improvement and to help in continual learning. Benchmarking and partnering with other organizations provide the baseline data needed to establish standards and to assess progress being made.

At the institutions in this study, professional development has progressed to the point where members know data should drive decision making. Several interviewees said that people now consistently bring data with them to meetings. We sensed that institutions are working hard to avoid intuitive decision making. Several people said that their institutions previously made arbitrary decisions and now decisions are based on data collected.

Although most of the institutions are in the process of developing measurements, we discovered that all of them view measuring the success of their quality efforts to be the most disconcerting aspect of data collection. For the most part, they have developed and implemented systems to make continuous improvement an integral part of the institutional culture. The difficulty lies in designing specific measurements that indicate improvements have taken place. One administrator described the measurement dilemma this way:

> When people tell me that we can't measure something, I ask them to identify how we know something is not working. If we know when it is not working, we should be able to determine when it is working. We know when morale is better. That can be measured statistically. Is there more resistance to continuous improvement efforts? If there is, that is good news because it means you are communicating. We have to quantify the quality efforts, but we also need to calculate in the unknowns. For example, every time we look at retention figures, we remind ourselves that one person may represent nine other people because you do not know what the dissatisfied students are saying to others.

Even in an institution dedicated to practicing quality principles and to collecting data, we were told that some decisions still are not data based. When data are not collected and used to improve decision making, decisions often end in failure. One respondent expressed the situation best:

> The business school decided to have four hour-and-a half classes a week
> instead of two hour-and-a half and three one-hour classes. We did that to
> provide better blocks of time for case studies with no class on Fridays. The
> evening program operates on a nine-week term and the business school
> preferred 14 weeks. But we did not survey our customers. The schedule
> did not interface well with the rest of the university and industry told us 14
> weeks is too long.

Typically, most institutions collect data randomly, when they have a
specific need. In contrast, the institutions we studied had systems in place that
enable members to collect data regularly so that they can make continuous
improvements. To illustrate that systematically collecting data is a change in
practice, one administrator told us this story:

> We surveyed everyone in the physical plant about what problems they
> perceived. The biggest response was: I have never been surveyed before in
> the physical plant. Many of the problems were small, and we could take
> care of them that day.

At another institution, the staff is surveyed annually. The president reads
these responses and provides feedback to the appropriate division. Another
administrator commented:

> The Office of Institutional Research did a staff survey that revealed that
> staff expectations were about the same as the executive officers'. The data
> enabled me to go to our oversight group for quality and say that if we blow
> this it will be a terrible shame because what you want for the university is
> exactly the same as what the staff want.

Data are useful and powerful in supporting decision making. Because of quality
initiatives, interviewees have become accustomed to collecting data. They
reported that without data, it is hard to know which decisions to make and if
decisions are effective.

There was a consensus among interviewees that they are better informed
after the quality initiative began than before. The decisions that are made
reflect the value of good data. The data are greater and richer; the decision-
making process is more meaningful because people have the data they need to
make decisions. Statements that illustrate this point include:

> We need to steel ourselves against emotional responses. We base our
> decisions on fact and not emotion. Without data, it is easy to make
> decisions based on what works somewhere else whether or not that place
> is like us at all.

> Our group leaders and department heads are much better informed, and
> they are working with much better data.

> We don't pretend to always make decisions based on data, but we know
> when we are not and we acknowledge that. We try to think about what we
> need to do in the future so that we are making decisions based on data.

Methods Used to Collect Data

Suggestion systems, surveys, and focus groups are a few of the methods used to gather data systematically. The easiest system to start appears to be the suggestion system. Although suggestion systems have existed for years, the difference is that because of continuous improvement people witness responses to their suggestions, which tends to feed the system. Instead of paying lip service to a suggestion box, the institutions we studied consciously try to implement suggestions and communicate the changes that are made as a result.

As we noted earlier, one business school has a system of suggestion boxes throughout the school with forms to be completed. A team reviews the forms and distributes them to the appropriate people. We were told that some items are straightforward (i.e., clean the bathrooms more frequently, replace particular light bulbs), while other suggestions are more policy-related and a team analyzes those suggestions. This school also has a weekly newsletter with a suggestion form attached. The goal is to make complaining easy so that improvements can be made. This feedback system is proactive rather than the typical reactive approach. When people observe actions being taken based on their feedback, we were told they are more likely to contribute with their ideas and input:

> The president instigated a Sound Off system where everyone can get a gripe off his or her chest. Around campus you will find boxes on the wall with forms in them. The president's most trusted confidant is the person entrusted to receive the suggestions and distribute them to the various other vice presidents so that improvements can be made.

"If we ask what we can do better, we get good ideas," said one administrator. By surveying students, institutions have improved processes on campus. Several institutions have improved the registration process, which directly improves student satisfaction. At one institution, both an administrator and a staff member told us how library service to students has been improved:

> We surveyed students, and they requested longer service hours. Based on these data, we surveyed people on campus to find out which schedule they prefer. We sent a letter to the director of the library asking for more hours. We have been able to cover the extended hours with the same number of staff through more student assistants. This semester we are doing head counts at different times and days of the week to determine how the hours are used or if we have to make changes.

> We ask every graduating senior to complete a student opinion survey. The one area in which student ratings have gone up dramatically over the last four years is the service in the library.

It was interesting that when interviewees spoke about surveying students, they repeatedly expressed how valuable the input has been because it was different from what they expected. For example, at one institution students said they wanted higher admissions standards and they wanted more learning. At another institution, students voted for a tuition surcharge. This feedback is not typical of the input received from students before quality improvement efforts began.

One institution requires students to complete a survey each semester before they can register for the next semester. The survey data are then used to make improvements in processes for the next semester. The president said that he reads every response. He wants to be included in the data-processing system so that he has more information about the kinds of changes that need to be made. Because students are aware that he reads their comments, he feels they know that their feedback is taken seriously and that he is committed to making quality improvement a major priority.

In one of the institutions, the admissions office has developed numerous systems to collect data. One of the most useful is a postage-paid postcard sent to prospective students who choose not to attend this institution. The survey collects data on the reasons they selected another institution. Several questions are asked, and then they ask for the names of institutions doing a better job in supplying personalized assistance. According to the director of admissions,

> This provides us with natural benchmarks. We don't benchmark who we want to benchmark. We benchmark who our students are benchmarking us against.

The data are analyzed looking for trends that are passed on to the appropriate areas.

At another institution, there is a system for conducting focus groups of graduate students each spring. Many ideas generated in the focus groups have been implemented. Often the suggestions are classified as "glaringly obvious" but are blind spots for administrators and members of the staff and faculty.

One of the institutions also surveys parents to collect feedback to improve decisions. This institution systematically surveys numerous stakeholders every winter, but different surveys are sent to various stakeholders—students, faculty members, administrators, and alumni—and one survey is even designed specifically for parents. The data collected are distributed to the appropriate areas so that processes can be improved.

We found another trend of collecting data from the community to determine the needs of industry and of students. Some of the institutions survey students one to three years out of college to ask them: What skills should employees have? Two informative examples of this type of data collection follow:

> We set up a phone bank with volunteers to call previous students who were not currently enrolled to find out the needs in the community. Out of these data we developed a prenursing program. We are open to looking for information in many different places.

> I teach an educational leadership course in the graduate school. We revised our program by going out to the local school systems and talking to principals and superintendents, asking them what kinds of things need to be included in the program. We built the program around the feedback collected. We also recruit students based on their recommendations.

Input from the community is received from surveys that employers of graduates complete. An administrator explained what the institution gains from this survey:

> We ask them, "What did our students need when they came to you that they did not have?" Based on their responses, we have made many changes in courses, in processes, and in the advising process.

These examples illustrate the power of understanding that members in the community are also stakeholders. They should have input into decisions that are made, and their needs should be taken into consideration when defining the vision, mission, and outcomes of the institution.

Even though we found several kinds of surveys being conducted simultaneously in some of the institutions, the response rates were reported as being high. It was explained to us that people appreciate having input into decisions, especially if they are able to witness the results of their suggestions on campus. In fact, many reported that the act of collecting data from stakeholders leads to a greater sense of community. Once stakeholders know that institutional members are listening and trying to improve, they are more likely to express their opinions.

In addition to surveys and suggestion boxes, institutions have become accustomed to conducting focus groups with stakeholders to obtain data for all kinds of decisions. We heard about focus groups of students, alumni, employers, faculty, staff, board members, and combinations of these constituencies. What made an impression on us was how comfortable the interviewees are with data and how it has become natural for them to think of collecting input before making decisions.

Institutions we studied are using data to start and redesign programs, to better satisfy stakeholders, to strategically plan, and to enhance fund-raising efforts. At a few institutions, the Plan-Do-Check-Act (PDCA) cycle is being applied to assess academic programs. Before starting a new program, a pilot program is started so that data can be collected and analyzed. Some programs are eliminated because of the feedback received, and others are adjusted based on data. As one faculty member reported:

We do not do things full scale until we see if they are going to work. We adjusted a program six times during the year based on feedback received.

Data help the institutions satisfy stakeholders. By collecting systematic data, it is possible to determine what is not working and how often it is not working. One administrator said they keep detailed records on defects to know where improvements need to be made:

One thing that we have found to be most useful is to think in terms of defects. It does not matter how many times you do things right. The customer is only concerned with the times you did not do things right.

We wanted to examine graduate student progress by determining the leverage points in the process. Our goal was to decide if all of the leverage points are necessary or if time around the points could be collapsed. Basically, we want to shorten the time to degree. In order to do this we formed focus groups of students, faculty, and staff. This was the first effort in the graduate school to examine a true academic question.

At one institution, data are gathered to be used in strategic planning. When we asked if and how the approaches of continuous improvement and strategic planning are linked, one administrator had this response:

I see the approaches linked in the data gathering that is needed to determine customer needs. These data should be fed back into a strategic planning process to determine the institutional priorities, and the priorities should be addressed through an improvement process model. It is a nice loop, and we are trying to do that at this time.

At another institution, data are being used to support the institution in the funding process. One president shared this story to illustrate the value of data:

This year, the legislation was shifted toward performance. This is a great threat to some institutions, but it is popular with the constituencies that we serve. Higher education is losing a battle of support with the public and with the legislature. Because of the data we collect, I can demonstrate the increased performance level of the institution; fewer staff, more results. It is rare to find an institution that can do that.

Decisions that seem trivial still have a financial impact on our institutions. Interviewees understand that data need to be collected in all aspects of the institution because of cost implications. No matter how small the decision, we were told that data improve decisions made. One administrator made the point that no decision is too small for the collection of appropriate data:

We are using cloth towels instead of paper towels in the bathrooms. We suspect that it is more cost effective, but we are still collecting data.

Data are useful for clearing up misinformation and incorrect perceptions. Because perception is reality in the minds of those who believe things to be a certain way, it is important to collect data so that misperceptions can be disproved. The following examples illustrate this point:

> Surveys are not only helpful in identifying the problems but in identifying what the perceptions are of the problems. For example, people in the purchasing department said it took too long to get the purchase orders processed. I knew that was not the problem, and data showed that 95 percent of the purchase orders were done the same day and 100 percent were done within 24 hours. But the perception was that it took days. I used data to indicate that their perceptions were incorrect.

> Student survey data indicated that students could not get stamps when they wanted. Yet, there is a 24-hour stamp machine. I wrote back to all students to make them aware of the stamp machine and to help clarify their misperceptions. We have never had that show up on a student survey again. We would not have known that students were unhappy about that unless we conducted surveys.

It is common for data to be systematically collected from the various stakeholders of institutions. The data help institutions make decisions that improve stakeholder satisfaction. Without collecting data on a regular basis, we were told that it is difficult to know if time, money, and energy are being used wisely. It is almost impossible to know if institutions are good users of public and private funds if the voices of stakeholders are not incorporated into the decision-making processes.

Tools Used to Analyze Data

An important component in continuous improvement is the use of quality tools. These tools either help to provide data, to collect data, or to report data collected. Several themes emerged about tools and their use: tools are only one aspect of quality improvement, people use tools only if they understand when and how to use them, and tools are used in a variety of situations. One common misperception is that using quality tools is equivalent to implementing quality improvement. We learned that there is much more to quality improvement than tools, but the tools help improve systems and processes (Deming, 1986).

Since systems, not people, most often cause problems, tools are used to analyze data and to determine the cause of the problem in the system. A tool is the means to a solution and not the end in itself. One administrator stated it this way:

> Even though the flowchart is the number one tool we use, a change of attitude is another tool. The attitude that the system creates most of the problems, not the people in the system, helps to improve decision making. People need to understand that unless they want to be part of a bad system

> forever and see their jobs continue to deteriorate, they have to find time to
> fix the system. Flowcharting seems to be the tool of choice for them.

Interviewees commonly stated that even though tools are used, they feel they still have much to learn. Since most of the tools are not complicated, they stressed how important it is for all members to be familiar with the language and the purpose of the tools. This point demonstrates the value of professionally developing members. As one staff member said,

> Brainstorming is the tool we use most. We probably had been doing it in
> the past, but just naming it helped to take the pressure off and to help
> people understand the steps in the process.

In the institutions in our study, the most frequently mentioned resources for information on tools are *The Memory Jogger* (Goal/QPC, 1988) and *The Memory Jogger Plus+* (Brassard, 1989). We found institutions moving to a just-in-time approach for teaching members about tools so that they would be able to use the information at the time it is needed. It was also stressed that quality improvement tools should be introduced without jargon to lessen resistance, and we were warned not to overemphasize the use of tools.

Interviewees shared a variety of examples of how tools are being used, from restructuring committees to changing the title of a course. Process mapping (flow chart), cause-and-effect (fishbone) diagrams, Pareto charts, and interrelationship digraphs were repeatedly mentioned as common planning tools used to determine what processes to improve. Brainstorming, nominal group technique, and affinity diagrams are common tools used to improve decision making. The most popular tools used by our institutions are defined in exhibit 1.

Process mapping (flow chart) was the primary tool mentioned by people from various positions within the institutions. Through experience, they found that mapping out processes helps remind them to constantly think in terms of processes and systems. Once the steps in a process are mapped out, i.e., once data have been collected, the objective is to make the process as efficient as possible. No-value-added steps are eliminated. This mapping tool provides the data to improve decision making when redesigning the process. One president refers to it as "a process where you stand back and reflect upon what you are doing and why."

Processes cannot be changed unless people are familiar with all of the steps in the processes. It was common to hear people say that they did not have a conceptual picture of the entire process before they mapped it out. Since a flow chart creates a visual illustration of the process, people understand the process much faster and discover duplicate steps and steps that do not add value. Only then can the processes be improved. One person said it well:

EXHIBIT 1

WHAT ARE THE MOST COMMONLY USED TOOLS?

Planning Tools

Process mapping (flow chart): a graphic way of using symbols to identify the operations involved in a process, their interrelationships, inputs, and outputs. Flow charting is usually the first step in understanding selected processes in an organization.

Cause-and-effect diagram (fishbone): a graphic technique that illustrates the cause of a specific outcome.

Pareto chart: a bar graph showing where scarce resources should be applied to reap the greatest gain. The rule of thumb is that 80 percent of problems arise from 20 percent of potential causes.

Interrelationship digraph: a graph that takes complex, multivariable problems or desired outcomes and explores and displays all of the interrelated factors involved. It graphically shows the logical relationships between factors.

Decision-making Tools

Brainstorming: a technique used to generate ideas. Most commonly used in groups, its object is to gather as many ideas as possible in a specific time frame.

Nominal group technique: a tool for generating ideas; solving problems; and defining the mission, key result areas, performance measures, and goals/objectives.

Affinity diagram: a tool for gathering large amounts of language data (ideas, issues, etc.) and organizing it into groupings based on the natural relationship between each item.

Source: *25 Snapshots of a Movement: Profiles of Campuses Implementing CQI*

> When the process is on paper, people can see the inefficiencies in the system without getting defensive about any of it.

For example, one institution charted the process of changing the title on a course, and the flow chart was five pages long. The flow chart revealed that people continued to add steps to the process instead of redesigning it for efficiency.

Another example was a flow chart of the process for users to access the computer system. The flow chart depicted why it took three months before someone got access to the system—it was 48 pages long! Using this process flow chart, they decentralized the procedure so that there would be a person in each department who could assign user IDs within days. This procedure resulted in a simplified flow and in a vastly improved process. One administrator explained the use of mapping tools this way:

> We have a quality improvement team inside the business school that looks at processes, and we are mapping our courses and administrative processes. We want to be process driven. But there is resistance because

people want to go back and focus on structures instead. Then we find something wrong, and they want to get rid of the person. The thinking reverts back to: the problem can be fixed if the person is changed. Our change to quality took place because the people are different and the mission is different. The university is more committed to process change, and we are moving closer to the university. But we are still learning.

The affinity diagram is an important tool used for gathering and grouping ideas. It allows a team to creatively generate and to organize a large number of ideas and then summarize the ideas into natural groupings. The process helps them understand a problem and identify solutions. This tool could also be used with data collected through a suggestion box system or survey. At one institution, the affinity diagram was used to develop the new mission and vision statements.

We were told that the primary reason people like to use the affinity diagram is because it helps diverse groups of people arrive at a consensus rather quickly. Reaching a consensus seems to be a constant challenge in higher education institutions because the employees and other stakeholders have a variety of perspectives and high levels of expertise in numerous disciplines. Key characteristics of the affinity diagram are the use of Post-it notes and silence during the grouping process. Discussion is not allowed until natural categories have emerged. A useful example of the affinity diagram was provided by an administrator who stated

> We asked the faculty the following question: What do we as a faculty want to do this year? We had a meeting to discuss this question and we distributed Post-it notes and used the affinity diagram process. We had the silent grouping where we were moving the notes around to determine categories. We had a vocal discussion to come up with the titles of the categories. The silence is an important part of the process to make people feel free to participate.

One president refers to the affinity diagram as "a public way to think in a creative way." Like process mapping, it is a visual tool used to get all of the ideas out in front of everyone so that each person can have input in categorizing the ideas. Because participants must remain silent while grouping ideas, egos and personalities do not get in the way. Ideas are depersonalized and a consensus emerges quickly. The affinity diagram facilitates thinking "outside the box" within a reasonable amount of time.

Two other tools used frequently at one institution, but less at the other institutions, are Plus/Delta and N/3. Because these tools are used extensively by members at all levels and because members attribute their use to improving efficiency and effectiveness, we are including them even though we are not aware of these tools being used by the other institutions in the study. At this particular institution, administrators, faculty, and staff repeatedly mentioned

Plus/Delta as the most helpful feedback tool to determine what processes to change and how to change them. This tool is described as having two major steps: People are asked to identify the things that are working and that should stay the same (Plus). Then they are asked to list the things that are not working and that should be changed (Delta). We were told that this tool is used in meetings, in the classroom with students, and "even after lunch or on lunch!" The ease with which this tool is used increases its use. Our interviewees stressed that it is an important part of their system of communication. At the end of a meeting or class period, people expect to be asked these basic questions so that the next time they meet, the situation will be improved based on the feedback received.

The second tool, N/3, is used to help teams or groups arrive at a consensus quickly. Users of this tool said that it works well after using nominal group technique or brainstorming. The number of ideas generated by those processes are divided by three and that determines the number of ideas each person would select from the brainstorming list. For example, if 15 ideas are gener-ated, every person selects 5 ideas. In a roundrobin fashion, each person states his or her top five ideas after which two or three ideas emerge as the most popular. Again, this tool could be used with data collected by other methods such as surveys. It is a way to prioritize any data list in a short period of time because items emerge about which there is some agreement without having to discuss every idea.

Benchmarking and Partnering

The fact that the 10 institutions were willing to participate in this study knowing that the goal was to share the information with others indicates that they understand the value of benchmarking. The practice of benchmarking is looking at other organizations to identify their best practices that can be used to improve systems and processes. Data are collected from benchmarked organizations to set standards and to measure improvements being made. Benchmarking reduces time on the learning curve for institutions striving to improve. Allowing us to visit campus and to interview people across the institution reflects another theme: people who participated in our study have a clear understanding of the value of helping one another. Throughout our interviews and in our follow-up work, there was a consistent pattern of an unselfish exchange of information: "if you ask, you will receive."

Over and over, from one institution to the next, people were gracious about supplying information and written documents that outlined their quality jour-ney, and it was common to have people suggest others who might contribute valuable information. We consider this spirit of cooperation evidence that they want others to learn from their successes and mistakes. Several told us that just having a dialogue with us about their experiences was also helping them learn and improve because it gave them a chance to reflect upon their efforts.

Because several of the institutions we studied have gained recognition for their quality improvement efforts in the literature, they are targeted by other institutions as sources of information, and they share documents accordingly. Within our sample of institutions, many have helped each other, and a strong network is emerging. We were told by interviewees in several of the institutions that if we were conducting another survey instead of visiting their campus, they would not have taken the time to share their experiences with us because they are inundated with surveys. We were impressed with their generosity in allowing us to visit campus and to interview numerous people about their improvement efforts. Their willingness to share information is a sign that they are not threatened and that they know the difference between a competitive mind-set and one of cooperation. They wanted others to benefit from their experiences, just as they had benefited from benchmarking other institutions or businesses.

One way an institution uses benchmarking is to ask service units and noninstructional units to identify a similar service activity, either in the university or not, that has fewer errors or a shorter cycle time. A faculty member provided this example:

> It was taking three months to get a university student report to determine if graduation requirements have been met. So people within an individual school figured out how to print the report themselves by accessing the university computer. It is difficult to find out a student's status. The pharmacy school has no problem whatsoever, so we need to benchmark them.

At another institution, front-line employees who interact with students call other institutions and role-play as customers. These employees are asked to benchmark the best customer service practices and to write a report of the best practices. This exercise is an attempt to walk in the shoes of the customers.

It was common for the institutions we visited to help one another get the quality initiative off the ground. Quality improvement coordinators often work together, present their results to others, participate in conferences by sharing their experiences, and form networks to encourage dialogue. In 1990, a number of community and technical colleges that were in the process of implementing quality improvement concepts formed the Continuous Quality Improvement Network of Community and Technical Colleges (CQIN). The purposes of CQIN are to assist member CEOs with active organizational transformation through outside-the-box learning and sharing of best practices, and to enhance active institutional learning for faculty, staff, and trustees. The organization meets twice each year, once for a summer institute at which a learning theme is discussed and a second time (for the CEOs) at which leadership issues are addressed and at which a particular subject related to learning organizations and continuous quality improvement is addressed. As of summer 1997, there are 22 institutions and 4 community college districts that are members of CQIN.

In addition to interacting with other institutions that are implementing continuous improvement ideas, the institutions we studied turned to business and industry to benchmark processes. They looked to businesses in the community recognized for their quality efforts (e.g., Procter & Gamble, Xerox, Kodak, IBM, and Kellogg Company). Reflected one administrator,

> I was at a meeting one time and discovered that the person with problems most similar to mine was the head of a medical center.

In industry, it is common practice for suppliers and businesses to form partnerships. This trend is starting to be seen in the higher education community as well. Our interviewees believe that the partnerships have helped to accelerate institutional learning about continuous improvement and that the relationships are helpful in funding internal professional development needs. For example, Kellogg Company gives money to institutions to redefine land grant institutions. We were told that executives from Kellogg are *asking questions* of institutions such as: How do you partner better? How do you listen to constituent groups? Again, industry is definitely driving quality initiatives. An administrator reinforced this sentiment:

> What choice did the Japanese have? Things were not good, they had to improve, and they turned to quality. Like General Motors . . . what choice did they have? Maybe higher education is nearing that point. What we are trying to do by implementing quality is to make sure we never get to that point.

Many people believe that these partnerships have contributed to more creative thinking within the institution. When they witness businesses changing the paradigm, it becomes easier to think about doing the same at their institutions. The partnerships also facilitate learning. For example, one institution created a learning network of quality-oriented organizations so that in addition to learning, the organizations could pool resources to bring nationally recognized speakers to the community. According to the president of this institution, the network functions as follows:

> The network consists of about 20 companies, none of which compete with one another. There is a membership fee, and every company puts together a senior leadership team of four or five people. The first year, each company did a two-hour presentation to the group on their best practices. We brought in one or two speakers. The pattern is we have an outside speaker who will give a two-hour lecture, and each one of the organizations can bring 50 people, plus we sell tickets. We will have 1,000 to 1,500 people for the lecture. Then the network will have lunch with the speaker.

> We have been known to spend three hours interacting and discussing the
> lecture. Because the event is held on campus, students do not have to pay
> for the designated student tickets. Speakers have included Stephen Covey,
> Peter Senge, Peter Block, and Joel Barker to name a few.

As this example illustrates, educational institutions and business organizations
have found ways to learn and to grow by working together. They have access
to resources that they would not normally have because of their creativity in
finding ways to combine their financial resources. It is a practice of cooperat-
ing rather than competing. The fact that the members are noncompetitive
enables a freer exchange of information. The importance of the partnering
concept was explained by one president:

> We are not alone in this quality movement. The whole community is
> partnering on this effort. We belong to the quality council, and 25 of us
> went to a Deming four-day seminar together with business, industry,
> public employees, the city manager, the public school system, and the
> private college in the community. The community continues to engage
> itself in improving the quality effort and moving to a quality paradigm as a
> community. Our institution is only one segment of a very large movement.

Another president had this to say about the value of partnering with businesses:

> I am eager to link up more with businesses in the area. It helps our people
> see the importance of continuous improvement. When students show
> that they are familiar with quality improvement concepts, employers love
> it. I want to extend our effort into the undergraduate experience more
> fully.

Developing relationships with businesses in the local communities is a win/
win situation many times over. Institutions and businesses win by sharing
knowledge and resources. Students and employers win because students have
the knowledge needed and desired by employers. Institutions further along in
the quality journey are well aware of the advantages of partnering and have
been proactive in establishing these business ties.

Collecting and Analyzing Data— Summary

While the institutions we studied are struggling to develop ways to measure
the results of their efforts, they are systematically collecting data to improve
decision making, to monitor stakeholder satisfaction, and to improve processes. Data are being collected by a variety of methods, including suggestion
systems, surveys, and focus groups. Rather than making arbitrary decisions
based on intuition, institutions are establishing systems to continually gather
data for use in making decisions.

Quality tools are being used to analyze data and to improve decisions in a
variety of situations. Even though the flow chart is the most commonly used

tool at our institutions, we learned that they also consistently use the cause-and-effect diagram and Pareto charts. Brainstorming, nominal group technique, and affinity diagrams are also tools used to improve decision making. We discovered that many people within the administration are educated well enough in the use of the tools that they use them in a variety of settings from developing mission statements to conducting team meetings.

Our findings indicate that institutions are beginning to benchmark other institutions and organizations. In fact, a number of interviewees said that they are willing to participate in this project because they want to encourage other institutions to pursue the quality journey, and they see this book as one way to do this. Institutions are also partnering with businesses in the communities as a way to share resources, to fund continued professional development, and to establish closer relationships.

When institutions are learning about quality improvement, developing and communicating about the vision and mission statements, developing the knowledge and skills of members, or collecting and analyzing data, they are simultaneously improving the overall communication system. Communicating effectively so that continuous improvement is a priority is the next system to be discussed.

SYSTEM 6: IMPROVING COMMUNICATION

All of the system changes need to be communicated across institutions. An effective communication system is a key to the success of having members across the institution improve processes. This particular system is broader than the system communicating the vision and mission statements—system 3. A crucial component of system 6 is improving how people interact with one another formally and informally so that the overall system of communication is more open and feedback is incorporated.

Several patterns emerged from our analysis of the communication systems at the institutions in the study: language used significantly affects the ability to communicate; systems are designed with the purpose of sharing information across all levels of the institution; members need to be able to communicate efficiently and effectively because multiple perspectives are involved in making decisions; several methods of communicating can be used; and within a continuous improvement organization, people cooperate rather than compete for information.

Language

When we asked about language, several themes emerged. One theme was that institutions continue to grapple with the language of quality improvement. The findings were mixed in terms of the words people are using. Several institutions are using "total quality management (TQM)" because they feel it accurately communicates what is meant by quality improvement to most people. It has also been a common term in the literature and popular press. In addition to TQM, "continuous quality improvement (CQI)" is another term often used in our institutions.

But whatever terminology is used, an important part of continuous improvement is helping people learn a common language. We heard statements such as

> I think it is just good management. We call it total quality management but it is about participative management and process improvement.

> We call it TQM because that is the common denominator for most people, but we do not press the language.

> I am convinced the word "quality" will go out of style just like the word "excellence." The concepts of empowerment, of shared authority and responsibility, of using teams, of getting input from people closest to the process, of putting the customer first are concepts that are here to stay.

Open Communication

The key to successful quality improvements is more than just language used, though. It makes no difference, for example, whether the term "customer" is used for students or not. What is important is that students are viewed as expert witnesses who can testify about the sequences of experiences at each step of each process. They are intelligent products who are able to talk to instructors all along the way. In business and industry where quality efforts have made drastic improvements in product quality and customer satisfaction, the products (i.e., automobiles, computers, hamburgers) are not intelligent products and therefore cannot provide constant feedback for improvement (Ewell, 1996). Given this advantage, it only makes sense to create systems of communication that integrate students as partners in improving the quality of education.

It was clear from our interviews that people understand the importance of open communication. We heard about senior leaders speaking all over campus and holding "town meetings" so that people from all areas of the institution can *ask questions*. Most of the institutions we studied had to redesign their systems to encourage two-way communication. People must feel comfortable enough to give feedback, and they need to see that their feedback is "heard" and then used to improve processes and systems. The degree to which channels of communication are open is usually a reflection of the institutional culture, which is why we designated creating a quality culture as system 1.

There was a pattern among administrators, faculty, and staff of giving information away rather than hoarding it for one's own benefit. Sharing information within the institution and among institutions is becoming the norm in the institutions we studied. We were told that members need to talk to one another about continuous improvement until it becomes the common language that weaves people together. Because every employee is a part of the system, communicating effectively at all levels is vital.

Interviewees reported that implementing quality principles changes both how and what people communicate. The change usually revolves around *asking different questions*, which results in different conversations. People are changing their perspectives and looking at situations differently. This new mind-set is reflected in comments such as the following:

> Quality means getting everybody to ask questions about how we do things, why we do things, and should we be doing different things.

> At research institutions, everyone is asking questions. Quality means continuing to ask questions about things rather than relying on history or tradition.

> My approach to quality is to ask questions. What do you want to do to make it better around here? What are your ideas? Who do you want to participate? Why should they participate? With questions, you get out of TQM-speak or jargon. It is important to think about how to communicate with the various audiences.

Interestingly, interviewees are acutely aware of the communication process. Once educated about continuous improvement, they have high expectations of the communication process. They appreciate effective communication, and they become frustrated with ineffective communication. The interviewees indicated that they continually evaluate the communication process. Since effective communication is two-way, feedback is an important part of the communication system. Members, however, are only willing to give feedback if decision makers are willing to listen.

The communication system breaks down when feedback is not incorporated to complete the loop. When feedback is not given, people feel left out. It is difficult for people to improve when they receive little feedback about their performance. Lack of feedback can lead members to fear what they do not know. Because of these difficulties, institutions are working hard to ensure that their communication systems are complete and continuous.

An incident in one of the focus group sessions illustrates the importance of feedback. One member was extremely concerned about what we were going to do with the information collected. We thought the concern was about confidentiality, so, as authors, we continued to reassure him that he could trust us, that we were not going to report anything that would identify him. As it turned out, he wanted to make sure that the administrators at his institution *heard* the information. It was important to him that his input be fed back to the administration. He stated it this way:

Will you please tell them what the problems are? Could this report be given back to the institution? I expect to be heard in this room, and I thought that it was going to be brought to the higher-ups' attention. I do not want to waste my time if they will not have the opportunity to hear what I have to say.

Fortunately, this institution was one of the first we studied. After this discussion, we changed our interview system to ask participants if they wanted us to report the focus group discussions to the senior leaders. We improved our system based on his feedback (data collection), and most of the focus groups chose to have a report sent to the senior leaders. As this story illustrates, feedback is viewed as an essential part of the communication system by all members of the institution.

But as one administrator said, "If you are going to ask for feedback, you have to be able to listen to what they have to say." Another faculty member stated that their administrators, like most people, do not like dissenting opinions but that they do listen. Most interviewees emphasized that they work on sharing information with others, but many interviewees stressed that when information is shared, it needs to be honest information for people to trust one another. For example, when leaders admit mistakes, the communication system is perceived to be more effective.

Methods of Communication

A variety of communication methods are used by the institutions we studied as part of the system designed to share information. Some of the more common methods include campus forums, meetings, newsletters, e-mail, informal and formal gatherings, and surveys. Each activity occurs on a regular basis so that people can rely on that method for information. Each of these methods will be discussed on the following pages.

Campus Forums. Campus forums are one way to keep the quality movement alive and to communicate what it entails. An administrator explained his institution's forum this way:

In the first year we had an all-campus forum in which there was a panel that the chancellor chaired. Several of the deans were on that panel. This was a perfect opportunity for anyone to ask questions. That was an exceptional day for me to listen to our people, to interact with them. They were well prepared, and they asked excellent questions. We have the forums once a quarter, and people are curious about what is going on.

Some leaders believe that it is important to have an all-campus convocation or an event to communicate where the institution is going, similar to a state-of-the-institution address. Campus forums are a common practice in many institutions, but what is different at institutions employing quality principles and practices is the atmosphere of the event. Interviewees often described these events as having a theme and a party atmosphere. One respondent provided a description of the event:

> We are starting to have two meetings each semester in which the whole university community is called together to hear what is going on. We are going to talk about the staff survey at the next one. We are going to ballyhoo and recognize people who have done an outstanding job on quality.

To communicate quality improvement success stories, several institutions host a one- or two-day event for quality improvement teams to showcase their projects and the changes that have resulted from their team's efforts. The atmosphere described to us is one of celebration and excitement. In addition to communicating to the college community how quality improvement efforts have benefited the institution, these events also provide visibility to the quality movement, encourage interaction among people at all levels of the institution, recognize the quality efforts of many people, and help people develop respect for one another. Some other indirect benefits are reflected in this quote:

> Our quality event put people who are hidden within the infrastructure of the university into the role of teachers. The whole university has the chance to recognize the quality work they are doing. We had positive publicity from the event. There were pictures in the paper of regents talking to custodial and information technology people.

As this quote illustrates, campus forums not only improve communication, but they also help highlight the players behind the scenes. Institutional members who are not usually included in the communication system are involved and recognized for their participation in the continuous improvement efforts. The forums were described as events that help build a sense of community.

Meetings. To improve the effectiveness of communication, some institutions are working hard to improve the effectiveness of all meetings. These institutions are making systematic changes so that meetings are more inclusive and occur more regularly. The primary focus of the meetings is to share information.

Many of the institutions we studied have regular joint meetings with various groups on campus. Traditionally, groups meet independently of one another, but we discovered a pattern of holding meetings with faculty and administration and/or staff. Joint meetings with faculty and deans are also common. Rather than having people meet by levels, some meetings are designed to create a more horizontal organization and to provide for a freer exchange of information. A useful example of how institutions are using several forms of communication was provided by an administrator who stated:

In addition to the forums, we put together a one-hour presentation that we are going to cascade out throughout the institution. Each dean has an hour meeting with each cabinet. We were going through a tough retrenchment time and some of this did not materialize, although many areas did follow through.

Running effective meetings requires changing thought processes and behaviors. People regularly said that in their meetings, they create ground rules or parameters on which the members agree so that there is ownership, accountability, and responsibility from the start. During the meeting, some interviewees use the concept called the "issue bin." If a topic comes up during the meeting but does not pertain to the discussion, it is placed in the issue bin, which means that it is written down on a flip chart or board. The purpose is to document the idea so that it is not lost but is dealt with at a more appropriate time. This simple concept keeps meetings on task.

The primary reason why institutions have systematically redesigned their meetings is to open communication channels. Quality processes and tools are used in meetings, and interviewees spoke enthusiastically about how meetings are more effective and more efficient as a result. Perhaps the strongest evidence to support the belief that quality principles improved meetings is that interviewees stated that people come more prepared for meetings than before the quality initiatives. They come with data in hand or with charts and graphs to illustrate data. A general consensus emerged that having data at meetings improves decision making.

Examples of innovative ideas that institutions have implemented to encourage communication include staff meetings attended by senior leadership of the department, college, or institution; all-college meetings (two meetings per year was common) for senior leadership to communicate with all institutional members; and minutes from meetings, particularly budget meetings, sent on e-mail so that anyone can read and respond to them. Other examples are training sessions to teach members how to conduct an effective meeting and the use of facilitators in meetings to encourage communication and to allow the chairperson to take a more active role.

Some of the institutions have the capital budget online so that this information is readily accessible. We were told that this is a powerful tool for opening up communication channels within the institutions. The following story illustrates how this small change in the system has significantly influenced how people communicate, which, in turn, influences the decisions that are made:

> The budget committee consists of faculty, administration, and staff, and the capital budget is online. At times, we have excess money in this account, but there are no secrets. Everyone has a chance to see everyone else's budget requests. We have vertically integrated meetings and we come up with proposals that are always more than the budget. But before

the meeting, everyone on the committee receives a copy of the proposed budget line by line. This opens up discussion from the start. We begin to ask questions such as, What is the mission of the college? What do we need to succeed? People usually decide what they can give up. We collaborate and share resources. The budget used to be a black box, and no one knew how decisions were made. Because of our commitment to quality, the budget is constructed in a logical fashion with input from all areas. The outcome has been people working together to decide how to save money. The creativity is unbelievable.

Perhaps the most important pattern that emerged in terms of meetings is the level of understanding and acceptance interviewees have of meetings. People were excited to tell us about the positive changes in their meetings. They feel informed and included. In essence, they feel empowered, and this feeling is reflected in their positive attitude toward meetings.

Newsletters. Newsletters are also commonly integrated into the communication system. Many of the institutions we studied publish a quality improvement newsletter that describes their efforts. These newsletters are typically used to develop a shared vision, to highlight quality efforts, and to share success stories. They also serve to continually educate all members about quality principles, practices, and tools.

The publication of these newsletters varies from weekly to monthly to quarterly, but the importance of the newsletters does not vary. Interviewees felt it was vital to have a system in place that consistently communicates the value of the efforts being made to improve processes and systems. Once institutions understand the significance of this type of communication, variations of newsletters are developed. For example, some departments have started their own newsletters to communicate with graduates. The driving force for this effort is the desire to keep alumni informed. It is also hoped that graduates will experience a stronger sense of connection to the department and that they will eventually become donors. In addition, the newsletters are another venue for collecting feedback from graduates regarding skills and competencies so that programs can be improved.

Maintaining the perception of positive momentum is challenging, and communicating internally about achievements in the area of quality improvements is difficult, but necessary. One respondent described the two purposes of these publications best:

We need an internal publication to keep everyone informed about what is happening on campus. We need someone to translate what is going on internally and to transport the information externally.

Although newsletters are being developed and incorporated into the communication system, we consistently heard from interviewees that more needs to be done in the area of internal publications. Most of our institutions are in the beginning stages of regularly communicating internally about their quality improvement efforts. The more effective the communication system is, the better the support for the quality initiative should be.

E-mail. E-mail is another mode of communication being used consistently in the institutions in this study as a way of encouraging anyone to talk to anyone else about anything. It was often reported to us that e-mail has helped to drive fear out of the organization because it facilitates communication across levels. People believe that the e-mail system flattens the organization by removing the hierarchical barriers that often cause fear. Members of the staff and the faculty frequently commented on how e-mail has made the top administrators, particularly the president, much more accessible and approachable. As one person said, "We can discuss the undiscussables."

A system that works well at one institution is a weekly report from the president. In this report, people are encouraged to ask questions of the president about whatever is on their minds. Every Monday on e-mail or hard copy the president responds to every question asked that week. The questions can be asked anonymously, but as the system continues, the president said that more people feel comfortable taking ownership and are not as concerned about anonymity. A general consensus among members of the faculty, staff, and administration was that the e-mail system of reporting has greatly controlled rumors that can negatively affect the institutional culture, in addition to opening up communication significantly. Several people referred to the report as "the rumor control report."

Similar to a newsletter, this weekly report keeps people updated on what is happening on campus: announcements are made, teams submit updates, new teams are announced, information is updated from the governing board, and people submit general items. While institutional newsletters are common in many institutions, this president's report is different in that everyone "hears" responses to every question asked of the president on a weekly basis. We concluded that e-mail encourages more communication and links people together, which helps reinforce the concept of systems thinking.

Formal and Informal Gatherings. Another method of opening channels of communication is the use of formal and informal gatherings. Even though these gatherings may be commonplace at most institutions, institutions we visited have intentionally incorporated them into their communication system as ways of encouraging more open communication among members. Getting institutional members together in order to share information and to collect feedback on how processes and systems are working is an important part of the communication system.

Presidents and top administrators are systematically integrating a series of gatherings to encourage more open and honest communication within the institution. At one institution, people are invited to breakfast so that senior leaders can collect informal data from members at various levels. Approximately 20 people are randomly selected for these breakfasts for which there is no agenda. Usually the group is a mix of faculty and staff members and administrators, and the intention is to maintain an informal atmosphere. It was described as a way to give administrators an opportunity to share success stories, to ask and answer questions, and to control rumors.

Although the goal of encouraging open communication is the same at all the institutions, another example of a good communication opportunity is a presidential tea. The people who attend appreciate the recognition and consider the event rewarding. We were told that there are three governing ideas: (1) to say thank you for work well done (at the tea, everyone is given a small gift such as a lapel pin by the president); (2) to define reality: vision, mission, and values; and (3) to discuss current questions in the system. In addition, the president wanted to collect data. Before one tea, people were asked to complete a card that had two questions: How does my job impact retention? What is the best thing going at this institution?

At another institution, the department chair surveys the faculty asking two basic questions: What do you need from me? How can I help you accomplish your goals? He takes people to lunch in small groups to talk about how to build more of a community within the department. He started a system of one faculty seminar per month to discuss teaching techniques, to share research ideas, or to informally interact based on the feedback from his colleagues. Formal and informal gatherings have worked well in the institutions in our study to encourage a more casual type of communication that can have an important role in creating a culture of trust and support. These gatherings also have contributed to a stronger feeling that everyone is on the same team working for the same goals.

Surveys. Another important component of the communication system is the use of surveys to collect data for decision making. Surveys are used to collect feedback on a regular basis so members feel they have consistent input into the system. Even though surveys are commonly conducted at many institutions, the institutions we studied differed because they have integrated the surveys into their communication systems. In other words, surveys are conducted regularly rather than randomly or sporadically. Institutions must continually monitor the expectations of stakeholders to determine the level of their satisfaction, and surveys are one of the best ways to do this. In the institutions we studied, they not only understand the value of collecting data, but they also know the importance of telling members what they "heard" from the data.

Completing the feedback loop is the key to opening up communication channels.

Faculty members determined to continuously improve in the classroom use a variety of surveys to collect data from students. These techniques are designed to open communication channels between the faculty member and the students. These surveys will be further explained in system 8 on improving learning and teaching.

Improving Communication—Summary

As these examples illustrate, administrators are changing their thinking about what constitutes effective communication, and their behaviors reflect this change in thinking. They are *asking different questions* of members, and they have found that this leads to different answers. The questions vary, but the goal is always to find ways to continuously improve systems and processes within the institution.

Quality principles and practices depend on open and honest communication. Learning about quality improvement terms and concepts allows members to communicate effectively. For the most part, members are involved, they share information with others, they stress the value of feedback, and they *ask different questions*. In the institutions we studied, the primary ways of communicating that emerged are campus forums, meetings, newsletters, e-mail, informal and formal gatherings, and surveys.

Sharing information with organizational members and opening up communication channels are common themes emphasized in leadership literature. The difficulty lies in taking steps so that this communication occurs. The institutions we studied are making this happen. The key element that connects all of the methods of communication is the fact that these methods occur systematically. Since engaging in quality initiatives, most of our interviewees said that communication happens more regularly and that information is more readily shared with more people. There is an intentional effort to facilitate communication among members on all levels. They felt that this effort has positively changed their institutional culture.

The institutions in our study are aware that more communication is usually better than less. They are continually looking for ways to keep the quality improvement efforts visible and to articulate progress being made. As one member put it,

> We must constantly look for new ways to communicate how people are working together in new ways to innovate processes and systems, and to communicate how they are using quality principles, techniques, and tools.

We discovered that people are communicating differently as a result of working differently. Teamwork and collaboration are quality concepts being practiced in these institutions. The next section, system 7, describes how institutions are developing and encouraging people to work in teams. Included are various examples of both project teams and management teams.

SYSTEM 7: DEVELOPING AND ENCOURAGING TEAMWORK

The institutions we studied are actively using teams to solve problems and to improve processes. Even though working in groups, committees, or task forces is commonplace for most institutions, working in teams is not. Using teams is a new approach to problem solving in higher education, which involves learning new behaviors and which changes the way people perceive their work. We discovered a pattern composed of this sequence of events: 1) data are collected usually from a survey or focus group; 2) issues emerge from the data; and 3) teams are formed to study an issue and to make improvements within financial limitations. In this section, system 7, we describe how both project and management teams are being used in the institutions in our study.

Building effective teams that include all levels is a priority for all the institutions we studied. Even though many interviewees suggested that their institutions still need to work on team building, cross-functional teams are becoming common. People stressed the value of including those members closest to the process. By involving people who are most affected by the process, teams have access to the information they need to make changes. As staff members related,

> The cross-functional part is the most enlightening. We included customers as members of our team.

> People were asked to listen to the other person's point of view without becoming defensive. Their input was valuable in helping us to understand the issues.

Teams are formed in different ways, but the objective is to include people who have useful input from every layer of the institution, from housekeeping to the president. Typically, team membership is voluntary and teams usually meet on institutional time. As people become accustomed to working in teams, they discover that anyone can set up a team to solve a problem. They feel empowered and supported by the institution. We heard interviewees say:

> Three administrators asked for a meeting with me and the vice president of administration. At the time, two of the groups reported to me and one to him. They wanted to be combined as an enrollment team. We asked when they wanted to do this and their response was, now. We told them to consider it done. Things happen in teams.

> When something is not working, you can form a team. People are willing to be included. It is important to note that you do not have to check with the higher-ups before you form a team.

I had made some suggestions about procedures, and shortly after that I received an e-mail message asking if I would like to be on the team.

Cross-functional teams even include people from the community. For example, one institution brought in executives from various businesses and used the nominal group technique to come to a consensus on what skills and knowledge the new hires need to have to be most marketable. As a result, certificate programs in customer service and quality leadership were created for people within the community.

Quite a few interviewees expressed the notion that cross-functional teams provide an opportunity for individuals to learn from one another and that the teams create a nurturing atmosphere. As stated by one administrator,

We view the person who sweeps the building as just as important as anyone else. If this person does not do quality work, the institution looks bad. Everyone needs to be involved in improving processes.

Another staff member shared this perspective:

We identified four critical processes in our office and assigned ownership of two of those processes to each associate director. This set some boundaries and gave us a better sense of who was doing what. The most valuable part of quality for us was assigning teams, getting sponsors, identifying things that need to be improved, and having the management working in our teams. We have people buying into quality at all levels. There is so much more sharing of information.

We heard of many successful teams at the institutions; however, many interviewees made it clear that professional development is required before working together on teams because of the new roles and new behaviors that are expected. Once people are educated in quality improvement concepts, it is best to assign them to teams right away so that they can use their training. Since true teamwork is not the norm in higher education, many people said that teamwork is a major cultural shift for their institution. One respondent said it best:

I heard about the team concept and I thought that was the way things should always be done. Then I realized that teamwork is not everyone's mode of operation. Teamwork is so foreign to some that it will be difficult to change their minds.

Because the members in these institutions have been educated on continuous improvement, most of them realize the significance of using facilitators for all kinds of meetings. Facilitators keep the team on task and help to ensure participation from all members. Facilitator development is one key area in which people are usually educated. One president provided this perspective:

I am a member of several teams. I resent not being allowed to participate in the discussion and then having the situation passed on to me to make a decision. It seems to me that if we are going to make a cultural change, that the president needs to be engaged in the discussion. I do not mean dominating the discussion, but to be a part of the team. There are going to be issues about presidential and collegial involvement, and I need to participate in the discussion. Facilitators allow me to do this.

In addition to facilitators, support from senior leadership is often critical to team success. When teams do not feel empowered and supported, the time spent working in teams is perceived as a waste of time. One staff member expressed the need for support this way:

Our team had upper-level management who were able to say, "We are going to do this." That was a crucial step in the process. The project improvement team came up with changes, but we were not sure we could get the changes implemented. But we recommended an action plan and the administration agreed. That is so important to the success of the team.

Once people are comfortable using cross-functional teams, more departments organize themselves as teams, taking the team concept back to their specific work areas. People expressed their growing desire to work with others because of their interdependence and systems thinking. Along this line, an administrator shared this experience:

At our institution, teamwork is taking place more at the natural work team level. What supports it is our coaching system that we have developed. It is totally voluntary, but people from various departments go through training and then are assigned as a coach to a team in another area. In a spirit of reciprocity, that team will send someone to coaches training to be deployed elsewhere in the institution. This indicates the interdependence within the institution and the desire to build cross-learning capabilities within the institution in order to understand other components than itself. We are forging interrelationships and cooperation instead of a constant culture of competition.

Using Project Teams

People within the institutions we studied have changed the way they work and how they think about their work. When members see a process that needs to be improved, they feel empowered to set up a team with a variety of perspectives, to find a solution, and to make the change. Most of the examples shared with us were project-based teams (a team with a goal of improving a process) established to improve internal processes. For example, a project-based team was set up to examine the time it took for a professor to receive a book from the library after it had been requested. The process took an unusually long time, but the team was able to reduce the time substantially. Additional examples of project-based teams accomplished the following:

- self-directed custodial work teams set up procedures to reduce grievances;
- team led by provost streamlined academic services;
- team examined ID card system for the entire campus: dorm access, food services, security;
- team analyzed internal building systems on campus;
- team reviewed policies and procedures manual for the school;
- team addressed the hiring and management of student assistants in the library;
- registration team piloted telephone registration;
- resource administration team studied moving from a mainframe environment to a distributed computer environment;
- team studied senior-level accessibility and made recommendations;
- system monitoring and renewal team identified and dealt with problems and processes related to the development, scheduling, and delivery of programs; and
- student service team worked on customer service, career development, and performance/accountability.

One particular success story involved a student services streamlining team that was asked to improve and to integrate many services including admissions, registration, financial aid, student accounts, and housing. They were to develop a one-stop shopping place for student services. The goal was to move student services closer to the students by having a centralized location. The idea emerged out of surveys that indicated dissatisfaction with student services.

All of the offices affected were represented on the team. They began by benchmarking with another institution. With the help of a facilitator, they met for two hours two days each week, for approximately three months. As the team was beginning, the members signed a covenant that required members to talk with the people in their areas about the deliberations on a regular basis so that these people were continually informed, and therefore, they would not be surprised about the recommendations.

Because the team consisted of front-line assistants rather than administrators, there was some initial resistance about who was on the team. But throughout our interviews at this institution, administrators and staff members consistently mentioned this team as a success story and expressed hope that the team would serve as a model for the future. They said the team succeeded because it was made up of the people who did the actual work and not the administrators who often made the decisions. One staff member of the team elaborated:

> I told my father about this team and he said, "You are telling me that every member on the team except the team leader is a secretary?" I had not

really thought about it like that. I viewed it as including people on the team who are on the front-line having to deal with the process. It made sense to me, but not to my father. He thought it was a good idea though, and said "I hope you realize that you work at a wonderful place." And I do realize this.

This team was eventually awarded the USA Today Quality Cup for education for their innovativeness in making quality improvements.

At another institution, a cross-functional team made up of students, student affairs staff, faculty members, and administrators was created to study retention. After analyzing data, they concluded that the greatest retention problem is at the end of the first year. They recommended a new position to the board of trustees, Dean of Freshmen. This position cuts across all boundaries, and this person tracks the freshman experience. Anything that happens to first-year students between when they register and when they become second-year students is in the jurisdiction of this dean. As reported to us, retention is improving.

Another example of a team effort to solve a problem involved studying the food service situation. The same food service contractor had been used for 18 years, and even though students would informally complain, their feedback was not "heard" until the first student survey. A team was pulled together of students, faculty, and staff members to analyze the situation and examine other vendors. (There were not any senior administrators on the team.) The team visited other schools and interviewed other companies. The team selected the highest priced contractor, but according to the administrator responsible for food service, "food service has dropped off my list of problems and concerns." About seven years have passed and based on student survey data, food service is not an issue for most students.

Using Management Teams

Other teams are created to be management teams, to manage a process. A staff member shared that at his institution teams and team leaders make 85 percent of the decisions within the physical plant. The teams understand they are accountable for the decisions, which in turn makes them more responsible. Team meetings are held weekly, and team leader meetings are held every two weeks. Another administrator offered an additional example of how a management team has changed the decision-making process:

My staff is now a self-managed team. They went through quality training, and we no longer have a department manager. The manager left and the staff made the decision to be self-managed, and it has worked wonderfully. They make their own decisions, write their own job descriptions, and they hire people themselves.

Additional examples of management teams include

- physical plant divided into teams by duties and jobs: steam team, craft team, office team, green team (grounds);
- leadership team in the business school made up of the provost, associate business dean, dean of music, and a stakeholder from the business community.

These examples indicate the variety of projects and processes for which institutions are using teams. Based on our data, project teams are more common than management teams. People are regularly brought together to improve a particular project.

Although there was a general consensus that teams take time, many interviewees told us they enjoy being on teams, and they believe it is a valuable use of time. They feel that teams are more action-oriented and more effective than committees. Once decisions are made in project teams, the teams disband and people move on to other tasks. They reported that it is rewarding seeing the results of their efforts reflected in improved processes.

Involving Students on Teams

We found a concerted effort to involve students in the quality movement by placing them on teams. As people recognize the value of student input, they are placing students on teams so that the students are involved in the decision-making process. In the institutions that systematically include students in their quality efforts, there was a general confirmation that the outcomes are positive. Quoting one quality educator:

> Developing teams with students and watching them get excited about quality keeps us excited about it. Students maintain the excitement.

Because students are being taught about quality principles and practices in some classes, it was common to find students actively involved in teams focusing on continuous improvement. One example was the continuous improvement committee, made up of students who identified opportunities for improvement within the business school. Within the courses that focused on quality concepts in the business school, student teams produced projects that improved processes in a business in the community or in the business school itself. One team studied the student MBA newspaper, conducting a satisfaction survey of 2,000 students, which focused on various aspects of the paper such as distribution and composition. With the help of the newspaper staff, the team redesigned processes. The result:

> Now they have a student newspaper that is very differently laid out with a different content and new ways of obtaining the content. For example, they print student papers recommended by professors. There are new sources for articles and a variety of articles.

One institution developed a series of seminars on quality improvement topics for student leaders on campus. Another institution encouraged putting together a student team within the classroom to collect data from other students to improve classroom learning.

Comparing Teams and Committees

Perhaps one of the most important points learned was that teams function effectively only when people have been taught the differences between teams and committees because the expectations are different. When members learn what it means to be an effective team member, all members share the responsibility for the assigned task. They take more ownership in the project, and they rely on the skills of everyone to accomplish the task. In contrast, a committee consists of several members who usually do not know each other well enough to know what skills members possess. Committees also do not feel the sense of shared responsibility, and therefore, do not take as much ownership in the project. People seem to "put in their time" in committees, regardless of whether the task gets accomplished. They know other committee members will be elected, even if they don't finish the assigned task.

There are other differences between teams and committees. In composing a team, people are usually selected because of their knowledge and interest in the project or process. In committees, people are typically elected by their peers, and they may not be the most appropriate members for improving the process. A faculty member illustrated this point:

> The dean formed an ad hoc committee on curriculum development recognizing that the curriculum needed to be reformed. He brought in faculty members from each department at the grassroots level. But he asked members to decide if they wanted to do this. They had the option to say no. The option to say no cemented the committee. His charge was: What are the elements of an effective curriculum? The list was not discipline-specific, but it cut across courses such as communication and team-building skills. The committee used quality tools in the committee process. This committee has been effective because it functions as a team.

Interviewees credited the professional development efforts for helping members understand that teams think, act, and feel different from groups or committees. We heard people describe the difference between committees and teams as follows: committees are "a waste of time" because they are notorious for being passive, yet time is spent in dreaded committee meetings. Conversely, teams are perceived to be an effective use of time because they solve problems and are action-oriented. Interviewees consistently regarded team meetings as more effective and more enjoyable than committee meetings. Several people stated that they even look forward to team meetings because they consistently see the results of their team efforts.

Developing and Encouraging Teamwork and Collaboration—Summary

It is one thing to talk about teamwork; it is another thing to practice team-work. The institutions we studied are using teams, particularly cross-func-tional teams, to solve problems, improve processes, and manage projects. There was a general sentiment that the teams being formed and used are a new way of operation for these institutions. People like the culture change because they feel involved, empowered, and energized. Committees can hurt morale because of the perceived inaction, but teams are uplifting because of the action that is a result of teamwork. Another significant point was that many teams are formed to improve processes, and once the process is improved, the team is dissolved. Our interviewees stressed that they like being on teams because they feel the time is productive and because improvements are made as a result of the team effort.

In addition, interviewees value the relationships that form when working in teams. One interviewee remarked that she knows more people and has better friends now because of a team experience than before she worked on the team. Interestingly, she has been with the institution over 20 years.

Professional development plays a critical role in teaching members how to function in teams. People learn the various roles needed in teams and how to run team meetings. At some of our institutions, students are learning about teams and are participating in teams to improve systems and processes.

The first seven systems discussed so far have focused on implementing quality improvement on campus, but for the most part, little has been said about using quality principles on the academic side of the institution to improve the quality of education. Since learning and teaching is the primary mission of higher education institutions, we wanted to know how quality improvement efforts have changed experiences in the classroom. We found that faculty members who have learned quality principles and practices or have been on a quality improvement team are changing their practices in the classroom. System 8 focuses on how institutions are using quality concepts to improve learning and teaching.

SYSTEM 8: IMPROVING LEARNING AND TEACHING

According to one administrator, "Continuous improvement is a blind spot for teachers." The recent literature on quality improvement in higher education confirms what has been commonly suspected: continuous quality improve-ment is moving more slowly on the academic side than on the administrative side. (Chaffee and Sherr, 1992; Coate, 1991; DeCosmo, Parker, and Heverly, 1991; Evans, 1992; Seymour, 1991; Seymour and Collett, 1991). This was also supported by our national survey. (Refer to table 7 in appendix B.) One reason for this discrepancy is that faculty members have not been professionally developed to the extent that administrators and staff members have been. Although our national study and the institutions in our detailed study reinforced this finding, we are encouraged by the progress being made.

Several themes emerged within this system. First, faculty members who have adopted quality principles and practices understand the power of shifting the focus from teaching to learning, from professor-centered thinking to student-centered thinking. They make a conscious effort to implement feedback mechanisms into the classroom environment so that continuous improvements can be made. Second, students are being actively involved in the learning process as the focus shifts from teaching to learning. Faculty members with whom we spoke are using interactive teaching methods so that students can take more responsibility for their own learning.

We also discovered a pattern of faculty members organizing at the grassroots level to improve learning and teaching. On several campuses, small groups of faculty members have formed to talk about how to improve the learning process for students. In addition, institutions have found ways to financially support teaching improvement through existing resources such as business departments that teach courses on quality management or through forming teaching institutes.

The first theme, the changing role of faculty, was described by faculty members who see their role evolving from being the sole authority figure to being more of a facilitator, coach, and guide. There is an emphasis on involving students and on designing systems so that students take more responsibility for their own learning. For many teachers, this thinking may not be new, but we found a renewed focus on improving the learning and teaching processes. One administrator said it best:

> The best teachers are those who say that continuous improvement is just common sense. All teachers should be practicing this. But the poorer teachers do not have that common sense. They need to learn these techniques.

Another administrator explained the situation this way:

> It is hard to find people who are receptive or familiar with quality because it does not characterize most of higher education. The most nonquality culture in America today is the graduate culture of existing Ph.D.s. It is hierarchical and authoritarian, and unfortunately the system of teaching assistants is not working. So when we hire new faculty, we have to reeducate them.

One institution has actively used continuous improvement concepts to change the teaching assistants program. Teaching assistants are paid a percentage of their appointment to complete a project that will improve the quality of undergraduate education. The ideas for these one-year projects come from input from departments and various faculty members. One year the teaching assistants selected the faculty evaluation instruments as their project and redesigned the process. Another year the project was to find ways to integrate more case studies and real-world examples into the classroom. This system has the support of the administration, and the faculty members indicated that they are pleased with the teaching assistant teams.

Continuous feedback and classroom assessment are examples of the quality principles being practiced by faculty members in the institutions we studied. Faculty members emphasized that a culture of trust has to be cultivated for student feedback to be honest and helpful. They stressed that they are *asking different questions* in the classroom and that asking these questions leads to classroom improvement. Interviewees often mentioned "minute papers," which are a series of short questions asked by a faculty member as a way to collect student feedback and reactions. This type of formative feedback is becoming common practice at the institutions in this study. As one faculty member said, "The data I am collecting from students indicates that they perceive me as challenging, but fair." Even though summative or end-of-semester student evaluations are still standard practice, we had interviewees from one institution tell us that as a result of their quality efforts, there was a question added to the student evaluation forms: "How did the learning and teaching process change throughout the semester?" This question implies that the institution expects the instructor to make continuous changes throughout the course.

According to one focus group of faculty members, "Often informal conversations go to teaching issues." They explained that this sort of voluntary emphasis on teaching was not the case in the past. They attributed the increased emphasis on improving learning and teaching to the quality initiative and professional development members had received.

Using quality principles and practices to more directly involve students in the learning process was another theme we discovered. In most of the institutions we studied, a core group of faculty members is thinking differently about teaching, and this shift in thinking is reflected in their assignments and decisions. For example, one engineering school has a first-year design course in which students work in teams. They solicit industry problems and identify customer needs in designing their project. Because the students work with actual customers from industry, the projects are realistic. The shift in thinking is reflected in the quote of one of the faculty members, "Students see the project as the goal; faculty perceive the process as the goal."

Another example of the shift in thinking is provided by an administrator. He related how the faculty members in math were concerned because some business students were having trouble in the math courses that were prerequisites for finance courses. It turned out that if the students were able to enroll in the finance courses without taking the math prerequisites, they were able to pass the finance courses anyway. The math professors analyzed this situation and concluded that either they were teaching the wrong content, or the students really did not need to take the math courses. This example indicates that faculty members are *asking different questions* to solve common problems.

Many of the faculty members did not necessarily attribute changes to continuous improvement efforts. In fact, many said that they make a conscious effort to avoid using the quality language so often associated with business and industry. Still, when faculty groups described the changes they are making in the classroom, the new behaviors are consistent with continuous improvement practices. Most of the faculty members with whom we spoke are comfortable with pedagogical methods such as collaborative learning strategies or classroom assessment, which are consistent with quality principles and practices. Many had not seen the connection between new methods of student learning and the concepts of continuous improvement before the quality initiative on campus.

At several institutions people referred to the "Seven Principles for Good Practice in Undergraduate Education" as published by the *Wingspread Journal* (Chickering and Gamson, 1987). These principles emerged from a study supported by the American Association of Higher Education, the Education Commission of the States, and The Johnson Foundation. According to this study, good practice in undergraduate education

- encourages student-faculty contact.
- encourages cooperation among students.
- encourages active learning.
- gives prompt feedback.
- emphasizes time on task.
- communicates high expectations.
- respects diverse talents and ways of learning.

These principles of good practice are similar to quality principles and practices. The emphasis is on gathering continuous feedback, sharing responsibility for learning with students, and encouraging a high level of interaction in the classroom.

Once faculty members developed an understanding about continuous improvement, they often became enthusiastic supporters. We found a pattern of small faculty groups forming to talk about how they can personally make changes to improve learning and teaching. This grassroots movement is usually voluntary, but the informal membership is growing.

Faculty members who participated in these groups shared that they feel a sense of camaraderie and cooperation. They learn from one another and do not spend time reinventing the wheel. Because the informal groups are often cross-discipline, it became apparent that faculty members have discovered a new meaning of the word "colleague." They have a better understanding of what it is like to work in a team to accomplish common goals by using everyone's strengths.

At one institution small faculty groups meet once a month. These groups are based on self-interest; they are self-directed, and the momentum is growing. For example, the institution started with one group and six years later there are eight groups of five or six members each. Members in the faculty focus group believe the groups should remain small, but encourage other members to form small groups of their own. One faculty member said that it took a few semesters to develop a level of trust among members, but once the trust is established, the open dialogue leads to synergy within the group. One group even wrote an article together, becoming a working group in addition to a group focused on teaching improvement.

At one of the research institutions, a teaching improvement program was initiated by members of the faculty. Since this program is operated by faculty members, it adapts to their teaching needs. The program focuses on what makes teaching valuable, meaningful, enriching, and motivational. Faculty members with whom we spoke indicated that given the context of their responsibilities where the emphasis is on research, the focus on teaching is a shift for them. They believed that because of the program, there is a feeling that quality teaching has become more of a priority than before quality improvement efforts. An ongoing dialogue about how to improve learning and teaching has been created, something that we were told did not exist before the formation of these groups. They perceived that faculty members are more excited about teaching in addition to their natural interests in their research areas. One faculty member described the program as "a series of questions since the program does not have the answers." We were told that even established faculty members who have not demonstrated an interest in improving their teaching in the past have been changing their behaviors and teaching strategies as a result of being involved in this program.

Although there is no pressure to become involved in the teaching improvement program or any specific rewards for participating in these groups, faculty members said they are motivated because they feel better about their teaching in the classroom. The cross-discipline aspect enables them to meet people they would not normally meet. Discussing teaching challenges and successes with people from other disciplines keeps people involved and interested in teaching. The programs are growing primarily through word-of-mouth. At both institutions using these groups, faculty members told us that the administration emotionally and financially supports the programs. They believe administrative support is one of the main reasons the groups have been successful. We had people tell us that improving teaching is a priority on which to spend time and energy.

Another institution has a teaching center that is a resource available to individuals across campus. The center sponsors informal sessions that focus on techniques to improve student learning. It also awards grants that support the development of teaching-related projects. Often the grants provide for release time to support faculty members in improving their teaching methods. As stated by the director, "We want to encourage people to think of teaching as a form of scholarship. We want people to do research on issues related to teaching." This center is another way of creating a dialogue across campus about the importance of effective teaching and of recognizing excellent teachers. We were told that it helps faculty members realize that effective teaching and increased learning is a priority.

It was common to hear people say that faculty members are receptive to teaching improvement issues. Therefore, to help them translate quality improvement in the context of the classroom, the focus needs to be on student learning. We heard faculty members *asking different questions*. The driving question was, How can teaching be changed so that learning is improved? At one institution, faculty members reported that they have Friday afternoon seminars to talk about teaching techniques. People share the exercises they use to improve learning and teaching. The key is to engage faculty in a dialogue so that they see the relevance of continuous improvement in what they do individually.

Involving Students

Involving students in decision making is a new practice for the faculty members we interviewed. The traditional paradigm is that the professors rule the classroom because they are the experts of the discipline. Our interviewees discovered that involving students does not lessen the faculty member's expertise, because the focus is on process and not content. One faculty member uses the analogy that it is the instructor who designs the product and assesses the final quality, but it is the student who needs to design the processes in order for them to be effective.

The institutions we studied are making efforts to include students in quality efforts, though many do this by focusing on improving learning rather than by teaching quality. We found students participating in determining the most effective teaching processes for courses. Collaborative learning strategies— teaching techniques based on team learning—are congruent with the concepts of cross-functional teams. Classroom assessment techniques— methods used to determine how well students are comprehending the course material—are similar to feedback techniques advocated in the quality improvement literature.

Throughout our interviews, we found institutions creating systems to involve students and to incorporate student feedback in decision making.

Faculty members and administrators are challenging students to become partners in the learning process by seeking their input for decisions and by encouraging students to accept more responsibility for their own learning. It was common to hear interviewees say that students are assessing their own learning, and that an intense effort is underway to involve students in decision making and to actually listen to what they have to say.

Another pattern was toward use of interactive teaching methods rather than the traditional lecture method. In one institution, students critique drafts of syllabi; in another, students design the evaluation forms for the various course requirements. We were told that giving students some control over their learning environment facilitates active learning. When students are involved in making some of these decisions, they more fully understand the requirements. Some faculty even involve students in setting the agenda for what takes place in class. Given that the instructor outlines what has to be covered in class, the question asked of students becomes, How should the topics be covered?

Several faculty members told us how they are using the classroom to coordinate and improve activities outside the classroom. For example, students are being taught teamwork skills and how to conduct effective meetings so that they can operate successfully in teams on "real world" projects. As one faculty member put it,

> We require students to do group projects without having the skills to successfully complete these projects. We want to increase the chance for success and not set them up for failure by not teaching the skills that they need.

By involving students, interviewees believed that understanding and learning increase because the mystery of grading decreases. By way of illustration, an administrator shared this story:

> A teacher required three drafts of a paper and the students resented having to turn in three drafts. Because of the resentment, she asked the students, "What would I have to do in order to determine if you did a good job?" They said she should require three revisions in order to give them feedback.

In other words, when students are involved in the process of making decisions about the learning processes, they better understand the significance of the specific assignments.

In fact, we learned that students who are involved in the learning system can be more demanding than the faculty person. Several faculty members have class discussions on what students have to do to receive various grades, for instance, What constitutes an A based on what has to be accomplished and how are these criteria different from those that constitute a B? Faculty members reported that students are tougher on themselves than they are.

Students are also more accepting of the amount of work that needs to be done in the course after participating in these discussions. According to a few of the faculty members, the downside to these discussions is that the course gets off to a slower start because of the interaction about the course requirements. Despite this delay, they believe that having students as active participants who take ownership in the class is well worth the extra time.

Faculty members had numerous examples of how they are involving students in the classroom. One faculty member videotapes students giving speeches and receiving feedback from the students. Students add to the tape throughout the course. They have to listen to the feedback and are required to write an outline for improving the next speech. Quality principles and practices are also being integrated in the classroom by having students work in teams on projects to improve the institution. For example, in one business school a student team called the Continuous Improvement Committee was created to identify issues and problems in the school. As part of their coursework, they work on projects where the results benefit the school. One team organized a used-book exchange after identifying the need for improvement in this area. Another team worked on establishing a partnership with another business school in the area so that students would have access to more courses.

One business school proactively has student teams work on continuous improvement projects with companies in the community. They discovered that students can add value to actual companies in a relatively short time (one semester). One faculty member stated that "every student team that engaged in an improvement endeavor has been successful at some level."

As these examples illustrate, these faculty members have changed how they teach because they are starting to perceive students as partners in the learning process. Some faculty members are establishing systems to help them determine the barriers to learning so that these barriers can be removed. Within the institutions we studied, this shift in mind-set is changing behaviors of faculty members in the classroom. Instead of an adversarial student-teacher relationship that impedes learning, many faculty members are involving students in the system of learning. We were told that faculty members are more aware of teaching effectiveness as a result of the emphasis on continuous improvement and that they are taking advantage of opportunities to improve the learning process.

Teaching Courses on Quality Management

Courses in which quality principles and practices are central to the course content are primarily being taught in the business and engineering schools as a response to industry demand. One engineering faculty member said that professors teach the quality concepts in their classes because their students are encountering continuous improvement concepts on their first jobs. According to one administrator:

> We have totally changed our graduate program in business. Now a quality course is required. The students complete two practicums and one is in quality.

Another institution is in the process of developing a certificate program in quality improvement within the school of business. The requirements for this program include coursework, participation in teams, and leadership responsibility in teams. These examples illustrate that faculty and administrators are *asking different questions* as a result of being educated about continuous improvement principles. They are seeking the input of various constituencies before they make permanent decisions and are improving their programs based on the needs of those constituencies, especially employers. They are much more aware of serving others rather than being self-serving.

At several institutions, employees are invited to participate in courses that emphasize continuous improvement philosophies and techniques. As a result, some staff members, administrators, and other faculty members attend courses on quality management taught by faculty members. Even members from the community are invited to attend. As one president stated,

> Staff members and people from the community attending classes with students has created a real sense of community—that we are all in this together.

A few institutions incorporate quality concepts into programs instead of teaching them in a single course or set of courses. A business school administrator provided this example:

> The best project we developed is a multidisciplinary project that takes place in the second part of the semester. Teams of students go into the community and work on a company project. They observe processes in production, distribution, and human resources. It is a practical experience that brings interdisciplinary faculty together. The feedback has been positive from the companies and from the students involved.

We repeatedly heard people express concerns about how to further teach students and to involve them in the quality movement. One president feels so strongly about connecting with students as stakeholders that he demonstrates his commitment by teaching a course in leadership for first-year students each fall. Many quality improvement concepts are integrated into this course so that students are introduced to continuous improvement as they begin their college careers.

Using the LEARN Model

One classroom improvement model that is being used in several courses at two of our institutions is referred to as LEARN. The model was developed by Kathryn Baugher (1992) and defines the teaching and learning improvement process as follows:

Locate an opportunity for improvement.

Establish a team to work on the process by defining team roles and setting ground rules.

Assess the current process using checklists and surveys to determine the issues of the particular class.

Research causes of the issues by utilizing cause and effect diagrams.

Nominate an improvement and enter the plan-do-study-act (PDSA) cycle.

The model was developed to improve the learning and teaching processes by removing barriers during the course rather than at the end of the course. In the LEARN model, students and instructors work together for maximum student achievement. Basically, a student improvement team is established during the course and is responsible for using quality tools and concepts to improve the processes within the course. The model helps students own their learning.

At one institution, this model is used so consistently across campus that one administrator said if a professor doesn't use the model, "some students will ask why the professor is not using LEARN." At this same institution, one administrator said that LEARN has improved the culture of the institution. The upper-class students speak so favorably about it that entering students ask about the model. For purposes of illustration, one faculty member shared this experience:

> I use the LEARN model in several of my courses. Each team meets once a week for 30 minutes. They do surveys and analysis, and it really works. It is nice to know in the second week of the class whether your teaching techniques are working. I receive immediate feedback. We get responses that range from the room is too cold to there are not enough left-handed desks, and then we send memos to the physical plant. If the student team does not receive an adequate response from the physical plant within a month, they send a memo to the provost. Students feel empowered and rewarded that they are contributing to improvements on campus.

According to one faculty member at this particular institution, the schools of education and pharmacy have had the greatest success using LEARN. Students in pharmacy are demanding quality teams and LEARN teams. Because of the success in the pharmacy school, that dean has requested that all faculty members try the LEARN model in at least one course.

LEARN is also being used to improve processes outside the classroom. At one institution, members of the promotion and tenure committee are using LEARN to improve the evaluation processes for faculty. A faculty member explained the utility of this approach as follows:

> We have been charged to design and implement a faculty development model that includes training in the LEARN process and quality improve-

ment tools. We are developing a mechanism to assess faculty teaching within the first three years of employment. In addition, we are developing a way to appropriately document the teaching performance to support data-driven decisions in the promotion and tenure process.

This model is based on having student teams use quality tools to improve the learning and teaching process while they are in the course. Students learn course content and improve the processes concurrently. The LEARN model is an example of educating people across campus to use quality tools in a variety of situations. It illustrates the value of people having the same knowledge base so that when the methods and tools are used students, faculty, administrators, and staff immediately understand and participate in the process. The common understanding translates into time saved and credibility granted.

Using Existing Resources

Another pattern that emerged was using existing resources within the institution to improve learning and teaching. People with expertise in teaching techniques, such as those in the school of education, are being called on to assist in the improvement process. It was made clear to us that faculty development should be on a volunteer basis, but that some faculty members are starting to use the services available. Establishing mentoring relationships was another way institutions are making the best use of their human resources. This process was explained by one administrator:

> AAHE has a mentoring process that we adopted. We have five pairs or 10 colleagues in the program. We pair up people on the same level so that there is not an imbalance of power between experienced and inexperienced (i.e., two assistant professors). They observe classes, read syllabi, and make suggestions, but it is purely on a volunteer basis. Next year each of the 10 will find new partners so that we will have 10 pairs.

We found institutions "thinking outside the box" to find solutions to their problems. The president at one institution allocated up to $100,000 for funding teaching improvements. One year it was used for instructional innovations. Another year, money was set aside for any kind of improvement, academic or nonacademic. This grant has become an annual activity. In a few cases there have been significant breakthroughs in improvements and the president passed out an end-of-the-year bonus. For example, one year the library staff received a bonus for improvements made. One administrator went on to say

> The money allocated to create innovative teaching methodologies stimulated a lot of syllabus revision, team teaching, media technology, and small group techniques. These new teaching strategies flourish in a quality culture.

As institutions begin to *ask different questions* about how to improve the learning and teaching process, they have been able to find resources to help them. A few institutions have established centers, the focus of which is to help faculty members improve their teaching. The centers were described as non-threatening ways for faculty members to get feedback and assistance. They are perceived as successful and the costs of the resources to the institution are minimal because the centers have been funded by foundations. According to one of the presidents,

> The center is a tangible indicator of the seriousness of our commitment to effective practice in the classroom.

Improving Learning and Teaching—Summary

Many of the faculty members who have had the opportunity to participate in professional development seminars or who teach courses that incorporate continuous quality improvement concepts have changed their thinking about teaching and their practices in the classroom. Some common themes emerged with these faculty members: Classes have become more student-centered, classes are more focused on learning than teaching, and faculty members have found ways to involve students so that students take more ownership for their learning. In addition, faculty members are systematically collecting feedback from students so that they can make continuous quality improvements for the students during the course rather than waiting until the course is over.

One pattern is the formation of small faculty groups to discuss how to improve learning and teaching. We perceive this movement as a real grassroots effort to practice quality principles. The faculty members who participate in these groups are highly dedicated to implementing quality principles and practices on the academic side of the institution. The LEARN model used by two of the institutions is another illustration of faculty members and students working together to maximize student learning.

The involvement of faculty members in quality improvement efforts greatly contributes to creating a different type of culture. Since the accomplishment of an institutional mission depends so much on the faculty, it becomes apparent how important they are to the success of a quality initiative on campus. According to one respondent, "faculty are key power brokers." It is important to engage faculty members from the start. They are critical to the accomplishment of any institutional mission.

Even if institutions have implemented systems 1–8 in some form, other obstacles remain. One of the main hurdles to clear is how to financially support the changes that need to be made to develop and implement these systems. The institutions we studied are looking for all possible ways to financially support their quality efforts. They understand that they have to look for new answers to old problems. In a time of tight financial resources, they have become creative, innovative, and assertive about finding financial support. Their methods are described in the next section, system 9.

SYSTEM 9: FINANCIALLY SUPPORTING QUALITY EFFORTS

The members of the institutions we studied believed that an institution cannot afford to ignore quality initiatives. They felt that their efforts have been worth the costs incurred. But despite the clear need, institutions often do not know how to justify the initial costs of supporting quality improvement when operating budgets are frozen or cut, even though other institutions reported that the cost savings from continuous improvement efforts ultimately help to cover the costs of educating people about quality improvement. Decreasing budgets just make it difficult for many institutions to allocate money to another cause, even if there is a potential for reward down the road. As one faculty member said:

> If the president had hired a continuous improvement coordinator at the same time as we were laying off teachers, it would have been a lightning rod for all of the people who want to do him in.

In our interviews, we learned that a strong dedication to continuous improvement unleashes unbelievable creativity within the institution. These institutions found innovative ways to learn how to improve, to develop members, and to support their quality improvement efforts. Because of the unique ways of covering additional costs of quality development, improvement efforts have been able to gain momentum without taking money away from the operating budget. This financial wizardry is politically important in higher education institutions:

> We do not want people to feel like we have improved the quality at the expense of other programs or at the expense of laying off people. We attempt to have the quality movement not function as an add-on but as the way we do business.

Many of these institutions do not have a formalized budget to support their continuous improvement efforts. We had administrators tell us that they allocate dollars from their budgets and that they allocate part of their time to keep the movement alive on campus. As people adopt quality principles and practices, they work hard to find ways to fund quality initiatives. The theme that emerged is reflected in the following statement: "We make quality improvement a priority." In doing so, other priorities have changed. This reallocation of funds and changing of priorities was best expressed by one president:

> Our library is full of quality information. As the interests of the college changed, the librarian changed what she was ordering: books, videos, and

> journals. We subscribe to all of the quality journals. The priority of what we were spending our money on has changed. People still travel to conferences, but now they would prefer to go to a quality or classroom conference. Our memberships have changed because now we are a member of the CQI Network and ASQC. We have changed the things in which we are interested and the dollars have been allocated accordingly.

At one institution when the president or other administrators receive honoraria for speaking, the money received goes into the "quality budget" to help them fund their efforts. Internal personnel educated in quality principles and practices can also be used to conduct seminars outside of the institution, where they are compensated accordingly.

Many institutions save money by using experts within their own institutions to design surveys and to analyze data. Using local talents and expertise facilitates data collection because the resources are available and affordable. Research institutions, for example, often have a research center that they use for the collection and analysis of data.

Many interviewees reported that they operate from the assumption that there is no extra money for improvement efforts, which is fairly realistic. In the institutions in our study, the amount of money allocated ranges from absolutely no extra money to a small fund set aside for quality improvement. As a result, teams learn to propose solutions that do not require significant investment. If money is available, many interviewees suggested that the financial limitations need to be known up front. When teams know the budgetary limits initially, it is easier to make proposals that stay within the limits.

As previously mentioned, most of our institutions have formed partnerships with business and industry to learn how to improve performance and to pool resources. Some institutions are more fortunate than others with respect to the location of their institution. According to one administrator, whose institution has an advantageous location,

> We sit in the middle of a quality paradise. We have AT&T that just won the Baldrige. We also have GTE, the first American company to win the Deming prize, in our area. Northern Telecom and Texas Instruments are companies in our area with which we have partnered. We even have a quality consortium in our area.

One administrator said it best: "We have been able to beg, borrow, and steal when it comes to developing employees." At one institution, people attended Deming and Ishikawa seminars because the business community sponsored these quality experts. An administrator at this institution believed that they have been able to take advantage of opportunities and resources because they have been on the forefront of quality improvement in higher education. He felt they have access to information and other benefits because of their leadership role in quality initiatives. According to the president,

We are doing a lot of development now, and it is a significant change from what we were doing several years ago. But we are doing it without taking a piece of the budget, which is important politically in terms of faculty and staff acceptance. In order to fund our quality efforts, we have focused on developing partnerships with businesses in the community. These partnerships have had many positive effects for us in other areas such as public relations and the recruitment of students.

The main theme that emerged when we discussed budget was that it is necessary "to think outside the box." Creatively finding ways to financially support quality improvement efforts is a necessity given the challenges from the external environment. So that continuous improvement efforts are not perceived as a way to eliminate people or as an effort that is too costly, people have found innovative ways to help the institution pursue quality improvement.

Even though few of the institutions in our study have a formalized budget for their quality improvement efforts, they have found financial support. Thinking creatively allows them to take advantage of opportunities either within the institution or within the community. For example, by using faculty members and administrators as "resident experts" to collect and analyze data or to teach other members about quality principles and practices, institutions have been able to lower costs. By making quality improvement a top priority, financial resources have been reallocated to support quality improvement efforts. By creating partnerships with businesses in the community so that professional development and quality improvement resources can be shared, institutions are able to implement continuous improvement at a minimal or reduced cost. The bottom line is that institutions cannot afford not to engage in the quality improvement journey.

CONCLUSION

It is the development and implementation of systems that integrate quality principles and practices into the culture of the institution. Because systems are continuous and interdependent, they have the ability to shift the culture to one that supports continuous improvement. Some of the systems being developed appeared to be operating more consistently than others and, therefore, were referred to more often in our interviews. A few of the systems are still being developed or are in need of further development and emerged less frequently in our conversations with members. We took this information into consideration in organizing the data.

After analyzing the data collected from 10 institutions, nine systems clearly emerged. First, quality improvement principles and practices create a culture of continuous improvement. People within institutions change their thinking and their behaviors as a result of engaging in the quality journey. We discovered specific decisions, actions, and events that institutions use to create a culture that supports continuous improvement efforts.

Second, for leaders to shift their thinking, which in turn changes their behaviors, they need to learn about quality improvement. This knowledge is used to develop, revise, and communicate vision and mission statements to members throughout the institution, which is the third system. The fourth system that emerged was how to professionally develop members so that they have the knowledge and skills to improve processes and systems. Fifth, because of professional development, members are taught to collect and analyze data so that decisions can be based on fact rather than intuition. Improving overall communication was the sixth system that emerged. Members remarked that for the most part, communication methods are more systematic and information is more readily shared with more members across the institution as a result of embarking on the quality journey.

We labeled the seventh system teamwork and collaboration because people reported that they have changed how they are working and how they think about their work. The next system, improving learning and teaching, identifies ways faculty members have implemented quality principles and practices in the classroom. The creative means institutions have found to financially support their quality initiatives is the final system.

As these systems indicate, the quality improvement journey is not easy, but it is necessary if an institution is to be prepared for these *different times*. Even though many of the systems are not new or revolutionary, we found that the institutions we studied were using new and different techniques to implement quality practices. The primary difference is that they are diligently integrating their practices into new systems or redesigning systems so that the practices become part of the systems.

We also learned that continuous improvement is a challenging and complex journey filled with benefits, obstacles, and surprises. Chapter 4 identifies the factors that act as barriers and explains how to overcome these barriers so that continuous improvement ideas can be used to improve processes and systems within higher education institutions.

CHAPTER 4

What Are the Barriers to Systems Development and Implementation?

Decreasing budgets, declining enrollments, and increasing competition from other institutions and from business and industry make managing a higher education institution a major challenge in these times. Many institutions are struggling under these conditions and wondering how they will survive as they see operating costs, particularly in the area of technology, skyrocket. Continuous improvement is one approach to addressing these challenges because it focuses on decreasing the costs of processes and systems while simultaneously stressing quality improvement and stakeholder satisfaction.

We wanted to determine the effectiveness of quality principles and practices in higher education and the barriers to implementation. A section of the interview questions dealt with obstacles to continuous improvement efforts. We asked members of the administration, faculty, and staff about the specific barriers to implementation and the general barriers over the course of their quality efforts. Their answers helped us determine the progress institutions have made in implementing quality improvement principles.

After analyzing the data, eight themes emerged as barriers to implementing quality principles and practices. First, we will discuss the obstacles that have the most impact on quality improvement efforts across the institutions we studied. Then the eight themes will be addressed based on our perception of their significance. These themes are institutional culture, leadership, professional development, data collection and analysis, communication, teamwork and collaboration, learning and teaching, and skeptics. Within each theme, several barriers often emerged. Interestingly, we discovered that these themes almost mirror the systems presented in chapter 3. When the system is initially being developed or is not as strong as interviewees would like, problems within the systems to enact quality initiatives become barriers themselves.

NEGATIVE IMPACTS ON SYSTEM DEVELOPMENT

When we asked interviewees about the obstacles that inhibit continuous process improvement, the primary obstacles mentioned were lack of understanding, lack of time, and lack of money. Interviewees were concerned about the time needed to sustain the efforts, and some interviewees mentioned that there is not enough money for adequate training, for incentives, and for funding improvement projects. As one administrator stated, "There is inadequate time and energy even more so than dollars."

Lack of Understanding

By far, the strongest theme that emerged was the lack of understanding about quality improvement. If members within the institution are educated so that they understand the quality initiative, they are more dedicated and the initiative gains momentum. This need for understanding appears to be the initial barrier to overcome. It is difficult to make any progress when members lack this knowledge. It became apparent to us across institutions that the level of understanding about quality principles and practices influences the success of the quality efforts on campus. This thought was best summed up by one quality coordinator:

> I don't see how anyone cannot agree with the principles of continuous improvement and be in education. They must not understand the concepts because if they really understood them the way I understand them . . . they would agree that quality principles and education are a natural fit."

Even in institutions where significant amounts of time, money, and energy have been allocated to professionally developing members, there is still a strong sentiment that even more education is needed to have a consistent level of knowledge and understanding within institutions. We learned that all members need to understand *why* the institution has embarked on a new journey. They need to be familiar with the different quality concepts and the new quality practices. The following quotes are representative of this theme:

> There is a lack of real understanding of what it takes to do quality improvement.

> We do not educate people about all of the philosophies of continuous improvement.

> We make too many assumptions that people already understand the concepts.

> People need to have a more prevalent understanding of the concepts if they are going to practice them.

Some interviewees believed that some members want to discredit continuous quality improvement when problems emerge. We concluded that this thinking reflects an inaccurate understanding about the essence of quality improvement concepts. It is clear from the next two quotations how this type of misunderstanding slows progress:

> It is easier to blame things on the quality movement when things do not work because it is the "new kid."

> People do not want to admit mistakes. Rather, they point their fingers at CQI instead of trying to find the reason for the problem.

When members do not understand the philosophy of continuous improvement, these misperceptions become barriers. One misperception that emerged was the thinking that the quality improvement approach to management is a fad rather than a long-term philosophy. Many of the institutions in our survey have been subjected to program after program in the past. So it was not surprising when interviewees informed us that there are members who consider quality practices and the development of systems as another "flavor of the month" management approach. Without a clear understanding of what quality principles and practices have to offer, people responded:

> Many management systems have come and gone and this is no different.

> They think this is another fad. Everybody brings up management by objective, and I try to explain that this is different.

We realized that some of our interviewees do not understand continuous improvement:

> Many tend to not view it as forever. They do not see quality as an ongoing process.

Others do not appreciate the simplicity of the ideas:

> They think a lot of the quality information is just common sense, and I ask them why we do not use quality.

These quotations show how damaging an inappropriate mind-set can be. People cannot practice concepts they do not understand. Interviewees told us that ignorance or inaccurate information has led some people to become cynical, pessimistic, and resentful—attitudes that run counter to continuous improvement.

One pattern that consistently unfolded was that institutions further along in the quality journey demonstrated a more in-depth understanding of systems thinking, which helped to overcome barriers to systems development. In these institutions, most of the interviewees were aware of how the numerous parts of an institution are interrelated and why systems thinking is an essential component for successfully practicing quality improvement concepts.

Since most management problems are system problems (Deming, 1986), the degree to which members understand systems thinking determines whether barriers continue to exist or if they are overcome. One administrator stated this thought directly:

> If I were going to give a generic illness of every organization, it is the system. The system won't let you take care of the customer or stakeholder.

The following example of a system breakdown describes a situation at an institution that prides itself on the professional development it provides for members:

> We have 48 seminars, but the employees need the signatures of supervisors before they can attend. If top management support the quality efforts, they need to create a new system that lets people initiate and participate without permission from supervisors. It is important that supervisors let people attend.

The lack of systems thinking was frequently pointed out to us as a barrier to overcome:

> Systems thinking is so difficult for faculty members because they often have little connection with the larger picture because they are independent entrepreneurs who work alone.

> There is a lack of understanding about quality improvement on campus. We know of pockets where people understand, but many people lack the conceptual view.

> It is a real hindrance when people do not understand the basic principles of continuous improvement. They just do not get it.

> The schools want to retain a separate identity. They don't have system-wide thinking.

It was clear that people do not truly understand quality principles and practices when they fail to change in response to outside changes:

> On the academic side, faculty have failed to recognize that the inputs (students) have changed, but teaching techniques have not changed accordingly.

State institutions have to work closely with state governments, and therefore, legislatures are also included as part of the system. As one president stated,

> Our major obstacles are the historical practices of the state. Their legislative mandates are based on bureaucratic thinking rather than quality

thinking. This causes a significant gap between the governor and our campus, and it affects our system and the decisions made.

A systemic orientation is critical to the success of the development of systems, but this mind-set is difficult to practice in higher education because of the strong traditions and historical practices. To enhance quality initiatives, we believe that this shift needs to exist before behaviors actually change and quality improvement efforts thrive. One administrator offered the following perspective on what happens when the mind-set does not change:

> Quality of life is better if you get involved in quality initiatives. People go into academe for all kinds of reasons, but certainly one reason is to share ideas and to be excited about ideas. The reality is that faculty members end up being pigeon-holed in a way that you try to avoid—the same reason they did not go into business. They did not want to be limited. They wanted a world that was expansive and could be enlarged. Because of the economics of it and the pressures of it, faculty members are driven into the same kind of narrow tunnel that they were trying to avoid when they went to graduate school in the first place.

Although a majority of the people we interviewed understand the philosophy of continuous improvement, they were candid about the barriers. One administrator said it best:

> One of the major problems with continuous improvement is that it identifies problems that need to be addressed. It puts them out where everybody can see them. It takes a lot to overcome the reluctance to do that. It is hard not to get overwhelmed by the negatives. But we have come a long way in understanding the philosophy of quality.

The development and implementation of systems can be hindered if members do not adequately understand the philosophy of continuous improvement. This lack of understanding is a major barrier to progress and inhibits a systemic orientation to processes. To overcome this barrier, it is imperative for all members to "be on the same page" so that everyone knows what is trying to be accomplished and *why* the development of systems is so important.

Lack of Time

A second overall theme that emerged concerned the time associated with the development and implementation of systems. For the most part, people were worried about the time it took to become familiar with quality practices, to learn the new systems, and to prepare for meetings. Using quality tools and techniques requires that people prepare for meetings rather than just attend. They stated that this takes time in the short run, even though it saves time in the long run. The time needed to prepare for meetings is not only greater, but initially the number of meetings also tends to increase while redesigning processes. Because of these factors and others, interviewees consistently commented that the time involved is a primary barrier.

Several people indicated that developing and implementing new systems adds more work to their already heavy workloads. Rather than saving time, they reported that they do not have the necessary time to implement quality improvement effectively. Some bad experiences with ineffective work teams and too many unproductive meetings have led some people to make comments such as

> Continuous improvement is time-consuming and perceived as inefficient and often nothing happens.

With too much time being consumed by meetings, we learned that people tend to revert to their old ways of solving problems:

> People know how to improve, but now people have to put out fires because of the work load.

Other comments, however, reflected the perception that while practicing quality improvement concepts requires more time, many participants feel it is worth it:

> Now people do not see quality as an add-on activity. The principles and tools have been integrated as a part of our own personal growth.

> People who think quality is too time-consuming do not understand that it is not about time because quality saves time.

People indicated that they are learning new ways to conduct business through the development and implementation of systems. Two remarks illustrate that members are changing their ways:

> In the beginning, quality requires doing your work two ways until you can get to the point where it is the way you do your work.

> Being committed to quality is a life-long learning process, and the important things do take time.

These comments indicate that the time involved is viewed differently based on the level of fundamental knowledge about quality principles and practices. People who practice quality improvement concepts realize that they require a personal transformation and paradigm shift. These people have changed the way they think about their work. Others who perceive continuous improvement as too time-consuming are personally not as far along the quality journey and have not shifted their thinking accordingly. This point was expressed best by one administrator:

> If you do not believe in and implement the underlying philosophies, and that has to do with how you treat people and how you listen to people, you

can use all of the tools and set up all of the quality teams you want and it is going to be a problem. People look at behaviors.

Lack of Financial Resources

It was not a surprise to have the lack of money mentioned as a significant obstacle by almost all of our interviewees. Across institutions, interviewees agreed that it is necessary to have financial resources to initially get the movement off the ground and to continuously support quality improvement efforts. Hiring consultants, developing members, and purchasing additional materials to educate members about continuous improvement requires an allocation of financial resources. Even though interviewees shared anecdotes that illustrate how they have found innovative ways to support their improvement efforts, there was still a general consensus that there are up-front expenses of which leaders need to be aware.

As explained in chapter 3, institutions have overcome financial obstacles by using faculty members and administrators within the institution to collect and analyze data and to teach other members about quality principles and practices. Partnerships have been created between institutions and businesses within the local communities so that resources for continuous improvement efforts are shared. Some institutions have established professional development centers that train people within the business community for fees that are used to fund the development and implementation of systems.

In addition to these general barriers to developing and implementing quality principle and practices, we discovered some specific barriers to implementation. Throughout our interviews, creating a culture that supports continuous improvement emerged as the system with numerous barriers. Because changing an institutional culture is complex, many obstacles hinder progress. In the next segment, these barriers will be discussed and ways of overcoming these barriers will also be explained so that institutions can learn from the experiences of our institutions.

INSTITUTIONAL CULTURE

Initially, continuous quality improvement is threatening to people because it focuses on the need for improvement. The inference is that processes need to be improved and that what existed before quality improvement efforts began is not of high quality. But as one administrator verified, "Once the quality movement became more of a discipline and part of the culture, it was much easier to accept."

Unfortunately, a quality improvement culture is not a panacea for all of the problems in an institution. Commenting on this situation, one president remarked:

When a quality culture emerges, there are just as many problems. First, one focuses on the transition to the new culture. When the culture starts emerging, the issues are still out there, but you approach them differently. There is just as much complexity as there is in a bureaucratic culture.

In creating a culture that supports quality improvement, the main barriers that emerge are difficulties in the areas of involving and empowering members, recognizing and rewarding members, driving out fear, and driving in honesty and trust.

Involving and Empowering Members

A serious barrier to creating a culture that supports continuous improvement is involving and empowering members. The idea of involving members is easier to understand than the idea of empowering them. In our study, a pattern emerged that led us to believe there is a misunderstanding of the concept of empowerment, which leads people to cross boundaries inappropriately. It appeared that most of the misunderstanding has to do with the constraints of decision making. When should people be empowered and involved and where should the boundaries be set? One of the college presidents who has studied extensively about how quality improvement affects the human side of the institution explained the concept of empowerment and the complexities involved in empowering others:

> Empowerment means authority equal to responsibility in the organization. There are decisions that people at various levels can make based on their authority. As a college president, there are things that I am held responsible for, therefore the authority rests with me. Employees confused wanting suggestions and input with implementing them. They felt they were not empowered. They need to understand there is a difference between the opportunity to give your input, which we welcome at all times, and always having your opinion be the prevailing opinion. We have had to refine some of our authority because we were on the edge of chaos.

She continued:

> We got carried away and caught up with the concept of empowerment and we thought that we could declare overnight that employees were empowered. The truth is, not everyone wants it. There are a number of things that have to be in place in the organization in order to have empowerment: driving out fear, being sure people have information and development necessary to be empowered, understanding the boundaries that accompany empowerment. This was our mistake early in our efforts.
>
> We have addressed some of these misunderstandings in our internal newsletter. Our goal is to push decision making and responsibility down to the lowest level, and sometimes the lowest level is the college president.

The paradox of empowerment is that "empowerment means letting go while taking control" (Baker, 1994, p. 62). According to the literature on empowerment (Freed, 1996; Freed, Klugman, and Fife, 1997), mid-level administrators are often the ones who have difficulty letting go of power in the traditional sense. They feel threatened when asked to share power, and they are accused of resisting change. It was common to hear interviewees say, "They don't seem to be able to let go." Commenting on empowerment, an administrator remarked,

> The middle-level managers have enough authority to make the change, and they can take the initiative, but they are also caught in the middle. It is a dilemma.

We found that people misunderstand what empowerment means and that they make inappropriate decisions. In the institutions we studied, people in leadership positions often do not want to give up power or people do not want to be empowered; they are afraid to accept the additional responsibility.

Empowerment is the goal, but we discovered that people often do not feel empowered or involved. The perception that empowerment exists does not match the reality in many situations. Empowerment means giving up power and not everyone wants to do that. Quite a few participants repeated this thought in different ways:

> The administration sometimes makes decisions that should have been made by faculty, and they are pretty sensitive when you point it out to them.

> People are being transferred without having any input. Two years ago they created a new department and people were transferred without asking to be transferred. This year people are being moved around and no one talks about it. This negatively affects morale.

> Decisions are still being made at the top without input from others.

As these statements indicate, members do not perceive that empowerment and involvement exists as much as administrators would like to believe. We learned that involving others is difficult to practice. If others are involved, the suggestions they contribute may be very different from what was expected:

> We would form a team and have them work on something without telling them what we had in mind. Then we would get back something totally different than we thought.

Involving others does not mean giving people free rein to make decisions, but it does mean outlining the constraints so that acceptable decisions can be made. This concept is where we found most of the confusion with empowerment. Leaders let members cross boundaries inappropriately, and then when their decisions are not implemented, members feel involvement is a waste of time and effort:

> People think they are empowered, but they try to make decisions they do not have responsibility for.

These examples reflect members' needs to have an accurate understanding of empowerment and boundaries. Through continual education, people can learn when it is appropriate to make decisions. As one staff member put it,

> Sometimes the people with the knowledge are not involved in making decisions. That is changing. Even though all of the suggestions from the various teams were not followed, at least they were asked, which is positive.

Other interviewees shared this same conclusion:

> Staff will comment that they thought we were involving staff and being good to staff, and then they will ask why they can't do something.

In contrast, we also had people admitting that they were scared of being involved. Others stressed that it takes secure leaders to involve and to empower others. As one faculty member said,

> Empowerment requires a lot of the individual. There needs to be open encouragement for people to want to accept the additional responsibility. It takes time to gain the skills to feel confident.

We learned that the culture of the institution influences whether or not people feel that involvement is worth it. A culture that supports continuous improvement is a culture that supports people in changing behaviors and in learning new skills. It encourages them to become involved in decision making and in accepting responsibility. As employees participate in making decisions, they feel more confident in their own abilities. Members develop their self-esteem so that they are willing to accept more responsibility.

Despite the difficulties in involving others, one staff member reminded us of the accountability that accompanies involvement:

> Involvement means having a voice and having a voice makes you responsible. If you have a voice and you do not use it, that is just as bad as not having a voice.

Recognizing and Rewarding Members

We also noticed barriers in finding ways to recognize and reward members. There was even a theme of no incentives being offered. Even though leaders felt strongly that people should be recognized for their quality improvement efforts, we found an absence of a reward system in many institutions. Interviewees stressed that new ideas and creativity are not systematically being rewarded as much as they can be. Basic psychological theories say that rewarded behaviors tend to be repeated. Since institutions want people to engage in continuous improvement, they need to find ways to reinforce quality principles and practices. They do not think that behaviors will change drastically if the reward and recognition system does not consistently acknowledge the new values. One administrator explained the dilemma:

> It is hard to tell if people are opposed or just not interested. I am not convinced we can put quality in place and have it work all of the time as long as higher education is the way it is. The rewards go disproportionately to the researchers. There are no rewards for service on process improvement teams. There needs to be a long-term incentive for involvement in the quality movement. We can't say we will fire you if you do not participate or reward you if you do participate.

Two administrators thought that the way to solve this dilemma is to build quality standards into the evaluation system. This solution also has problems:

> Right now there is no merit pay and compensation is very flat. Overperformers are under-rewarded; under-performers are over-rewarded. This system undermines the quality movement.

> We tried merit increases in the past, but they did not work because we did not have an effective evaluation system. Flat increases have not worked either because of market value.

Added another administrator,

> If we were really using the philosophy of quality, we would build up people's strengths and not their weaknesses in the evaluation process. The current promotion and tenure system almost guarantees that we are shoving weaknesses down people's throats and not building on their strengths. People have different strengths, and we should be trying to find the best way to utilize their skills. Some people are better teachers than researchers and vice versa. We should have a system where everyone can excel.

Not only do institutions vacillate on what to do about incentives, but their members are often not receptive to whatever means is used. We found a pattern of members being highly skeptical of any incentive, reward, or recognition. This pattern reinforces the significance of developing a culture of trust. When people do not trust the leadership, the reward system is not perceived as effective. At one institution, plaques are given and icons are awarded to add to the plaque. These next two comments are from people who have received such awards:

> I feel embarrassed with my association with continuous improvement. The awards and recognition system does not feel good because I feel let down with the whole system and the people in charge of the system.

> People walk around the building and look at the icons and look at the people who do not have icons or they do not even have walls on which to put their plaque. I think the whole system is a political gesture.

One of the difficulties in recognizing and rewarding members is that teamwork is a basic quality principle. Quality improvements are often accomplished because of the combined efforts of people working together. When this type of effort is the case, it seems inconsistent to reward individuals. When discussing this topic, one president responded with the following example:

> The district has awards for outstanding college innovator, teacher, manager, and support-staff person. About two years ago, we decided that their system was inconsistent with what we were doing, but we did not want to boycott their process. So we nominated the entire college for innovator, all faculty members for teacher, all administrators for manager, and the entire support staff for support-staff person. We had a lottery and we selected someone from each of the groups to receive the award. We wanted to participate, but on our own terms. This example indicates that we operate in a different paradigm.
>
> This year we selected an outstanding team of trainers, faculty, administrators, and support staff, and they became our outstanding people. Now the district has moved from innovator of the year to innovation of the year to recognize that teams innovate. The district has a team studying rewards and recognition.

These barriers can be overcome when systems keep the quality improvement efforts visible to everyone. The institutions we studied have found ways to communicate progress being made around campus. An idea being implemented at one institution is a quality improvement wall where photos of teams and their charges are being displayed for all to see. Several commented that the wall attracts attention from visitors and prospective students, which often leads to conversations about the quality improvement efforts on campus.

At another campus recognized for its horticulture program, the institution plants trees in the names of people who are outstanding employees. When walking across campus, people report that they see the trees planted with plaques under them identifying the employees and their accomplishments. One respondent described this system as a life-affirming way to recognize people at all levels.

Driving Out Fear

We also found that the presence of fear in the culture inhibits continuous improvement. Deming conceptualized the concepts of quality improvement and developed his Fourteen Points as explained in *Out of the Crisis* (1986). The eighth point is Drive Out Fear. It is important to drive out fear because it is like a cancer that destroys an organization's long-term growth and viability. Fear inhibits the implementation of quality principle and practices.

Throughout our interviews, we learned that fear has numerous negative effects on an institution and on employees. It limits employee involvement and the contribution of ideas. Fear hinders communication and breeds problems associated with low employee morale and lack of teamwork. Fear perpetuates old behaviors, actions, and thinking, which limit abilities to change.

We discovered many fears that prevent members from achieving their highest potential. Fear manifests itself in many different forms: fear of the leadership, fear of retribution, fear of speaking against those in power, fear of losing jobs, and fear of continuous improvement. In general, people fear change. Interviewees particularly expressed a fear of failure and reprisal. The following quotes show how fear limits people from performing at their highest level:

> You will go through development or you will lose your job.
>
> If you do not use the tools in your job, people feel that it is used against you in evaluations.
>
> While there is no rank in the room during a meeting, there is always rank in the organization.
>
> People will be very vocal in the department and within the teams, but when it comes to confronting the administration, only the brave speak up. The people who speak up the most are new to the institution. The people within the department know who they are dealing with, and outside of the department people are less sure.

Even administrators demonstrated a sense of being afraid to communicate and hesitated to be honest with members when it was logical to do so:

> The administration is taking a defensive position with enrollment decreases. They are afraid to talk with us and to bring the issues out.

It was not surprising that fear of losing one's job emerged as one of the strongest fears. Similar to business and industry, some institutions are restructuring or contemplating doing so, which contributes to people fearing they will lose their jobs. When people are not told otherwise, continuous improvement is often perceived to mean layoffs and downsizing. In some minds, quality improvement translates into fewer jobs for fewer people so that the system works more efficiently. One administrator stated the fear directly, "Continuous improvement will wipe out your jobs. Quality efforts are wonderful, but watch out."

We were told that it is hard to drive out fear when institutions are restructuring and jobs are being cut. As one staff member said,

> In the back of people's minds, they see IBM winning all of these quality awards while they read that IBM simultaneously laid off 500 employees. So quality at whose expense?

It was common to hear, "Members who quit or die are not being replaced." In addition to attrition, some tenured faculty members have lost jobs as departments merged or were eliminated. Many of these changes are in response to the strong forces in the external environment such as decreases in enrollment, increasing costs, and declining federal and state funds. Several comments emphasized this point:

> The quality movement is shaky because we are reorganizing again. Even though we are refining the structure, people get nervous. There is tension in the air, and the fear indicators are going up.

> We had layoffs in the spring, and people fear outsourcing. Nothing will drive in fear as fast as replacing people with contract labor.

> Continuous improvement is not a way to eliminate positions, but members perceive it that way because we are doing it without meaning to do it. We are not replacing people as they leave.

> Since we have been involved in the quality movement, there have been retrenchments where positions have been eliminated. We are trying to improve processes with fewer staff and this adds to the frustration with continuous improvement.

The fears expressed in these comments are barriers. As people associate continuous improvement initiatives with lost jobs, they are less interested in understanding the underlying philosophies of quality improvement. Given this unstable environment, their apprehension, lack of motivation, and lack of devotion are logical and understandable.

People fear more than just losing their jobs, though. To practice quality concepts is to embrace change, but our data affirmed that people fear change of all kinds. The challenge is to help people accept change. We heard interviewees repackage changes by referring to them as "opportunities for improvement" in the hopes that people will be more accepting. The following quotes illustrate this fear of change:

> People fear change. They need to have permission to be who they are, but we have to provide opportunities to let them change at their speed. This is not easy. The key is to put them in positions where they feel comfortable.

> Even though the quality movement gives people a voice, they fear it is destroying the academic structure by replacing it with the service sector.

> People have a natural tendency toward inertia and so do institutions. An institution of higher learning is, by its nature, resistant to change. They

believe they do not have time to practice quality, particularly when money is tight.

One administrator shared this story to make the point that people at his institution are afraid of change and usually prefer the status quo:

> I am reminded of an incident when Kansas won the NCAA championship under the leadership of Larry Brown. They won big over an opponent rated higher than they were. An interviewer asked what Coach Brown told the team at halftime to get the team going. The response was: "Don't be afraid to win." We in higher education are so afraid to win that we do not want to let go of things that hold us back and weigh us down.

A lack of knowledge about the philosophy of continuous improvement fuels the fears and slows the momentum of quality initiatives. People lose faith that the institution can support quality improvement efforts because of cutbacks in personnel, equipment, and supplies. Several quotations illustrate this point:

> How can we have quality when we are cutting back. We can't produce quality when we do not have sufficient facilities.

> When the majority of our faculty are tenured and there is not any new money to allocate for supplies and expenses and equipment, what is the sense? I call this a lack of clarity about what we mean by quality. People do not understand what we are trying to accomplish.

> It is hard to break down barriers between departments when resources are tight.

To overcome these fears, institutions should help members understand that continuous improvement does not mean that they will automatically lose their jobs. As one staff member pointed out,

> The administration has to reassure them that there is plenty of work to do or that quality means you are going to be doing your job better.

When members trust senior leadership, we were told that less fear exists because they trust the motives of the decisions made. But the institutions we studied still have work to do in creating a culture that supports quality practices. Developing trust was said to be the hardest part about changing the culture. This evidence confirms that fear still exists in the culture and inhibits people from performing at their highest level. Lack of trust is a barrier:

> If you do not have trustworthiness, you have nothing.

> There is an attitude here that says: Tell me what you want but I still have to make a decision. There are people who still do not trust.

> We have to watch out for people who have all of the vocabulary down, but they do not act on it.

If institutions are to survive and grow, individuals must be able to grow. To overcome their fears of continuous improvement, they must feel comfortable and be able to trust members within the institution.

To overcome those elements in the institution that instill fear, members need to have a better understanding of quality improvement so that they realize *why* certain decisions are made. Additional education combined with a system to continually communicate quality improvement successes helps to diminish fears. Encouraging people to openly discuss their fears in hopes that changes can be made to improve the situation is another way institutions are trying to drive out fear. The quality improvement process and the process to remove fear from the culture are similar journeys. When institutions work on driving out fear, they also move toward creating a quality culture.

One of the institutions in our study held a Drive Out Fear Day as a way to create a quality culture. Their objective was to "discuss the undiscussables." According to the president,

> We identified fears through an anonymous survey of employees. The results were interesting. The top fears were fears of people who want to do a good job. The number one fear was that "the amount of work I have to do will keep me from doing a good job." Another fear was that "another person's inability will keep me from doing a good job."
>
> We had an all-college meeting with a consultant. He conducted a seminar on what fear is, what it looks like, what the symptoms are, and the damage that it causes. We divided into small groups, and we gave them different fears on which to do cause-and-effect diagrams. The steering team reduced most of the fears and summarized them as, "I may not be able to do a good job and there is too much work to do, how can we get it all done" (i.e., copier is always broken, people stand and talk around my desk, not enough computers). We analyzed the results, and we conducted staff development seminars on the giving and receiving of feedback so employees know how to talk with one another. We studied the repair record of the copier and ended up putting a sign that says "This machine functions properly 95 percent of the time" to counteract the perception that it is always broken.

When we asked how the day could have been improved, the president had this reply:

> Even though I feel that I would not do it over again, I talk about it in presentations and people are amazed. But we need to talk about trust and not fear. We need to discuss the "undiscussables" or the things that are going on in the organization that people are afraid to talk about because of fear of repercussions. The consultant encourages people to talk openly about the things that are discussed around the water fountain. He contends that as long as there is fear in the organization, it will be difficult to have creativity, innovation, teamwork, and empowerment. If the

undiscussables continue, they become part of the culture, and they give people a sense of helplessness.

At our institution, the fear of losing a job was the last fear. People do not worry about being fired or laid off. My goal is to drive out fear, not drive out standards.

Numerous interviewees confirmed that even though Drive Out Fear Day was stressful for everyone, it was healthy and they appreciated the opportunity to be open and honest with the administration. Commenting on this situation, a faculty member remarked

We filled the flip charts with fears. The president was visibly shaken. A few years ago people would not have said anything. Now they have gotten past that and they feel free to say what they think. We have changed from a hidden fear to a culture that is more positive and open. As people talk about fears, many are being resolved.

Driving out fear is a significant part of creating a culture that supports quality. The following quotations from other institutions indicate that they also recognize the detrimental aspect of fear and continue to work on developing a culture in which people feel comfortable to make improvements and to offer suggestions:

Our president deserves credit for driving out fear.

We have a decrease of fear in the organization.

As president, I have talked about helping people reflect on their work. That is a more acceptable term in higher education. Quality is about making public your private assumptions and testing them. It is about making your fears public. We are focused on driving out fear.

Interviewees said that creating this culture free from fear is not fast or easy. It takes a conscious awareness and deliberate efforts to influence how people feel, behave, and act. Removing fear from the culture so that people feel comfortable to make continuous improvements and contributions is one important aspect of creating a quality culture.

Our interviews revealed that institutions vary in the degree to which this type of culture has been created. Across institutions, we heard numerous people describe the culture as having pockets of commitment or as having islands of success:

Quality grew like a virus, it did not grow in all areas.

Some places on campus make it easy to implement quality while others do not.

Continuous improvement is a whole philosophy to be taken on, and I do not see the whole philosophy being bought into here.

> Culture is not changing as quickly as in quality improvement teams. In teams, we collaborate based on mutual respect. The overall culture is counter to continuous improvement values and work processes because it is competitive rather than cooperative.

Developing a quality culture is a continual process for the institutions we studied. People commented on what an accomplishment it is to have created subcultures of quality, but the hope is that the positive outcomes of the new culture will fuel the momentum. According to one interviewee, "Leaders need to change their behaviors for people to lose their fear." In the transition to creating a culture free from fear, management beliefs and attitudes must be supported by management practices that in turn are reinforced by systems and practices within the institution. Although driving out fear is a major goal, we were reminded that driving out fear does not imply driving down standards. Continuous improvement requires people to feel that they can make improvements and perform up to expectations.

The effectiveness of most systems is dependent upon actions and decisions of leaders. It is the responsibility of leaders to create and support an environment that eliminates fear and encourages the development and implementation of systems for continuous improvement efforts.

LEADERSHIP

Strong leaders drive the development and implementation of systems, but at the same time, leaders can be fundamental barriers to the development and implementation of processes and systems. When leaders do not thoroughly understand the philosophy of continuous improvement, when they do not know who is accountable for the quality initiative, when members become skeptical and do not trust them, when they are unable to communicate effectively, or when decisions are made that are perceived to conflict with quality principles, these leaders are barriers to quality improvement. To illustrate, one interviewee had this claim:

> The greatest impact of quality has been related to leadership and to the development of an understanding about quality within the department.

A prerequisite to being an effective quality leader is adequate knowledge of the underlying philosophies of quality principles and practices. For leaders to drive the process, they need knowledge so that they can educate other members about quality improvement. The following anecdote describes one approach to developing this understanding and overcoming this barrier:

> The president wrote a brilliant article about the student as customer and the provost wrote about servant leadership. Our administrators have a deeper understanding than most would have about the quality principles.

Having key people write journal articles about continuous improvement efforts is one approach that several institutions have found to overcome this barrier. Writing is viewed as an appropriate approach because people in higher education are accustomed to learning new material through reading. Articles are more respected because people do not feel they are being "sold" an idea or an approach if they learn through the written word rather than through personal interaction.

Another leadership barrier results when there is confusion about *who* is responsible and accountable for the progress or lack of progress. Most interviewees look to the president or top leaders for guidance. But that is not always clear to everyone, as one staff member stated, "Who owns the quality movement? To whom should we give feedback? Where are we going with this quality movement?" An example of how influential leaders are perceived to be is illustrated in the following remark, "Our institutionwide quality efforts are essentially on hold pending the arrival and interest of the new chancellor."

Even though members who have adopted quality practices may be present within the institution, it was reported that the future of the quality journey is dependent on who is hired into the top position in the institution. An administrator expressed this similar view about the importance of effective leaders:

> Quality has not permeated the whole university. It spreads in almost exact proportion to the leadership of the unit. There are several schools where there are leaders who are prepared to take quality and run with it. There are other schools where the leadership is just not into it.

Leaders need to continually communicate what the purpose of the new systems are and *why* the development and implementation of systems are so important. This message can be communicated through traditional sources such as institutional newsletters, but we found leaders at all levels looking for "windows of opportunity" when they can articulate how quality improvement helps the institution address the challenges they are facing. These opportunities may be in the form of town meetings, convocations, or just casual conversations. Reflecting, one president said, "It is important to have honest conversation about the purpose of our improvement efforts." We cannot stress enough how much senior leaders influence the success, failure, and momentum of the implementation of quality improvement practices. Hiring the most appropriate people for these leadership positions is critically important.

One of the strongest themes that emerged is the lack of trust between faculty members and the administration. Some of our interviewees doubted the dedication of senior leaders to quality practices, particularly college presidents:

> I am disappointed and I think the movement has died. The whole thing has been about enhancing the president's résumé.

> I think the president has sold out and that is a major problem.

Throughout our interviews, we found a lot of skepticism of the leaders' actions and decisions:

> The team senses that top administrators are ambiguous about the quality efforts.

> Are administrators interested in quality because they believe in it or because they think they should be doing it?

People who are seriously disgruntled with quality improvement efforts often resent others who favor it:

> I am trying to make things better and I am criticized for being a cheer-leader for the administration.

Some interviewees expressed that they even prefer the old, traditional style of management (command and control) if effective quality leadership is lacking. They question whether leaders really "walk the talk." As one person said, "At least you know where you stand under the old style of management." These comments indicate the skepticism and cynicism that exists in some institutions.

Another barrier is leaders who don't support a culture of open and honest conversation, a culture built on trust. People in leadership positions cannot communicate too much information or too often. Interviewees made it clear that they need to be informed about major issues at the institution, and that they are aware of when leaders are trying to openly communicate. Since understanding the logic behind decisions helps members accept decisions, leaders must make the communication system a priority. To overcome this barrier, leaders should articulate compelling reasons for decisions and should provide evidence that decisions are made based on data.

It was common for leaders to be criticized for not listening and for not communicating effectively. Because of professional development people expect clear communication from senior leaders, and they find unclear communication to be a primary barrier to improvement efforts. Continuous improvement is based on continuous feedback, yet some leaders do not want feedback on their decisions:

> The top people do not ask for feedback. They do not ask so we do not have a chance to tell them what we think.

Others ask for ideas and feedback, but do not appear to use them:

> The administration will listen but not really hear. We can tell them our concerns, but they will do what they want to anyway.

A pattern emerged indicating that members watch the behaviors of leaders. We found that the more knowledge members have about quality principles and practices, the higher their expectations for leaders. When leaders fall short, members' disappointments are magnified because reality did not match what they learned in their professional development seminars. When behaviors and attitudes are consistent with the philosophy of continuous improvement, leaders gain credibility, which enhances their effectiveness. When behaviors and attitudes are not consistent, members are not understanding and not very forgiving. As one respondent put it,

> In team meetings we use the quality principles. Yet in meetings with administrators we often do not use the principles, and it is a culture shock. Quality is being perceived as a delegated function because of the lack of use by administrators.

Because continuous improvement efforts affect how decisions are made and who is involved in making the decisions, bad decision-making processes were repeatedly cited as barriers to the quality initiative:

> Quality practices are used when it is convenient. Administrators use them when they want to use them, otherwise autocratic decisions are made.

> Quality is being viewed as a managerial process instead of a philosophical approach.

> We talk CQI and then we go back and do the same old thing.

> The major decisions are made without using quality practices.

As these comments suggest, leaders play a powerful role in leading the movement. Their actions, decisions, and behaviors are continuously monitored by members. Members expect leaders to consistently use quality practices and are discouraged when they do not.

Our research indicated that for leaders to drive the movement, they need to understand the underlying philosophy of quality and to take ownership so that people feel a sense of accountability. When senior leadership positions are open, hiring people who practice quality concepts enhances the quality initiative. Leaders whose behaviors are consistent with what is being communicated within the institution about continuous improvement gain the most credibility. If leaders are striving to create a culture free from fear and based on trust, they are perceived as more effective. Quality leaders listen to the wisdom in the voices of members.

Leaders need to understand that changing how people think, feel, and act is a monumental undertaking. They need to begin by realizing how influential their own actions and decisions, or lack of, are in driving continuous improvement on campus. In the institutions we studied, it was essential for leaders to thoroughly understand the philosophies underlying the continuous improvement and quality practices. Their demonstration of this understanding in combination with their consistent implementation of quality practices helps to overcome these barriers.

The key to leaders developing an understanding about quality principles and practices depends on the system for professional development. In fact, the level to which all members understand the philosophy of quality improvement, quality language, and tools is a direct reflection of how members are educated.

PROFESSIONAL DEVELOPMENT

According to one administrator, "Higher education does not practice what it preaches. We do not typically educate faculty and staff." Although the norm is for faculty members to attend conferences and conduct research in their fields, it is not the norm to continually update their skills in other areas. Developing staff members is often even a lower priority.

For quality principles and practices to become an integral part of the institutional culture, professional development has to be the number one priority because the other principles are dependent upon the knowledge of members. Helping people to develop individually is essential for them to work effectively alone or in teams. Education is vital for understanding what is meant by continuous improvement. One administrator views continuous improvement as "a cultural mind-set change." Professional development also provides members with a common vocabulary within the institution. This is not the case when uniform education is not provided for all members of the institution. The main barriers in this system revolved around the questions: How much training and development are needed? When should the development take place? Who should conduct the training? How should the development costs be covered?

We found that the degree to which individuals are developed through education determines whether they have a thorough understanding of continuous improvement. If institutions are devoted to professionally developing members, then it is more likely that people will understand the underlying philosophies of the quality movement. Once educated, members tend to adopt quality principles and practices so that quality improvement is no longer an add-on to their existing jobs, but rather how they do their jobs.

The cost of and timing of professional development can be barriers to the system. For the professional development system to be effective, it requires a constant commitment of financial resources, and it needs to be continual. Whether institutions have in-house educators or if consultants are hired, development is costly, but crucial. The timing of development is also a vital consideration. We discovered that several institutions are moving toward just-in-time development. When people are developed at the time they need the information and skills, they are more likely to retain the information.

For the most part, people across the institutions we studied felt fairly satisfied with the professional development efforts. Realizing that education and training is a continual process, most of the interviewees believed that the early stages of development are being sufficiently covered. In fact, a few mentioned that they are "getting kind of burned out on the first-stage stuff," which usually involves an introduction to quality concepts such as customer service and tools. We believe this burnout is an indication of where the institution is on the quality journey. If members know and understand the initial concepts of quality improvement, they need to move on to more sophisticated development to further their understanding of the philosophy underlying continuous improvement.

In retrospect, people generally feel that sessions on customer service have had the most dramatic impact and that they probably spend too much time on quality improvement tools before having the opportunity to directly apply them. Too great an emphasis on tools at the beginning of professional development often leads to the misunderstanding that quality improvement is about tools and techniques rather than about a personal transformation and personal dedication to continuous improvement.

A strong sentiment that was frequently repeated was "if you do not use it, you lose it," or, as referred to by one of our presidents, "the evaporation effect." One staff member reiterated,

> I think you have to use quality improvement in order to understand it. If they have not used it successfully, then they do not see the value.

Development becomes a barrier if people are educated and then not assigned to a team or allowed the opportunity to use their newly gained knowledge. When this occurs, they become disillusioned with quality improvement. To overcome this barrier, it is best to educate people as they have the need to utilize the information, or just-in-time.

Our findings also suggest that people tend to set high expectations for all of the systems (i.e., culture, leadership, development, data collection, communication, and teamwork) as a result of professional development. In these development sessions, philosophies and theories are explained as the ideal, and people expressed disappointment if their reality does not match what they learned in their training and development. Such a situation causes people to be skeptical of the movement.

Being cognizant of this barrier is one way of overcoming it. The important point is to be aware that development establishes clear expectations. Living up to these expectations is difficult, but the very fact that the discrepancy between what has been learned and what is actually in place causes frustration indicates that members have changed their mind-set.

Another barrier caused by education is the time it requires people to be away from their normal work responsibilities. This theme was repeated continually:

> People are out of the office too much for development. The time would be better spent in the office.

> We have done a lot of continuous improvement, but it is bogging people down. People are less willing to invest the time for learning the concepts.

To overcome this time barrier, some institutions have tried to find ways to pick up the slack when people are absent because of professional development. Institutions are looking for ways to fund temporary personnel to replace personnel who need to work on special quality improvement projects or who need to meet in process improvement teams.

Across institutions we studied, people firmly believed that education cannot be forced upon members. Although many of the committed members would like to make professional development mandatory because they believe it is critical, most stated that it should be voluntary. Many noted the dilemma between wanting members across all levels to be educated and trying not to force development upon them. Only one of the institutions we studied requires professional development for all employees. Since most members appreciate continuous education, we did not find many members at this particular institution resenting the requirement. The other institutions appeared to be consciously aware of not wanting to be perceived as forceful. We heard this in several ways:

> We provided a lot of educational activities, but we have not pushed it. It is a slow buying-in sort of thing.

> There is a strong willingness to participate in development. People want to go through the sessions because the word has spread that it is a worthwhile activity. Our development sessions do not have openings.

One of the ways to educate members without forcing them is to let people adopt quality principles and practices naturally. This is only possible if education and development are available and easily accessible to all members. A willingness to be educated on the part of members is an essential component for this system because education increases the level of understanding about quality improvement. As one respondent stated,

> Individual development should become part of the job so that people have to gain a certain level of knowledge and understanding.

The implication is that professional development should be an integral part of every position. This ensures that everyone has a certain level of knowledge about continuous improvement. When professional development is considered part of the responsibilities to fulfill and therefore part of the system, resistance to professional development is lessened.

Another barrier that emerged has to do with relying on consultants for educating instead of having in-house educators. Some of the institutions in our study have their own development staff, and others hire consultants. These trends were also apparent in our national study. (Refer to table 4 and table 6 in appendix B.) Interviewees across the institutions said they strongly prefer having people within the institution teach and develop other members in quality improvement. As some of the interviewees observed, they are there when you need them most, they are members of the institution, which helps to decrease costs, and they are able to keep the momentum going because they understand the institutional culture:

> I can see a real advantage in having an on-campus educator who would do all of the development sessions in any department that needed it rather than hiring a high-priced consultant to develop the senior level hoping that it filters down. People resent the cost of consultants, and then they are not on campus when you need them.

We found that institutions not only are using more just-in-time development, but that they also are realizing that the one-size-fits-all model of professional development is not as effective beyond the basic introductory stage. Within the institution, people have different needs to address, processes to improve, and problems to solve. Therefore, a more appropriate model is to tailor professional development to specific groups. One person made this point:

> Our initial efforts at development assumed that all work cultures throughout the university are the same. I think it is time to begin customizing the development sessions.

One of the important aspects of development seminars is the teaching of quality improvement tools and techniques so that members can perform more effectively and efficiently. As stated previously, interviewees stressed not to overemphasize the tools, but at the same time, they were adamant that collecting data and using quality tools improves decision making. This next section will describe the barriers in the area of quality improvement tools and data collection and how to move beyond these barriers.

DATA COLLECTION AND ANALYSIS

Most of the interviewees in the institutions we studied expressed that measurements are needed and that data collection is the bottleneck of the journey. The three primary barriers are the overreliance on tools, the large amount of time needed to collect and analyze data, and the defensiveness and fear about measurement. We found these barriers are linked together. An overreliance on the tools leads to the perception that quality improvement is too time-consuming. People expressed a fear about measurement because they tend to think data collection is for accountability rather than for improving processes and decision making.

Although continuous improvement involves much more than tools, we discovered that institutions reported spending too much time on tools initially. The emphasis on tools and data collection often leads to a misperception that equates quality improvement with tools and techniques rather than with a shift in philosophy and personal transformation. One administrator said it this way, "We come in with the tools, and we miss the boat."

For the most part, interviewees believed in the importance of collecting data for decision making, but they warned us that it is easy to fall into the trap of overemphasizing the tools and collecting excess data. For example,

> There were hundreds of surveys circulating all over campus. I must have done 10-15 myself. Many of these were fairly meaningless paper exercises. We wasted money on paper and copying not to mention the time involved. We ended up hiring an outside person to do interviews which cost us money.

We were told that using quality improvement tools takes more time in the short run, but saves time in the long run. Unfortunately, we had interviewees who have not made the continuous improvement transformation and who perceive the tools as too time-consuming. They felt that they are collecting more data and keeping more records with the help of fewer people than in the past. Because of reduced staff and time, tools are not used when they should be:

> Tools are being used less in meetings because they are so time-consuming.

One person even admitted that occasionally reports are written saying that tools were used when they were not:

> Sometimes I will write up something and make it sound more formal than it was because I have to make it sound like I followed the rules.

Fear and defensiveness are other barriers to data collection. Many people fear measurements and become defensive when asked to think about establishing indicators of quality improvement. This fear reinforces the importance of creating a culture that supports quality efforts. According to one staff member,

> Every time I would ask for statistics, people would act like I did not trust them; as if I did not think they were doing a good job. Since they had been working hard and not being appreciated, I said that I wanted to let everyone know the work they had been doing. Now, they are working hard, and I think they know they are appreciated because we have the statistics to prove it.

To overcome these barriers, data need to be collected at appropriate times and need to be used to improve decision making. When people know the most appropriate times to collect data and for what purposes, they overcome the hurdle of collecting excess or inappropriate data. As one administrator stated, "Most of us use tools without knowing we are using them. It has become automatic."

Tools should be used to improve the effectiveness and efficiency of processes and systems. Data should be collected to improve decision making. When members understand the purpose of collecting data, they will save time by not overemphasizing tools, and they will be less threatened because they will know that the focus is on improvement, not criticism. This understanding is based on open and honest communication. In reality, communicating effectively is not easy. This next section will explain the barriers to communication and how to make improvements in this system.

COMMUNICATION

After members have acquired knowledge and understanding about continuous improvement, they know the value of it. They are able to use quality tools and techniques to collect necessary data and to improve the effectiveness of their meetings. As important as these systems are, the communication system is the system that influences how the other systems function and are perceived.

Ineffective communication is a barrier. What is communicated, how it is communicated, and the language used in communicating emerged as key factors to consider in the design of a system that supports quality improvement efforts. People are aware when the communication system is working and when it is not working. Largely because of knowledge gained, members expect communication to be different, more effective. One staff member had this to say, "We are impressed with how the administration uses information from the teams to open up communication channels."

Any communication breakdown is a barrier because it can damage the institutional culture. Ineffective communication leads to a lack of trust and to the withholding of information. Because of the complexity of this system, it is the system that most interviewees cited as needing to be continually improved. Once people are educated about continuous improvement, they expect to be included in decisions and to know *why* various decisions are made.

The main communication barriers mentioned were a lack of sincere listening, a lack of trust among employees, a need for better methods to communicate about continuous improvement, and a use of authoritarian language. These elements damage the institutional culture and inhibit continuous improvement; people do not feel comfortable making suggestions and improving processes. When fear permeates the workplace, quality improvement efforts are thwarted:

> We do not communicate well at all. There are a lot of secrets. The day-to-day information that impacts how people work is not shared, and we do not have input.

> We are learning how to listen, but it is not an easy thing. We need to observe and listen.

> We need to have more vehicles to find out what people are doing. People want to know. We lack social events or newsletters to inform people and to keep them current. We lack a system and facilities that encourage people from all areas to get together.

Numerous people said that a common problem is finding out what is going on within an institution. They said they feel left out and powerless when information is not freely shared. They are uncomfortable with the unknown, and this lack of knowledge leads to rumors and misinformation. Oftentimes, what members consider to be unimportant information is communicated, but information that is vital for the institution is not. As one staff member said, "They are good about sharing information that we are not interested in, such as information about the governing board."

Unfortunately, a general belief in the institutions we studied is that when direct, open, and honest conversation is needed the most, the system tends to break down. When institutions experience challenges such as a downturn in enrollment and people perceive a strong need for communication, the communication system does not work as effectively as it should. We found the focus to be on the disappointments in the system rather than on the negative factors affecting the institution. Statements such as, "a lack of communication from senior management," "a lack of communication about quality between the administration and the faculty," and "responses from the president are not empathetic enough" indicate that people become extremely critical of the communication system because they have high expectations.

Our interviewees not only criticized *what* is being said (or not said) but they also were quite sensitive to *how* the message is communicated. Interviewees were often critical of administrators, accusing them of not being as open or as honest as members would desire. A flattened, more horizontal structure helps support an open dialogue among members. The communication system should continually reinforce the importance of trusting each other. Reflected several administrators:

> Administrators need to practice what they preach. They need to continue to have an open door policy, even if it is painful.

> We need to work on communicating our achievements. We need to communicate to people how the teams are using quality practices effec-

tively. We need to let the organization know about the continuous improvement successes. People need to be reminded to keep the momentum going. There is a tendency to revert back to old habits.

Dissenting opinions need to be allowed, otherwise resentment and frustration occur.

A staff member agreed:

You can solve so many problems if you just communicate with each other.

We also heard people in senior positions share stories about how simple it sounds to openly communicate with institutional members but how difficult it is to practice. At the same time, they also agreed that their attempts to open communication channels and to learn how to accept feedback have changed the cultures within their institutions. One president concluded by saying that he continues to simplify the language by *asking people one question*: "What is keeping you from doing what you need to do?"

Language

In the literature, one of the major barriers to effective communication is the language associated with quality improvement efforts. Explained a staff member, "We are student-centered, and we always have been. But there is animosity toward quality improvement language." Since people often get "hung up" on the quality language, we wanted to find out how the institutions in our study overcame this obstacle of terminology.

One theme we discovered was that people, particularly faculty members, are suspicious of jargon and are "turned off" immediately when buzzwords are used. We were told members do not like the words "total" and "management" because of the business orientation, which they find unappealing and inappropriate in the higher education community. Academicians are proud of the fact that they are not in business and industry, and words associated with business are not preferred. As a result, some institutions have made a conscious effort *not* to use total quality management (TQM):

It is hard to get people to accept buzzwords like TQM.

I do not like to use TQM with the faculty because it has a negative connotation. Total quality? Everything we have done in the past is not quality? Once you set it up that way, people are automatically defensive. The language can set a negative tone.

We don't use TQM as an acronym, but we talk about continuous improvement and sometimes continuous quality improvement. There are messages in the TQM initials that do not feel good in higher education. There is also a fundamental difference between what we are trying to do and TQM. "Total" has a certain hubris when you are talking about higher education and "management" is not really right. What we are talking about is leadership.

A group of Canadians came to observe, and they said to not use the term TQM because it has a bad perception among various groups.

Another pattern of language usage was a strong movement *away* from the use of TQM in favor of continuous quality improvement or CQI. The preference for the word "continuous" reinforces the systems perspective and implies a feedback loop. The following quotations are representative of this trend:

The faculty kept asking where is this total quality management? Whereas CQI is constant, always seeking, and people can better understand this term.

We don't spend any time talking about TQM. We spend a lot of time talking about continuous improvement or how to improve. We talk about how to use our skills and abilities to continuously improve.

Others said they moved away from acronyms altogether for many of the same reasons: too business-oriented and the perception of being too trendy. To overcome this barrier, several institutions refuse to use any kind of acronyms:

We learned early that the message sent by the initials TQM made people feel like it is the program of the month, so we try to avoid any kind of initials.

We use continuous improvement because it is not so market-oriented. I think most people want to improve no matter what they are doing.

The question of what to call quality initiatives on campus is an early barrier that slows or prevents the practice of the quality principles before the efforts even have a chance to get off the ground. One way some of the institutions in our study have overcome this barrier is to not give their improvement efforts a title. In fact, one president reported, "I try not to use any of the quality words." He prefers to communicate through changed behaviors. People learn about quality improvement by observing him as he strives to "walk the talk." The following statements echo this perspective:

You can almost see people close down when you use the jargon. So we have focused on using good commonsense procedures and never call them anything, and I thought that was very beneficial.

I will go a whole day without saying the word "quality." You do not need to say it if you are doing it. You need to make sure that you are asking the fundamental questions that are at the core of quality. What are the indicators of success? Use the tools to answer core questions.

> We have tried to downplay some of the business-oriented language. We talk about improvement, about improving quality, about being more reflective about our work.

Yet another administrator said

> I am not calling it anything. I think it is a way of thinking. People will call me and ask me how I have time to practice quality. They do not feel they have time to have team meetings. I ask them if they have meetings, and the answer is always yes. Then I tell them that the quality principles are a new way to have meetings. It is a whole other way of thinking or another way to manage the work that is done. It is more efficient, it is going to save time in the long run, and it is probably going to save money. I do not think it has to be called anything.

Institutions farther along in their quality journey have clearly moved past the language barrier. Initially, it was common for institutions to use TQM, but the trend is to move away from TQM and acronyms in preference of continuous quality improvement and process improvement. Some institutions prefer to not even use the word "quality." Even though some institutions have created their own names and titles for their quality efforts, the institutions that demonstrated the highest level of understanding about continuous improvement are moving in the direction of not using any labels. They avoid the typical quality language and focus on improving processes and systems throughout the institution by *asking different questions.*

Students as Customers

People within the higher education community value and treasure words, and we discovered that the word "customer" is a significant language barrier for most of the institutions in our study. Our findings corroborated this hurdle that is frequently mentioned in the literature (Seymour and Collett, 1991). Time and again, members of the administration, faculty, and staff admitted that viewing students and others within the institution as customers is a challenge and often hinders the momentum of quality initiatives on campus. When students are viewed as customers, faculty members often perceive a surrender of expertise and authority. Faculty attitudes often are "Who are they to tell us?" or as one faculty member stated, "The inmates are running the asylum." To view students as customers, the thinking needs to shift so that the focus is on learning rather than teaching.

Even though many people expressed resistance to the term "customer," several were aware that the term does fit some characteristics or actions of students:

> Faculty do not like the term customer. It may not be like a retail customer, but students are paying customers. If they are not satisfied, they can go somewhere else.

Viewing students as customers and other faculty members as customers emerged as obstacles to effective communication. Only when these communication problems were overcome, could the communication system enhance quality initiatives.

Leading by example is one way institutions are trying to communicate the message of serving others within the institution without referring to members as customers. Individuals who have adopted quality principles and practices hope that their behaviors will help others buy into continuous improvement efforts. To do this, institutions have changed the rules, which indirectly changes the system. One person said it well:

> Quality customer service involves eliminating dumb rules that exist because of history.

Faculty members were careful to point out that they were more receptive to the quality concepts than they were to the quality language. As one faculty member said,

> We already had some quality improvements in teaching taking place. If they had come in and said continuous improvement is the new thing, you have to do this and call it that, it would have been a disaster.

One administrator stated it this way:

> We had assessment (quality indicators) in the classroom, and continuous improvement helped with the administrative side of the institution. You can do many things without ever using the vocabulary and still practice quality principles. The concepts are not new, but now they are being articulated.

The institutions we studied had distinct divisions between people who are engaged in quality improvement and people who are not. Administrators and staff members who are devoted to continuous improvement become extremely frustrated with faculty members who resist getting involved. As one staff member commented,

> I want to tell a tenured faculty member that even though you are tenured, your merit this next year is going to be coupled with how you are relating to and treating your students. That is something on which we can get measures.

Our data reinforced others' findings that accepting the word "customer" and understanding the concept of customer orientation is much easier and faster on the administrative side than on the academic side of the institution (Seymour and Collett, 1991; Seymour, 1991). A story best illustrates the resistance to the language from the academic side:

> A design team was established to write a plan for the whole university. When the report was finally released, we aimed it at the administrative

and business sides of the university. Our thinking was that if we can foster the notion that faculty and students are the customers of those units, through various successes we can create a more fertile environment for other changes. We ended up changing the language somewhat and talked about "those people we serve" instead of customers.

Another commented,

> The faculty felt that the president was trying to turn the academy into the University of Kmart. They understood customer to mean that if the students did not want to have Friday classes that there might not be any Friday classes. They feared that expectations would be lowered. What if students want less homework?

Our interviewees said many faculty members are concerned that if students are thought of as customers, they will be given what they want rather than what they need. That is not what the customer concept is all about. It is about paying more attention to customer satisfaction, which has beneficial effects on costs and perceived quality of programs and services. The difficulty in communicating with faculty members about the customer concept is reflected in the following example:

> The college of arts and sciences faculty got together and voted something like 47 to 1 against the idea of viewing students as customers. And the president said, "I don't care what you call it. As long as you realize that if they are not here, we are not here." Now we often talk about those we serve. We emphasize that in higher education viewing the student as customer does not mean that the customer is always right.

Faculty members who are practicing quality concepts and who understand that students are customers agree that students are usually not qualified to comment on course content. These faculty members do believe, however, that the students have every right to tell them if they understand the material or if the faculty member can change something to improve the learning experience. The following analogy was used to explain the customer relationship with respect to students:

> It is similar to a customer going to a bank for a loan. The customer has to be the right customer for that bank. Therefore, the customer has some responsibilities to the bank. When the customer signs the loan contract, or the student enrolls, he/she has agreed to certain conditions. If the customer wants the loan, or the student wants the degree, this is what the person has to do.

Education is usually the key to helping faculty members shift their thinking about students and to overcoming this language barrier. An administrator provided us with this explanation:

When the student is interacting with the administrative office, the student is the customer. In the classroom, the professor is primarily the customer and the student's job is to satisfy the professor. But when the professor gives the student an assignment, the student is the customer. The job of the professor is to make sure the student understands the assignment. When the assignment is turned in, the professor is the customer again.

The key becomes finding a way to move beyond this obstacle:

We spend a lot of time on educating people about the principles. Our principles are respect for people, managing by fact, satisfying those we serve, and pursuing continuous improvement. We have had problems with the term "customer." Sometimes in the education process, we suggest that if that word is bothersome, replace it with a word that works such as "client," "patient," "patron," and "end-user."

Some institutions have moved away from the term "customer" and are using different terms. As explained by one president,

I don't use "customer" on campus now. I have moved to "social contract." I saw that the liberal arts faculty would understand clearly what a social contract was. I stress that we need to rewrite our social contract. It is figuratively signed by students, faculty, administrators, and funders.

Since faculty usually resist the terminology, we try to teach the concepts before any specific terms are introduced.

When students are considered partners in the learning process, it is natural to collect feedback from them and to be concerned about their satisfaction and growth. One faculty member stressed that the professor has some degree of responsibility if the student does not succeed. This perception contrasts the traditional view that if the student does not succeed, it is not the professor's fault because the student did not work hard enough, was not properly prepared, or was lazy. The distinction is that quality improvement requires the instructor to have some responsibility for the student's success. For example, this faculty member now asks what can be done to improve the situation when students do not do well.

As people begin to communicate differently, they start to behave differently. Changing the language used changes actions and behaviors. One of the ways people change their behaviors is in the way they work in cross-functional teams. They understand the value of collaboration, and they appreciate being included in decision making.

TEAMWORK AND COLLABORATION

Teams that work effectively enhance the quality movement because decision making is improved and because people feel their participation and input are valued. Yet we learned that teams often restrain quality improvement efforts because they do not know how to collaborate. Members need to work together in redesigning improved processes and systems. Cross-functional teams (representatives from various areas form a team) revolve around using multiple perspectives to make improvements. We discovered that the successful use of teamwork is highly dependent on the degree of professional development within the institution. Again, we found that teamwork and collaboration are being used more successfully on the administrative side of the insitution.

In higher education, working as a collaborative team requires new patterns of thinking. As described by one president, "There is a built-in hostility to collective work in higher education." Faculty members are granted autonomy to work independently, and they consider this characteristic to be one of the incentives of working in an academy. When this independence is infringed upon, they become resentful.

Because faculty members are conditioned to work as individuals, it is difficult to develop the new behaviors required to work well in teams. To illustrate the dramatic shift in thinking needed for effective teamwork, one president used a personal example:

> The facilitator told me I was the most independent person he knew. It took me two weeks to figure out that that statement was not a compliment.

Most faculty members not only have trouble working in teams in general, but they also have a particularly hard time working in cross-functional teams. Cross-functional teams, those that involve combining faculty members from various areas, are usually used to improve processes. In higher education, however, faculty members and staff have a strong identity with departments or disciplines. In the institutions we studied this independence was a barrier to working in cross-functional teams. Interviewees gave several reasons for this problem, but the primary reasons have to do with specialization and expertise. Faculty members generally do not value multiple perspectives from people outside their area because they do not think their time is well spent when they are asked to be on a team outside their area of expertise. Two quotations illustrate this point:

> On a campus, the barrier is turf and specialization. There is the perception that people outside the area or discipline cannot contribute. We have been able to build better teams in nonacademic areas for this reason.

> Cross-functional changes have been hard to make because they require the cooperation of people across the lines in the traditional administrative

chart. People need to overcome their attitude regarding the interest of their own unit.

Even though working in teams is difficult for many people, our interviewees particularly commented on how faculty members are the source of the strongest resistance to teamwork:

> Faculty act like they know it all. They do not need others as much, so they do not know how to work in teams. They do not need each other to obtain the information they typically need for their classes.

> The president decided to start the quality efforts in the administrative area and let it ripple down. The thinking was that faculty would buy into it later. Faculty are like independent contractors, and they have trouble thinking of themselves as members of teams.

Many reasons were given as to why faculty members are apprehensive about participating in teams as part of the quality improvement efforts. Consistent with the traditional nature of higher education, faculty members are not as attached to the organization as they are to their disciplines. Faculty members do not see their role as making the institution better; they feel their role is toward making contributions to their fields. They do not view themselves as working on the same team as everyone else in the institution, preferring to work independently.

Because teams require new behaviors, we found people initially uncomfortable with teams. As one person said,

> Some people are threatened until they get into the team thinking. When they do, it raises their self-esteem. Until then, they just stay inside themselves.

> When the quality movement first started, it was just a word, just another fad to a lot of people. Through the financial aid office, people started buying into it. The fact that the staff was so involved was really unusual so people thought there were hidden agendas. People thought that management had already decided what they wanted, and they only had the teams for show.

These statements emphasize the value of professional development in implementing quality principles and practices. Unless people understand what the new behaviors are and why they are important in the process of continuous improvement, behaviors and actions do not change. Continuous education of all members helps them understand the new roles, behaviors, and thinking that are required of team members. Faculty members should be included in continuous improvement efforts from the beginning, and they should be educated at the same time as administrators and staff.

Some of the people we interviewed question the amount and timing of development. Many felt that there was not enough time spent on development, and/or they had participated in team development but had not been selected for a team. For example,

> We were pulled into teams without adequate training.

> We have been trained, and many of us are not on a team. Do we even still have teams?

> I could not use quality tools today if my life depended on it because I have not been on a team.

> I have volunteered, and I am still not selected to be on a team.

As with any other skill, working in teams takes practice, and members need to practice the skill of collaboration because these are not natural skills for most people in higher education. The sooner members use the skills gained in development, the sooner skills are reinforced and the sooner the value of them is recognized intellectually.

Another barrier is using teams when they are not necessary. Several people claimed that teams are used excessively. According to one interviewee,

> There is a question in people's minds about how much you can do by a team and when it is appropriate for the director to just make a decision. There are issues that we have talked rings around, and I think there are some people who would just like to tell the director to make a decision.

Because working in teams is time-consuming, people feel that too many teams have been formed when the situation did not warrant a team effort. Some leaders treat teams as a new approach that must be used in every situation, whether or not it is necessary. One staff member said it this way:

> I do not think it should be the case that everybody should have input into decisions that are made. There are many decisions that should be made by management, and teams slow the decision-making process.

Others believed:

> There is a misunderstanding about continuous improvement. Not all decisions can be made by a team. I can see where some people perceive these decisions as not quality.

> Teams should not be put together for any old problem. Rather, teams should be used to solve the important problems because of the time involved. In addition, the assignment of teams needs to be more selective in order to make the team effort cost effective.

Time is another barrier to working in teams. Time away from the office or primary work responsibilities to attend team meetings was repeatedly stated as a factor that interferes with jobs. It was common to hear people say that teams involved too many people having to coordinate their schedules:

> Our team has not met because we cannot find a time when we can get together.

Some people indicated that time constraints of team meetings not only inhibited team effectiveness, but it also negatively affected customer satisfaction because members attending meetings are not there to serve others:

> People are taken away from work areas, and customers are not served.

Because teams take time away from jobs, they are not always considered cost effective, especially when it is perceived that an individual could make as effective a decision. Depending on the scope of the decision and the expertise needed, teamwork should be encouraged but not overdone. The costs of having members away from their primary job responsibilities should be considered. This cost depends on how the work is covered when team members are away at meetings:

> Teams have not been cost effective because we have had to hire other people to cover the area while everyone is gone and involved.

> A lot of people had to step in and make up the time when the front-line people were meeting with the team. In one sense, it made the others appreciate you, but I still feel the team was worth it. It seems like the team process takes a long time, but then suddenly everything falls together.

The questions of when teams should be formed and who should be on the teams often become barriers. Because of an effort by leaders to involve others rather than make all decisions by themselves, we heard interviewees criticizing leaders for not making decisions. Sometimes people are also assigned to teams inappropriately. An administrator shared this perspective:

> I found myself on some teams that I should not have been on because the teams had to do with things that I was not directly involved in or I did not have knowledge about. Those teams were particularly annoying to me.

Professional development helps people understand how and when to use teams and who should be on teams, but communicating *why* these decisions are made helps people conceptualize quality principles. Why teams are needed, why people are selected, why teams have constraints are questions that need to be answered to overcome the barriers to teams functioning effectively.

It is crucial that teams know about any restrictions up front. We heard numerous accounts of team efforts that did not work because they were not aware of the time or budget limitations from the start. Explained one administrator,

> One of the big mistakes we made was that whenever we could find a group of people willing to work on something, we would appoint a team. But these cross-functional teams did not work well because we did not tell

them up front how much money they had to spend. They came back with proposed solutions that cost more than we could spend, and they got discouraged. Since limited money is a major factor for most institutions, I see this as a problem unless the financial constraints are discussed at the beginning of the team effort.

A common and damaging mistake admitted by many of the institutions in our study is when the leaders do not implement a team recommendation for no apparent reason or because the constraints were not shared initially. These actions disempower teams and discourage members, especially after investing the time and energy involved in teamwork. Establishing limitations and articulating them to the team before work begins on a project are the keys to a successful team project.

Using incentives is one strategy to overcome some of the barriers mentioned in building effective teams. In order for behaviors to change, interviewees said that incentives are being used to encourage change. What kinds of incentives and rewards are being implemented? As noted previously, institutions struggle to develop a system of rewards and recognition that persuade people to embrace change and to work in teams. Interviewees described methods that have been used with mixed results. Because most of the resistance comes from the academic side of the institution, interviewees believe that administrators and faculty members may need different incentives. People have to want to improve, and incentives do not always work:

We have no way to make faculty adopt quality practices. There is even a difference between wanting to teach about quality and wanting to use it.

Teambuilding is important, but we do not have consensus at the department head level. Everyone is overworked. We have large expectations for teaching and research. In their minds, they do not have time to be in meetings about quality. The only way to get people in meetings is to mandate it, and that goes against quality. You have to convince faculty that continuous improvement is going to make them better teachers or better researchers.

Finding ways to interest faculty members in quality improvement is crucial to the success of the quality journey. A vital component of this journey is having them understand how continuous improvement concepts can enhance their teaching and research.

The institutions we studied have taken different approaches to involving all key stakeholders, especially faculty members, in the quality improvement process. Several institutions hold an annual event in which process improvement teams display exhibits of quality projects undertaken during the year. Two events were described in detail. Several positive aspects were specifically mentioned about one of the events:

The initial reaction to the quality event was resistance because of the additional work to be done. We thought we would have a dozen exhibits, and we had 58. The impact was great. The event put people who are generally hidden in the infrastructure of the university into the role of teachers. The whole university could see the results of their quality efforts. About 2,000 people attended the event. Attendees evaluated the event greater than 4 on a scale of 5, but exhibitors evaluated it even higher. We had pictures in the paper of regents talking to custodial people and information technology people. There were door prizes from the area merchants with a grand prize of two free tickets anywhere in the United States if the evaluation form was turned in.

As the administrators and staff members in this institution processed this event later, they discovered several barriers built into the existing system of the event that should be changed in the future if a similar event is held. We heard comments such as

The vice presidents were evaluating the other projects, which should not be. The projects were requirements for middle management, while the vice presidents did not have projects but evaluated the projects of others. The process is anti-quality because it encourages competition.

There was a feeling that if a project was not done that you could not display it. This led to an emphasis on the end and not the means.

The quality fair had too much of a carnival atmosphere.

The timing of the event was poor in that there were no students or faculty around. In addition, the memos were sent out late.

Even though this event wasn't totally successful, these comments illustrate how people at this institution have changed their thinking about competition. They have come to prefer cooperation, and they are thinking about working in teams. They want the focus to be on process improvement rather than on specific projects.

The second event at another institution was a fair where teams were available to explain their quality improvements. It was described to us as an incentive because the team projects brought people closer together and because the members "found new respect for one another." The project teams met for two hours each week for eight weeks on company time, so the message they inferred was that this project was important. Interviewees indicated that they found the event rewarding because they learned what others were doing in their institution and because they could showcase what they had accomplished.

We were impressed that the people in our focus groups had processed these events thoroughly. These examples indicate that they are beginning to understand the true essence of what it means to be a learning organization.

They are thinking in terms of systems. They are demonstrating new ways of thinking, feeling, and acting. Interviewees are questioning the current practices and are realizing that some existing systems are barriers to continuous improvement. At the first event described, interviewees had fully processed the event. They identified ways to change the system so that the event could be more effective. Through numerous conversations about this event, it became clear that the focus is on continuous improvement and continuous learning. They are continually looking for ways to improve.

Since personal transformation is the heart of the quality movement, the fact that members are striving to improve themselves and the processes they use is evidence that quality initiatives have made progress at these institutions. One administrator said it this way, "Quality improvement is all self-driven." When enough people reach the conclusion that quality practices are the way to function and are intrinsically rewarding, then institutions are creating a culture that supports continuous improvement.

LEARNING AND TEACHING

Despite the evidence presented so far about faculty resistance to continuous improvement, faculty members can actually enhance the movement when they understand the underlying philosophies of quality. In fact, faculty members have the potential to influence the academic side of the institution the most because they are directly responsible for providing a high-quality education. Unfortunately, without a doubt, we discovered the strongest barrier to most of the systems is faculty resistance. This sentiment was strong among administrators, staff, and faculty alike. As one administrator put it, "You can't push faculty up a hill." Likewise, we discovered the preexisting conflict between members of the faculty and administration that is a norm in so many higher education institutions. We concluded that some of the faculty resistance to continuous improvement efforts is based on the "this is just another administrative fad" perception.

When we asked about continuous improvement in learning and teaching, faculty members repeatedly commented that they struggle with how much time they should devote to learning about continuous improvement and implementing quality practices. As one staff member put it,

> Faculty do not think of themselves as managers, or even about being managed. They perceive their job as one of teaching and conducting research. They do not think quality is relevant to them. At the department level they can see it. At the dean's level they see it clearly. Faculty are proud of the fact that they manage their time their own way.

Another staff member noted how critical faculty members are to the success of the quality movement:

> That is the Achilles heel of the whole issue of quality in higher education. The product is what happens in the classroom between the faculty member and the students. And the rest of us are ancillary to that and support the effort here and there. No matter how highly tuned we are to quality and no matter how exhaustively we practice it, if the faculty are not into it, the heart of quality is lost.

Our findings support the findings in the literature (Seymour and Collett, 1991; Seymour, 1991) that note that continuous improvement in higher education usually begins on the administrative side and that the academic side is slower to get involved. One of the main reasons for this discrepancy is that faculty members with whom we spoke are ambiguous about their mission. They are pulled between allocating time to teaching or to research because of their limited time. Since they perceive quality efforts to be associated with teaching, if applicable at all, faculty members at research institutions are less willing to give up the time to learn and practice quality principles. Interviewees consistently told us that faculty members have been reluctant to get involved in improvement efforts because they do not understand their role in the process. Faculty members are often the last people to be developed, if at all. One faculty member articulated the problem faced by faculty members well:

> I work in a research institution and the primary mission is research not teaching. Teaching is a part of the mission, but it is not the core. For faculty, the motivational structure is not there. Motorola felt a crisis and until higher education institutions feel that crisis, the quality principles are not priorities.

Because of a lack of development, faculty members often are not conscious of the processes and systems that could be continuously improved. They are usually uninformed about how continuous improvement can be used to improve the processes of learning and teaching.

Based on our interviews, we discovered that another reason faculty members are particularly suspicious about continuous improvement is the corporate analogy. Many reject the quality improvement models because they do not believe business models fit the culture and traditions of higher education. Traditional systems, such as tenure, protect academic freedom while at the same time encourage independence rather than interdependence. Tenure also facilitates stability in jobs, stability that does not exist on the administrative side of the institution. Therefore, faculty members are more isolated than administrators from economic variables, and they do not feel a crisis as quickly or perceive continuous improvement to be as relevant to what they do.

Faculty members are often described as skeptical, cynical, and individualistic. They naturally resist working in teams and working with people in other disciplines. We concluded that part of the difficulty is that the characteristics that attract faculty members into the profession in the first place—independence, autonomy, discipline specific, and stability—contradict many of the new behaviors needed to adopt quality practices. One respondent said it best:

> Faculty are used to being the teachers, and they find it hard to be the learners. They are extremely defensive about quality issues. They resent course evaluations because they are not willing to listen to constituents. They do not even like the word "customer."

The quality improvement journey is a paradigm shift for most members, but it became clear to us that the required shift is most challenging for the faculty. In the institutions in our study, this challenge is one of the major barriers. According to one administrator, "Faculty are still an obstacle. They still don't get it, and they may never get it."

Recognizing the problems with introducing continuous improvement to members of the faculty, the institutions we studied use one strategy to engage members of the administration and staff while another engagement strategy is used with faculty members. Unfortunately, separating the groups causes a vicious cycle of resentment and further resistance. Because faculty members are perceived as resistant, they are not involved in the training and development process as early as administrators and staff. As a result, they are not as informed, and they do not have a similar level of knowledge as members in other parts of the institution. This lack of knowledge and understanding causes faculty members to be even more resistant, perpetuating this damaging cycle.

Knowing that many faculty members will probably resist quality improvement efforts, institutions have selected various strategies so that efforts can progress with or without having the faculty engaged. At one institution, the president made a conscious decision not to include the faculty because of the perceived strong resistance. The decision was made to proceed on the administrative side because it was believed that this area was where most of the gains could be made in the shortest amount of time. The hope was that the successes made would have a trickle-down effect with the faculty. The other institutions in our study began on the administrative side because of the more natural connection between business approaches and language and administration. Yet, we found a pattern that there is a recognition that these strategies have not been as sucessful as if faculty members would have been educated from the start.

When we asked about obstacles to quality initiatives, we were repeatedly made aware of the faculty resistance. Some stated that faculty members feel that continuous improvement is a threat to academic freedom. Others mentioned that it is the time commitment that makes getting faculty members involved so difficult. Another administrator offered this perspective:

> Any naysayers create excuses. Unproductive faculty or marginal members are the most reluctant to change. Most of the people in whom I have the

greatest confidence will be receptive and leaders of change. They are the people who are productive both as teachers and as scholars. People who are open to new ideas in their own fields are open to new ideas of administration.

A faculty member clearly articulated this barrier:

> Faculty can always say that they cannot utilize the *7 Principles of Highly Effective People* in their classes when they have classes of 40 or more. Rather than thinking about how they can promote cooperative learning or active learning in a class of 40, they just throw their hands up and say they can't do it. They also do not want to talk about quality when the institution is cutting back faculty. If there is ever a time to think about talking about quality it is when you are cutting back faculty.

Even though faculty members were cited as primary barriers, we did hear people differentiating between senior and junior faculty members in terms of their resistance to quality improvement efforts. We were told that it is easier to engage newer faculty members in continuous improvement than it is to involve senior members. Evidence of this pattern is reflected in these two statements:

> We are frustrated with the older faculty who are not as interested in the quality movement when the rest of us are practicing quality concepts.

> The older faculty members are very skeptical. The younger members do not have the sense of history. They feel more ownership and more empowered. The newer people know the direction the institution is taking, and they credit the administration with it.

The institutions we studied have realized that it is difficult to overcome faculty resistance by changing their attitudes and behaviors. Several institutions are making more of a conscious effort to hire people with attitudes and beliefs that match the vision, mission, and goals of the institution. For example, they have developed questions derived from their governing principles that are used in the interview process to assess whether the person will fit into the new culture. As one president told us, "With each person who is hired, you have a chance to influence the culture positively or negatively."

What institutions learned along the journey is that the faculty should be involved from the beginning. From experience, we heard senior leaders admit that the best way to engage faculty members is to encourage a more open dialogue with them about the philosophy of continuous improvement. Many interviewees believe faculty members are intellectually interested in the idea of continuous improvement, so the goal should be to get them talking about quality improvement concepts early in the journey.

Finding some quality champions on the academic side to assist in creating change is another way to overcome faculty resistance. Members on the faculty who are implementing quality practices demonstrate their enthusiasm in front of their colleagues. Because faculty members are accustomed to reading and discussing philosophical ideas, another pattern emerged of creating faculty discussion groups to converse about quality improvement and of having faculty members write about the concepts and how quality practices can be used to improve learning and teaching. These are powerful strategies in engaging faculty members. As one faculty member commented, "If we never talk about quality improvement, the prospect of faculty participation is pretty minimal. I think there is real potential if we would begin to talk."

A general consensus among interviewees was that faculty resistance can be overcome when they understand how the practices facilitate effective teaching and research. Using the testimony of faculty members who are cognizant of how time can be saved when processes are improved and work is more effective is another way to engage them. The key is to help the faculty make the connections between what they see as their mission and the goals of continuous improvement. We heard this theme in several ways:

> Faculty are reluctant because they do not see the joy and fun in quality. They think productivity is to go out and write a book by themselves. They need to understand that it is not an administrative issue, but rather an issue of how to teach and to conduct research better.

> Faculty need to understand the competitive circumstances surrounding higher education institutions. They need to know that if it ain't broke, keep fixing it. There is not anything that cannot be improved.

In recording the perspectives of those directly involved in practicing quality concepts, we realized that the institutions further along the quality journey are involved in self-revelation and reflection. They think about what they are doing, and they ask how things can be performed better. They are *asking different questions,* which results in receiving different answers through the collection of different data.

Continuous improvement cannot be imposed on anyone, and particularly not on the faculty. For the most part, a better strategy is to help faculty members intellectually appreciate the value of quality principles and practices. As we were told,

> It is not very effective when the push comes from administration to faculty particularly where there is strong faculty governance. They are not inclined to embrace the concept. The bottom-up approach is the effective direction for faculty acceptance.

> You can't impose quality on faculty because they would refuse to do it.

Because of the pressure from AACSB, the primary accrediting association for business schools, more courses and programs on quality management are being integrated into business curricula. Since these quality courses are being integrated into business and engineering curricula, we hypothesized that faculty members within business schools and engineering schools would prac-tice what they teach. This scenario was not the case in the institutions in the study. Even some faculty members who teach courses on quality improvement seemed reluctant to practice quality principles. We discovered that there is a difference between teaching quality improvement, talking about it, and prac-ticing it.

When we interviewed faculty members in business schools, we found that although they are knowledgeable about quality principles and practices, they are not leading the efforts and are often behind the rest of the institution in their quality improvement efforts. This lack of support was also true for smaller institutions with business departments rather than business schools. By way of illustration, the following remarks support this finding:

> Most in the business department probably do not buy into it.

> The current stance seems to be that the business school thinks they will ignore quality and it will go away.

> The quality efforts are less pervasive among the business school faculty than the rest of the university.

It was ironic to discover that business schools or business departments are not the areas leading the quality initiatives on campus. We were surprised to find that they usually follow other groups in the institution rather than being at the forefront. Even though they teach courses in quality improvement, many faculty members in business in the institutions in our study are not as enlightened about continuous improvement in the classroom as faculty mem-bers from other disciplines.

SKEPTICS

We were not surprised that there are people within the institutions we studied who oppose the quality improvement efforts. Because continuous improve-ment is essentially about continuous change, we found that some members often resist the changes that are necessary. Opponents are barriers to the momentum of the movement.

We discovered skeptics (cynics, detractors) among members of the admin-istration, staff, and faculty at all of our institutions. These are people who do not perceive any significant positive outcomes as a result of improvement efforts. We requested that some skeptics be included in our interviews because we wanted their voices to be represented in developing a more accurate picture of the quality improvement journey. Some of their comments follow:

> Nothing has really changed.

> We thought that quality improvement could really help us to become a better institution, but it is not true.

> We are perpetuating a system that is not one of quality improvement, yet everyone in the district has been educated in the concepts of continuous improvement.

> Three years ago I went to a continuous improvement meeting. We were told these were things we needed to do, that we have to get going on this. I went to a meeting just a few weeks ago and I heard exactly the same things. There is no impetus.

These people are barriers to quality improvement efforts because they speak out against it, refuse to be a part of it, or do not get involved in improving it. They fear the unknown and favor the status quo. One way of overcoming their threat of opposition is to turn it into an opportunity to communicate the value of the quality initiative. Their comments and questions require those involved in continuous improvement to continually articulate quality principles and their benefits. The challenge for leaders is to help skeptics to understand quality principles and practices by explaining *why* they are important to the institution and its constituencies, but not to force them into complying. A staff member expressed this view:

> Some people have been against quality improvement from the start. I have left them alone, and eventually I have seen most of them find something that they really cared about, and then come into the process. It does not work to force people.

There was a general consensus that people in opposition cannot be forced to believe in quality principles and to engage in quality practices. Most interviewees felt that the best way to defuse the resistance is to lead by example. Again, the resistance is usually from the academic side of the institution.

In the institutions in our study, the people who have adopted quality practices are extremely frustrated with people who resist becoming involved in the continuous improvement efforts. They become impatient:

> I believe in consensus building and democracy and participation, but I am an impatient person. I hate floundering, stalemate, and inertia. I fight against being authoritarian and wanting to force people to believe in quality improvement.

Impatience, however, is not the best way to deal with detractors. As noted earlier, skeptics or detractors require the leaders of quality improvement efforts to continually articulate the philosophy, to explain quality practices, and to convey the value of continuous improvement to higher education. Two administrators commented on the benefits of patience:

> Sure, there are detractors, but they can be valuable. You would fail to overlook issues that they cause you to examine. They are a genuine blessing. We do things better because of the skeptics. They force us to think harder, longer, and better about how we are going to get where we

want to go. We have better processes and solutions because of the detractors.

Too many people want to approach the quality movement with a cookie cutter mentality. They want to cut out something that is nice and neat with predetermined programs, and I am not sure that it can be done effectively. We do not force quality improvement down anyone's throat. They come to the table willingly and in greater numbers. Quality improvement cannot be imposed, but people need to be exposed to the information and principles. Ultimately, they make the decision.

Other people shared examples of how people who had opposed quality initiatives are now proponents of continuous improvement. One president provided a story of successfully dealing with a skeptic of whom he is proud:

We have a custodian who was a shop steward when I first came to the university. He was always stirring up trouble. So I got him involved in the quality movement. Now he is giving quality improvement speeches all over the state and nation. I saw him the other day and he had attended a quality conference for front-line people in the system. He told me how he only had one reservation. He thought we were leaders in the movement, but now he thinks we are in the stratosphere. In his own thinking, he had moved so far out that he could no longer communicate with the other people at the meeting.

As this story illustrates, overcoming opposition by involvement has proven to be a successful strategy.

Another president described one of his key administrators as "pessimistic and certainly not customer-oriented." Various interviewees consistently remarked how this key administrator has been "born again" because of his involvement in improvement efforts. He has become a change agent for continuous improvement because of the change in attitude he continues to demonstrate. In our interview with this "born again" administrator, he confirmed that being involved in practicing quality principles has transformed him professionally and personally. In his words, "I am a different person." We found that people who are deeply loyal to quality principles and practices have made personal transformations.

As the quality initiative has grown within our institutions, we were told that some of the skeptics have become uncomfortable with their position and elected to leave the institution. They believe they no longer fit with the direction of the institution. As one administrator concluded, "By attrition some of the obstacles will go away."

CONCLUSIONS

Barriers to the effectiveness and momentum of most quality systems exist at all the institutions we studied. Institutions are working to overcome these barriers. This section of the book emerged from answers to questions asked about obstacles to the development and implementation of systems. Our analysis of the data reveals that the overall barriers are lack of understanding, time, and money. We also found barriers to implementing the following systems: institutional culture, leadership, professional development, data collection and analysis, communication, teamwork and collaboration, and learning and teaching. Skeptics, people opposed to continuous improvement efforts, are also an initial barrier.

The factors that enhance the quality movement when present or strong often are the same factors that become barriers when absent or weak. Although many of the barriers do not seem overwhelming, it is important to be aware of the hurdles that can prevent progress from being made. Sometimes paying attention to the timing of activities or to who is included in projects and in improving processes can lessen the impact of these barriers. Most of the barriers can be addressed with effective communication complete with feedback.

The dominant theme can best be summed up by saying: People are *asking different questions*, but not everyone is comfortable with the different answers that are generated. The issues may be the same, but institutions pursuing continuous improvement are looking at everything they do from a different perspective, one that is based on the premise that everything can be improved. Developing and implementing new systems is difficult and takes time. We were told that a systemic approach is essential. One person said it this way:

> I was a real skeptic, in fact I'm still a skeptic only because I think the whole nature of quality means that you keep asking questions about quality, about processes, and about improvements to be made. So it is about asking questions.

Another succinctly stated

> Continuous improvement is still worth it even if it is not perfect.

The question driving our research was, What is working or not working about quality improvement in higher education institutions actively engaged in practicing the quality principles? Chapter 5 outlines specific themes that emerged as a result of trying to answer the question, What are the results of practicing quality principles?

CHAPTER 5

What Are the Outcomes of Adopting Quality Principles and Practices?

Quality began for us as an emphasis, progressed to a methodology, and now it's becoming a culture. What we're really interested in now is norming the culture so that it becomes our instinctive response to each situation.

Continuous improvement is ultimately about improving the way we solve problems, treat people, and operate organizations. To show improvement, performance must be measured. In higher education the most important performance to measure is student learning. Measuring continuous improvement, therefore, must include measuring the institution's contribution to student learning.

Traditionally, the excellence of an institution of higher education has been based on that institution's reputation, which was often a reflection of inputs—admission test scores, number of volumes in the library, size of endowment, and percentage of faculty with Ph.D.s. These data are relatively easy to obtain, but they tell us nothing about how people within the institutions solve problems and treat others, how the organization operates, and if there has been any value added by the education process.

The performance of any institution is enhanced by continuously improving the efficiency and effectiveness of operational processes. To determine whether a higher education institution's performance has improved, we measure whether value has been added or talent has been developed through the education process. This means that institutions must monitor the degree to which customer needs and expectations are being met. The system must be held accountable for improvement, and members of the administration, faculty, and staff must be committed to improving student learning and achieving other positive outcomes such as greater revenues, increased stakeholder satisfaction, lower costs, higher productivity, and superior services.

To determine what improvements have been made at the institutions in our study, we asked questions about major benefits they attributed to their quality improvement efforts. We asked interviewees to tell us not only the major successes that resulted from continuous improvement efforts, but also how they measured these successes.

Eight distinct themes emerged as positive outcomes of using quality principles and practices. Many of these same ideas were also found in our national survey as well. (Refer to table 8 in appendix B.) Improved leadership was cited frequently as the improvement that sets the tone for quality improvement in an institution; many interviewees stated that leadership style has changed from a relatively autocratic style to a more collegial style. A second theme that emerged was improved coordination among members of the institution, including an increased amount of interaction, a less-hierarchical structure for the institution, and an increased sense of cooperation rather than competition. The fact that these institutions base their decisions on fact rather than on intuition or assumptions also emerged as a positive outcome. Improved communication among members was a fourth outcome linked to quality improvement efforts; information that once was considered confidential is now more widespread. Another outcome that was mentioned frequently was that processes have improved and problem-solving activity has increased because members are working together in teams. A sixth theme was increased pride in the institution and increased morale associated with involving the members of the institution in making decisions. Improved stakeholder satisfaction evidenced by improved processes, innovative ways of serving stakeholders, and improved learning and teaching was emphasized as another positive outcome in our interviews. Finally, the interviewees stressed that there has been an overall culture change within the institution. Each of these themes or outcomes will be discussed in more detail in this section.

MORE COLLEGIAL LEADERSHIP STYLE

Leaders create change and set the direction in which the organization moves. Before the implementation of continuous improvement, many leaders in the institutions we studied operated without a focus on stakeholder expectations; they did not know the needs of those being served because data were not collected. They based their decisions on intuition rather than on data. In the quality cultures that are being created, leaders receive information on stakeholder expectations. They understand how to empower others and how to build a supportive culture. Leaders create environments in which innovation is encouraged. To do this, they convince faculty and staff members and administrators to take risks to improve processes within appropriate boundaries. Quality leaders are aware of their actions and are careful that a consistent message is conveyed to their constituents. They are bringing many of the subgroups of the institution into alignment with the mission of the institution.

The preceding accomplishments are consistent with a leadership style that is more collegial than autocratic. Our national survey also showed that leadership style in the institutions became more collegial as a result of adopting continuous improvement. The presidents of the institutions in our study were described by their colleagues as collaborative, persistent, visionary, and caring. When we asked about the presidential leadership style before continuous improvement efforts, the styles were mostly described as authoritarian and more directive. As stated by two administrators:

> I came to the institution two years before the quality movement started on campus with the charge of academic intensification. The school had long concentrated on building structures. The president saw we needed to shift the emphasis. So the quality movement fit my emphasis. The previous two presidencies had been very autocratic, this might have been fine for building structures, but it caused the school to be very top heavy.

> The leadership style under the past president was much more autocratic than now. Our current president's style is conducive to quality improvement, to the sharing of information. We began to feel empowered immediately. People felt they could have a hand in shaping the future of the institution.

Another administrator commented that his president "becomes ill with layoffs, he cares about their lives." Still another administrator said, "My president was so focused that he never allowed himself to be diverted from the quality course." A third interviewee commented, "I think our president has been working all along to make things more participatory and collegial."

Many of the largest changes and greatest improvements in management style are seen in the middle-level management positions. These changes are all the more impressive given the nature of some middle managers:

> The middle management people are the most resistant. . . . They find their security in narrow, rigid boxes, and continuous quality improvement breaks the boxes. Then they feel vulnerable and exposed.

As a result of persons in those positions practicing continuous improvement, staff are made to feel they are significant members of the organization:

> Our institution previously was very autocratic, especially in reference to how staff were treated. We've been trying to build trust, we have staff meetings every month, people now feel they have some power and a lot of access.

Upon seeing the positive results due to changes in management style, many middle-level managers have been convinced that continuous improvement is worthwhile for their institutions.

In a time when effective leadership is crucial to continuous improvement efforts, our findings show that the leadership at all levels of institutions improved as a result of using quality principles and practices. For the most part, interviewees reported that their leaders are moving toward a more participatory and inclusive style of management. This management style encourages members to place more trust in leaders, to point out problems to them, and to share ideas for improvement with them. Our results indicate that quality improvement helps to influence the behaviors of leaders so that they are more receptive of members' ideas and treat all members with respect. This behavior is crucial because leaders are important drivers in the quality effort; they set the tone in a culture and are able to promote quality principles and practices in all levels of the organization. All the other outcomes are dependent on effective leadership at all levels, particularly at the senior level.

IMPROVED COORDINATION AMONG MEMBERS AND SYSTEMS

In the quality improvement paradigm, the culture enables people to share the vision of the institution. It helps them understand the significance of the institution operating as a system rather than as a collection of isolated parts. Because of past management practices and experiences, it is difficult for people to think in terms of how their actions affect others within the institution and how changing what they do will benefit the institution. Identifying all the players within a system and improving the system through simplification is a challenging task. In the process of defining and mapping out systems in our institutions, however, many discoveries were made:

> Quality helps us identify systems; we can put things down on paper; we are able to see why we can't serve everyone.

More successes and an awareness of those successes come with more experience in dealing with systems:

> The quality system is an intentional system based on stakeholder information and produces results. . . . Our systems are continuously improving over time. . . . Instead of looking in a rearview mirror and asking what happened, we are hearing that the system leads to results.

One result that frequently was mentioned in our interviews is that interaction among members in an institution has increased due to the implementation of continuous improvement. We found evidence that new relationships are being built, interrelationships are being acknowledged, the structure of the organization is becoming less hierarchical, and a sense of cooperation rather than competition is beginning to exist.

Within traditional higher education institutions, people tend to work independently of one another, to be concerned with their own success rather than with the success of the institution. Departments or divisions act as barriers in these traditional organizations. People interact within departments or divisions, but rarely overcome the invisible barriers that separate those departments or divisions. Barriers foster competition for scarce resources. We found that quality improvement efforts changed these attitudes because people are brought together, are educated in how they need to work together, and discover that they share the same ideas and hopes as other members of the institution. Faculty, administrators, and staff agreed that quality practices create an awareness of others and an interdependence on others:

> The quality efforts bring people together. Campus seems smaller because we know each other. I worked a long time, and I did not know half of the people. Now I know almost everyone, even the guy mowing the lawn.

> I now know infinitely more than in my first 25 years in the district about how interdependent everybody is just because of the past three years. . . . I have to work with people across this campus . . . teaching, an occasional meeting, maintaining an occasional office hour, in the classroom, coming back to my office. I didn't understand how the success of my class is directly related to so many different people on this campus. It's not just me on the center of that stage.

As people begin to recognize each other as individuals rather than as members of certain departments within the institution, they begin to think about how their decisions affect those they know in other areas of the institution. They look for and are conscious of how the decisions they make impact others. This awareness leads employees to work for the good of all rather than just for themselves. As a result of this attitude change, relationships among departments and programs on campus improve. Increasing communication by increasing the frequency of interactions among people on campus is an outcome that members attribute to quality initiatives:

> I came from a small college. The second day here I saw that we had separate fiefdoms here, no unity. The quality movement has improved interaction between departments. We meet as equals. That's the biggest benefit I've seen.

> One of the biggest successes was just getting people who work on the phone with each other all the time to meet and talk about the problems from both sides.

Researchers have found that one of the results of bringing people together to work on teams and to solve problems is a flatter, less hierarchical organization. Our findings support this research. The institutions we studied do have a more horizontal organization as a result of implementing continuous improvement concepts. According to people from across the institutions:

> Continuous improvement has been a leveling factor. Now there is a more even playing field.

> This has encouraged a dialogue across rather than imposing from above.

As organizations become more horizontally structured, members realize that they are more nearly equal within the organization. This understanding is necessary for empowerment and for persons to feel comfortable working with each other on teams. As expressed by both staff and administrators:

> I was really impressed how we were all looking at each other as equals, not management and support staff. A different view of us—a team. That was great to see.

> Ours is a much more inviting environment now. It is easy to go to the top administration with concerns and ideas.

> Certain kinds of decisions are now made at the department level that weren't before. It is much easier to ask for certain issues to be reviewed.

Much is gained from this cooperative attitude. One president said, "The hopes and dreams of constituencies are in alignment . . . the institution is feeling better, gaining a sense of alignment and pride." Another administrator stated that at his institution there is "evidence that the administration and faculty have moved beyond tolerance to pride that we are doing something that is different." People are excited about and proud of an institution in which all members are working toward a common goal. Two examples of the benefits of cooperation follow:

> The discussions are very different today than they were four years ago, much more sensitive and much less territorial. We changed the whole structure of the college. The associate deans were constantly griping about lack of budget information, that a budget transfer was made without their knowledge, we spent much of our time dealing with that. We don't ever hear that anymore. The structure has changed to force them into being less competitive and more cooperative and that alone changes the discussions. This is evidence that this is the way we do business now.

> There is a history of anti-administration feelings at our institution. We did not welcome change. The faculty survey last year revealed that 13 percent of faculty said colleagues respect each other, that 2 percent of the faculty feel that our students are excellent. The newer people are more receptive to change and the ideas of quality improvement. The administrative culture has changed. We work together more, we cooperate, there is a more egalitarian attitude, the mind-set is different. How can we make it better for the students? We now think of serving other offices.

Although it is always important for people within an organization to cooperate with each other, in these difficult times of declining enrollments and budget shortfalls the need for cooperation is magnified. Within the institutions we studied, more interaction takes place between members, organization becomes less hierarchical, and cooperation, rather than competition, exists between individuals and departments. These characteristics make institutions more inviting as places of employment and provide enjoyment to their members. In these challenging times when salary increases are small or nonexistent, having a satisfying place to work is perceived to be intrinsically rewarding.

DATA-DRIVEN DECISION MAKING

In traditional higher education institutions, decision makers do not listen to the voice of the stakeholder. Data are not gathered to determine whether the institution is fulfilling its primary mission of educating the students. Because of continuous improvement efforts, leaders at the institutions in our study understand that the quality of the goods and services provided by their institutions needs to be measured to provide information on continuous improvement. People within these organizations systematically keep track of how their organization is doing and the resulting information is readily available to all persons within the organization.

In the past, decisions often had been made intuitively or had been influenced by personal impression, anecdote, or complaint. In contrast, we found that leaders in quality improvement organizations more frequently base their decisions upon facts, upon data collected for a particular purpose. It takes time to gather information, and at first, people resent that additional time commitment; however, the positive results convince members that using data is the best way to make decisions. As an administrator stated:

> Continuous improvement takes more time, but the results are better and are validated by data. You have a better chance of making a better decision.

Although many examples of collecting data and basing decisions on data were given, the following four examples show how simple the procedure can be. One of the institutions we studied was developing courses on customer service and quality leadership. To make these courses as relevant as possible, they brought in 10 executives from companies in the surrounding area. The executives gave input on new skills needed in organizations that are moving toward a more horizontal structure. These skills were incorporated in courses.

At one of the institutions, it was discovered via a survey that people thought the culture was too serious. A team was created and charged with making the institution a more joyful workplace. Some of the ideas that resulted from this team are dress-down Fridays, Halloween costume day, and bringing in a laughter therapist. These events have helped people to "lighten up" with respect to continuous quality improvement.

A third example of data improving decisions comes from the library administration. Students asked that the library be open for more hours. The administration surveyed everyone on the campus to find out what schedule they preferred. As a result the library hours have been extended. The same number of staff cover the longer hours with the help of additional student assistants. The administration is now gathering data to determine which days and hours the library is most and least used for future decisions that may need to be made.

At one of the institutions, people learned to perform various jobs in response to information that was collected. Originally, persons were prepared only for the jobs they personally performed. When employees were absent, their jobs were not done, resulting in down time, or the jobs were done poorly by substitutes. In addition, people resented being called on to fill in for another employee. It became obvious that back-ups were necessary for the different jobs that need to be performed. Data were collected on when back-ups are needed. An administrator related:

> There was no back-up system, people who were gone or sick had a job that did not get done. We created a seasonality chart and identified point people who can back up others. People now feel good about pitching in and helping out.

Because the solution to the problem was arrived at by a group effort and because the decision was based on data collected by the workers themselves, they were pleased with the results and were willing to follow through and to help their department. This example also emphasizes the importance of systems thinking; in this case, viewing the work group as a system rather than as a number of independent people who just happen to work in one location.

Professional development in most of the institutions we studied included education on how to use tools for data analysis. The tools are not an end in themselves, any more than gathering data is the end of a process. Members we interviewed found that using the tools to analyze data leads to improved processes and systems. Although the tools appear awkward at first, one administrator acknowledged that with time the tools seem to be a natural part of the process, "Most of us use tools without knowing we are using them; they have become automatic." Once people feel comfortable with data collection and analysis, some of them apply these skills in other areas as well. In fact, one individual remarked:

> I use some of the tools I've learned here with my two kids at home. I look at everything differently. My wife and I have changed some things in our

> relationship as well. Quality really helps you look at the other person's viewpoint. You don't just brush people off. You think about other people's rights to information and explanations.

This comment reinforces the ideas that quality improvement requires a personal transformation, that quality principles and practices can be used personally as well as professionally to improve, and that culture change is dependent upon individuals within organizations changing the way they think, behave, and act. The culture of the institutions we studied changed to support the efforts to carry out the mission and to achieve the organization's goals.

This transformed culture is exemplified in organizations that have won federal and state quality awards. These federal and state awards have been created to increase interest in quality and to stress its importance. The best known of these is the Malcolm Baldrige National Quality Award (MBNQA), created to reinforce America's interest in quality for business and industry.

Being a recipient of an award such as the MBNQA or a state award can influence funding and can have a positive impact on the public's perception of the institution. It can improve the reputation of the institution and increase the institution's visibility in the community, the state, and the nation. In addition to these benefits, these awards are also external forces that help drive the quality efforts for some of the higher education institutions that have adopted continuous improvement. Several of the institutions in our study collected data specifically for applying for quality awards. They were interested in seeing how well they were doing using the impartial MBNQA guidelines. More than anything, the institutions wanted to be judged objectively. An administrator at an institution that submitted a report as part of the MBNQA pilot for educational institutions in 1995 explained:

> We learned a lot; it was hard work. The results were much more meaningful than an accreditation report. We have people who have been through Baldrige training, people who are examiners. This is not fluff; you can't fluff. They score it; this is not storytelling. We needed to report on a system of data.

Since the MBNQA criteria require institutions to self-assess, some institutions have used these criteria as the basis of accreditation reports:

> It appears that we will be able to do the seven steps of the Baldrige criteria, extract information from it, and send that as part of our accreditation application. There might be a whole lot more buy-in if faculty can see that the award criteria apply so closely to the accreditation process.

Two other administrators saw additional rewards for the institution:

> We're a closed society here, Baldrige will be a really good reality check. It forces people who go through their daily lives without thinking there could be anything negative to look at our failings.

We are getting a fresh read about ourselves by using the Baldrige criteria.

Regardless of whether or not the data were collected in connection with a quality award, many of our interviewees realized that decisions are improved with data. Although collecting data seems like a natural process, it does not follow traditional practices in higher education. Before changes are made in processes, it is necessary to collect data to determine what changes will improve those processes. After a change has been made, data collected over time allow the institution to determine whether the change is moving in the direction the leaders intend. Data collection is reported to be time consuming in the beginning, but the people in the institutions we studied found that, with time, people automatically collect data before they make decisions and realize that the resulting decisions are better.

IMPROVED COMMUNICATION

People communicate differently with one another after quality improvement is implemented. According to the literature, a quality culture is one in which there is open and honest communication based on a climate of mutual trust and support. We found members now expect that information will be available to all; they realize that secrets lead to rumors and dissatisfaction among the members. Open communication among members, especially between administration and other employees, is highly prized.

In contrast, traditional higher education institutions have more confidential information, and only upper-level administrators or those who are "in the know" possess these tidbits of information. Before continuous improvement was implemented in the institutions we studied, information was power, and members who did not have access to the information were considered powerless. Most of these institutions realized that they need to improve their efforts in this regard and have made improving communication a primary commitment. In several cases they have been rewarded with large improvements. One staff member related:

> One thing that has been really positive about the program is how we can improve communication, not only inside but outside the administration.

Two faculty members stated:

> Communication has vastly improved between faculty and administration; it has been a conscious effort.

> Communication is better. In the past we were given no justification for things that were done. It may not be perfect now, but there's a 200 percent improvement over seven or eight years ago. There were people who were denied tenure, but couldn't tell why, because there were no standards to be met. It's much better now, and I credit a lot of that to continuous improvement.

These statements indicate that members of the institutions are pleased with results of the improvement process and recognize that much effort has been expended to improve communication.

For example, the budget process is a private process in most institutions. After practicing quality principles, budget information has been made available to members of some of the institutions in our study. Two faculty members specifically commented on the improvements in budget communication:

> The budget used to be a very closed process, and now that's different. You didn't really know what any other area had, and now you can find that out.

> I think initially they were real resistant to letting information out. You knew what you got but didn't know what anybody else had. Now they're much freer with information that's needed to make decisions.

When people lack information in the budget process, they tend to believe that they are much worse off than anyone else. Such a belief leads to lack of trust in others and a resentment of them. Providing information on the budget to members of the organization gives them accurate data and prevents them from wasting time speculating on how poorly their departments are doing compared to other departments. The information clears up misconceptions and jealousies among members of the institutions. When institutional members are not so concerned about budgetary matters, they are able to spend more time and effort on improving the organization. When information is available, it enables members to cooperate and to work together to solve issues and problems. Open communication helps them develop a conceptual perspective of the institution as a whole rather than as many independent parts that compete with each other.

While financial information can be shared, some pieces of information cannot be shared. For example, in many cases, personnel issues cannot be openly discussed. Therefore, it is imperative to clarify expectations so that employees understand why certain information is not shared. An administrator stated:

> Personnel issues are confidential. People are used to getting information, and personnel issues cannot be shared. This causes frustration.

When people understand what information cannot be shared with everyone in the institution and why, they do not feel as though information is being hidden from them. Again, the change is toward open and up-front communication whenever possible.

We found that although it was not easy, administrators are more willing to share information and that this sharing results in improved communication. In addition to sharing information, leaders are making a conscious effort to listen to their constituents. Leaders learn a great deal from their constituents when the leaders are open-minded and allow all opinions to be stated and discussed without being condescending or intimidating. At one institution, a staff member confirmed the importance of listening, "Resentment and frustration occur if differing opinions are not allowed."

When people realize that they are free to comment and to provide suggestions without repercussions, expectations increase and dialogues begin. An administrator at one institution noticed, "When people realize that you are listening, they start complaining more. Things appear to be working better." This comment demonstrates that a culture has been created in which people feel comfortable to complain or to point out areas that need to be improved. As a result, processes are being improved, and interviewees report that the institution as a whole works better than it had before quality initiatives.

Communicating information on what is and is not working in the quality efforts is important to the health of the initiative. Valuable time and effort are saved when information on both failures and successes are passed from one group to another. For example, one faculty member provides others in his department with information on classroom improvements. He commented, "I am trying new things and reporting back on what's working and what's not working."

Some of our institutions publish weekly, monthly, or quarterly newsletters on the successes and failures associated with their quality efforts. Although all the institutions recognize the importance of publicizing results, some are unable to do so because of lack of time and staff. An administrator at an institution with no internal quality publication admitted:

> That is probably one of the things we have done least well, the communication effort, publishing success. We haven't done a whole lot of that. What little we have done wasn't effective.

At another institution, a staff member realized that she really did not know what was happening at her institution with respect to the quality efforts because her institution had no formal way of disseminating information on continuous improvement efforts. She stated:

> I have learned a lot in the last couple of days. I think it's great that you came because it made us take an inventory of what is going on.

Several of the institutions in our study communicated the successes of teams at quality fairs, events at which teams presented their results. These fairs serve to bring people together to educate them on continuous improvement and to help to spark interest in the quality effort. In this environment, members of the staff, faculty, administration, and, in some cases, people from the outside community come together to celebrate the efforts of teams. A staff member commented:

> The education level of the audience is improving. They know something about what you're talking about. Two years ago we were entirely defensive. They've learned now from teams they have seen operating in their workplace, and they see the support for it. The quality fair improved visibility.

As part of learning how to communicate more effectively, most of the institutions in our study educate their members on how to conduct meetings. In general, the results of this education are perceived to be positive. Several representatives of the administration, faculty, and staff agreed that meetings are now more focused, more efficient, more productive, and more positive. Participation is greater, and meetings start and end on time. Dialogue and discussion now take place in meetings.

Many improvements were made in how meetings are conducted. We heard people report that meetings no longer took place without preparation and that the meetings have to have a purpose. Meetings have an agenda and time limits (often with time limits for the separate agenda items). At one institution they dispensed with *Robert's Rules of Order*, which helped bring consensus to their meetings. At another institution the president commented on the freedom of expression at meetings:

> The new meeting environment is such that the staff member could tell the supervisor that the agenda was not the agenda of an effective meeting as they had learned it; the supervisor responded and said she would try again.

Above all, meetings have become a time to interact with and to distribute information to others on campus.

Communication influences how people interact and how they feel about one another and about the institution. Even though the communication system continually needs to be improved, people we interviewed at all levels of the organizations confirmed that quality principles and practices improve communication.

TEAMS AND IMPROVED PROCESSES

Articles on continuous improvement almost always emphasize the use of teams to make decisions. In the institutions we studied, individuals consistently are organized into teams to encourage participation and to gain additional perspectives. We also discovered that departments and divisions often function as work teams. These teams contrast with campus committees that typically function as groups of individuals who are burdened with administrative tasks and who often do not have specific goals or time limits for accomplishing goals. Using teams to collaborate effectively involves learning new behaviors and changing the way people perceive their work. The quality teams that accomplish the most are empowered to address specific problems, are action oriented, and have studied a problem with the goal of improving the system.

We learned that a good way to think of a team is as a process rather than as a product. Forming a team is the process of gathering a group of people who are able to lead, act, and think together. As one faculty member expressed it:

> Team members have knowledge and understanding; they have a purpose, an aim, goals, they know why they are there. There is less success when this piece is missing.

Teams are used to accomplish goals. They are composed of individuals who work together and who bring together a variety of perspectives.

Many team members claimed that they observe differences between the committee work of the past and the teamwork of the present. As members of a team, they work together to improve processes, they use tools together, and they see successes. They believe teams create a sense of community by allowing them to meet new people from all parts of the campus. Members of teams exchange information and ideas; these actions help individuals gain respect for others and their opinions, all of which contribute to creating a quality culture:

> It helps a lot to know how the processes work together. After listening to people, I have trust in how they do their jobs. It's increased my respect and trust for people. Teamwork involves building relationships with people you only knew over the phone or e-mail. We have the opportunity to educate one another. After you've worked with somebody on a process, it's hard to just dismiss them and their opinions.

> Cross-functional teams have been a wonderful experience in understanding the limitations of what other administrators feel. There is much more interaction, enhanced understanding, and appreciation.

> Cross-functional teams have improved relationships a great deal. New people know each other, and it is a natural process to get input from other departments.

Many successes were related to us by team members. In one case, three groups were set up to review programs, two of those were set up as committees and the third as a team; the team was perceived to be more effective. In the team, members knew how to collaborate, understood processes and tools to use to accomplish the task at hand, and were familiar with how to conduct effective and efficient meetings. In another case, the recommendation of a team led to the creation of a new position at the institution:

> We created the position of Dean of Freshmen because we found that our greatest retention problem was at the end of the freshman year. We conceptualized it as a quality team; there were students, student affairs

staff, academic and administrative representatives. The job now cuts across all of those boundaries. This person can track the freshman experience wherever it leads. Anything that happens to the student between the time he registers and the time he becomes a bona fide sophomore is in the jurisdiction of this dean. It's a horizontal job, not a vertical job. . . . Retention is improving. We now have a network that can respond to the potential dropouts before they do drop out.

In the institutions we studied, teams bring people together to solve problems. In some cases, these teams consist of people from a particular department who need to solve a problem within that area. If the goal is to improve an institutionwide process, they include people from many different departments. Typically, teams include people from different ranks, but ideally these ranks are set aside in the team meetings. The ideas of all members of the team are considered, and decisions are made only after the ideas have been explored. Teamwork and collaboration result in better decisions, an increased understanding of problems and processes in the institution, and an enhanced respect for other members within the institution.

INCREASED INVOLVEMENT OF MEMBERS IN MAKING DECISIONS

Empowerment means delegating decision making from leaders to members of the organization and involving members in the operation of the organization. People who work within the system have the most insight into how the organization works and the changes that should be made to improve it; therefore, it is logical to involve them in making decisions. It is the responsibility of leaders to set the tone for empowering and involving others in the organization. Once included, members will likely take personal responsibility for their jobs, and they will have a sense of accomplishment that otherwise may be lacking.

Interviewees pointed out that many people employed in their institutions are able to solve institutional problems. These individuals are much more knowledgeable about the day-to-day improvements that are needed than are the people in top-level administration. When people at the operational level are given the opportunity to improve their institutions, they are proud of their contributions. When employees are not involved or their knowledge is not used, this lack of involvement becomes a major source of frustration to them and leads to other problems in the institution such as lack of trust in leaders and communication breakdowns.

For the most part, leaders at the institutions we studied learned that giving up control helps to gain control. They indicated that this realization was not an easy lesson to learn. They first feared that they would no longer be in control, that the workers would not perform their tasks as they should, and that mistakes would be made. Two administrators validated the difficulty:

> Several of the deans say they do not feel empowered. It's a two-way street though. To feel empowered you have to be willing to empower others. And sometimes when you try to empower people, they don't want it. This takes an investment.

> We must recognize that if we do this, it will take enormous energy and commitment from the senior leadership of the institution. If they're not committed to empowerment throughout the institution, it won't happen. It doesn't require the president to cheerlead it, but he has to support it. The senior officers have to commit.

At another institution, an administrator observed that the chief academic officer of the institution was "having a hard time letting people run with their ideas. The president wants to control."

Middle managers sometimes had the greatest difficulty letting go of their power; they felt that they would not have a job if they gave away their power. To remedy this situation, it was suggested that the role of middle managers be redefined so they become an integral part of the quality team. They need to be empowered so they have power to give to others.

Once those who are in the traditional positions of control consciously relinquish some of that control, members who want to be involved must take control over their own jobs. Members become involved when the environment is supportive and when the culture of the institution is perceived as fair. Members accept power by being willing to make decisions, to give opinions, and to be involved in the institution. From the eyes of the president of one of our institutions:

> The culture is changing, and I think it's very noticeable. There is a much healthier willingness to make a recommendation and not be cautious or fearful about one's employment. I don't think of myself as a vindictive person, but there's a lot of deference paid to the person who is in my office, whoever it may be. A lot of that has broken down; I don't feel unappreciated or abused in any way; I just think people treat me more like a human being and are more ready to ask why this or why that or will I consider this or that. I think there is a greater expectation of information sharing and involvement now. It would be difficult to go back now.

Empowerment allows people at lower levels in the institution to have more responsibility and the freedom to exercise it. Employees need fewer approvals and have more autonomy in making decisions. In turn, they tend to trust and respect each other to get the job done because there is less supervision and more reliance on cooperation. Employees are proud when others listen to and implement their ideas:

> I am excited about the concept of empowerment. I have more input into decisions; I am now being consulted more.

> There is a sense of satisfaction both for students and staff. People who would otherwise be passed over see their ideas put into action.

Employees perceive that they are involved when input is sought of all members within departments and no distinction is made between the ranks of individuals. A faculty member expressed that this situation exists in his department:

> I'm encouraged to try anything I want. I can discuss anything. There is no differentiation between a professor, an assistant professor, or an associate professor. If you have an idea, you can bring it to the group, and if it makes sense, we do it; nobody is berated.

Staff morale improved as well because they have been recognized as valued members of the organization:

> Employees who get the most out of team participation are staff. The continuous improvement team is empowering; people leave status behind. They feel they have an equal voice; they don't often get to be on committees with faculty and administrators. A staff person told me that the only activity they look forward to each week is to go to quality improvement team meetings.

> Staff feel like they have some power, access, that they count. They are treated as colleagues.

> Support staff say they feel more empowered. From the beginning, it was not a management thing. There is no rank in the room, all the development has been faculty, staff, and managers together. There are no artificial barriers; everything has always been vertically integrated.

It is not enough to ask for and to collect input from members. When people give their ideas, management needs to listen. If management does not listen, the tenuous trust that has been built between manager and employee is broken. A complaint we heard repeatedly is that there have been breaks in this system. We learned that *listening* rather than just *hearing* is essential to complete the system. An administrator stressed this by saying:

> The only way you can make people believe in this, is to demonstrate that when a team makes a recommendation, that you do it. It doesn't sit on the shelf.

Several team members told us that they were upset that their ideas were not put into practice. An administrator commented that the reason some ideas were rejected is they required additional financial resources that the institution did not have. In many situations, teams were not informed that their recommendations were not supposed to cost the institution additional money.

In contrast, when people are truly included in making decisions, the constraints for team results are set up front so there are no surprises. Some institutions put a limit on the amount of money that can be requested as part of a recommendation from a team. One of the institutions in the study has a panel that decides on recommendations for allocating money to one-time projects:

> Previously, administrators would just make the decision. The panel has universitywide participation. Money was not budgeted; this is windfall money. Previously, we'd say we need a new roof on this or that building, and the provost would look at things like that and we'd just do whatever he decided. Now the panel decides.

At another institution, decisions on equipment are handled by letting employees suggest what they need rather than have a supervisor make those decisions. When employees are given this power, they understand that leaders trust them to make reasonable decisions:

> The employees are now asked what they need to get the job done where before the supervisor made those decisions on equipment. When they tell you and you go get it for them you develop trust.

Because of the challenges of empowerment, employees become successfully involved in some areas of the institution, but not in others. Several administrators confirmed this trend, "There are islands of success within our institution." Even within areas of institutions where there had been successful empowerment, some people are involved while others are not:

> Not all the staff feel empowered, some staff feel overly empowered. Some of the staff if they are asked will venture an opinion, but they will not venture out of their little world to voice their opinions if they aren't asked.

We found that, in general, people want to work in an environment in which they are involved, open communication exists, and leaders appreciate the members' input. In this environment, members flourish on the job, they exercise self-control, and ultimately they provide quality service. One staff member stated, "For the first time, it is fun to go to work."

Despite the benefits mentioned so far, we found that empowerment is a very difficult concept to implement in an organization. Leaders need a great deal of self-confidence to give up power to those who are beneath them in the organization's structure. Members also have to change their thinking. Unless members believe they have worthwhile ideas and that they themselves are valuable to the organization, they do not participate to their fullest.

When trust exists a great deal can be accomplished. The front-line employees take great pride in their accomplishments, and the leaders are proud of those who present new ideas and work on solving the problems. Empowerment and involvement increase self-esteem and pride in the organization, in one's job, and in other workers. As a result of empowerment, the organization performs better because leaders are allowed to lead rather than to manage every detail and because members are allowed to make decisions within their areas of expertise.

IMPROVED STAKEHOLDER SATISFACTION

We found that stakeholder satisfaction improved in institutions that are implementing quality principles and practices. Institutions that adopted quality improvement concepts collect information on stakeholder expectations and use that data to help them continuously improve their processes. In addition to collecting information on stakeholders at these institutions, the processes themselves are studied thoroughly and the data gathered are used to design new processes. Data are then collected again to determine whether restructured processes are better than the old processes. Data must be gathered on both academic and nonacademic processes to improve stakeholder satisfaction at all levels of the institution.

Several of the institutions in our study are participating in assessment programs along with their quality initiatives. The assessment programs are primarily concerned with measuring academic outcomes of the institutions, but quality initiatives and assessment do not differ drastically from one another, as one administrator stated:

> Quality improvement and assessment have common themes. They are compatible. We take a continuous improvement approach to assessment rather than following a model based on quality improvement.

To determine if processes and systems have improved, measurements are taken. It is only when data show that there has been improvement over time that our institutions can be confident that the new processes are better than the old. At institutions that recognize this need for careful data collection, members are working constantly to improve, and there is an intense focus on gathering data and on measuring the outcomes. What is being measured are indicators or signs (evidence) of quality improvement. Even though institutions are struggling with what the specific indicators of progress should be, we found a pattern of members *asking different questions* to determine these indicators. How institutions decide on quality indicators depends on the goals of the institution:

> What are you trying to accomplish? First identify the goals and then decide how you evaluate the movement with respect to those goals.

We were informed that the indicators must be developed from within and that they must be agreed upon by members of the institution, but we were warned that this may be a difficult task:

That's the next exercise I need to have with my team, the creation of quality indicators. They need to develop those on their own. It's no different from goal setting.

It is very difficult to agree on what the indicators will be. Some departments have graduate students and TAs and want those counted differently than, say, Art or Music. Some want the music lessons counted. Whatever measurement we come up with, one of the colleges feels it's unfair to them, and they're right. It becomes a political issue.

Sometimes it is easy to determine what needs to be measured; at other times this issue presents difficulties. These difficulties, however, should not keep an institution from evaluating itself, as one administrator said:

When somebody tells me we can't measure something, I say, we know when it's bad, don't we? Why can't we know when it's good? Even when it is subjective. We know when morale is better. Are we improving? That can be measured statistically. Is there more resistance? If there is, that's good news, because you're communicating. We've got to do all the things you can do with numbers, but we also have to figure in the unknown and unknowables. That's what puts you out of business. Every time we look at retention figures, we remind ourselves that one person may represent nine people, because they're telling people, "I don't like this place."

As this comment suggests, there was not a consensus about what the particular measures should be. Despite the confusion over indicators and measures, we are encouraged by the fact that we consistently discovered that *different questions* are being asked now than had been asked before.

Based upon our interviews, we found improved stakeholder satisfaction in three main areas: improved learning and teaching, improved services to faculty members and students, and improved academic programs. Improvements in all of these areas affect the amount of learning that can take place, and therefore, they all fit the primary mission of the institution, to increase the amount of learning that takes place for each student.

Improved Learning and Teaching

On the academic side, a pattern emerged of increased attention being focused on the improvement of learning and teaching by faculty members. With an understanding of continuous improvement, faculty members begin to realize that if improvements are made in teaching, increased learning will take place in the classroom. Members of the faculty and administration from all our institutions stressed that their institutions have "good faculty members who are willing to try some things." The three options that faculty members most often pursued to improve their teaching are participating in teaching improvement groups and institutional teaching improvement centers, changing classroom teaching methods, and requesting and acting on feedback from students.

Although the proponents of these activities were originally few in number, the number of interested faculty members involved in these activities is constantly increasing.

In several of the institutions we studied, completely voluntary teaching improvement groups meet weekly or monthly with the primary purpose of discussing how to improve classroom teaching. One faculty member described what occurs at a teaching improvement meeting as faculty members ask a series of questions that are discussed and for which suggestions are made; no attempt is made to provide definitive answers to the questions, and discussions continue over time. In one institution, the discussions are only part of the activities of the teaching improvement groups. As members of a group, faculty members attend actual classes and act as peer evaluators for other members of the group, bringing suggestions on ways of improving to the group. One faculty member reported that it required a large amount of trust to allow other faculty members to come into his classroom and evaluate him, but that the information provided to him has been valuable.

Several of the institutions in our study have instructional development services that faculty members can use to assist their teaching improvement efforts. The way in which one of these centers serves the faculty was described to us by a faculty member who uses its services:

> I know when I teach my class, one of the employees comes into my class, she collects data from the students, she observes, and she has a meeting with me to discuss the results. . . . She is looking at my teaching process and figuring what could work better, getting information from the customers. I adjust my process, do something different. Then I can ask her to come back to my class to help me decide if my teaching has improved.

This service is entirely voluntary; faculty members have to invite these people to come into the classroom; however, it was stated that if a large number of complaints are associated with a particular faculty member, the dean can request that that faculty member make use of the service. Faculty members who participate in the teaching improvement groups or who make use of the teaching improvement centers commented overwhelmingly that they are pleased with the improvement they see in their teaching and in their students' grades.

We found that teachers are willing to try teaching methods that are new to them to increase the amount of learning that takes place. Faculty members at several of the institutions we studied pointed out that they are concerned that their students do not all learn the same way. A particular teaching method may work well for some of the students, but other teaching methods may help students with other learning styles.

The methods that are used most frequently include interdisciplinary or team teaching and collaborative learning strategies. Both of these methods take more time than the traditional way of presenting material, the lecture method, but faculty members who use these methods are adamant about the improvements they see in their students as a result of using these new techniques. We found that faculty members who truly understand continuous improvement are more willing to spend the extra effort necessary to change their methods so that more learning takes place.

Interdisciplinary team teaching has been used successfully by a number of faculty members at the institutions in our study. Team teaching breaks down the lecture technique, increases the amount of information that can be presented in a course, and improves the students' understanding of the topics under discussion. In a course that is team taught, the student is presented with more than one approach to a particular problem or issue and gains additional insight into how to solve problems from several perspectives. At one of the institutions, the general education program is almost all team taught. Team teaching does not mean that each member of the team is in charge of a certain number of class meetings and needs to attend only on teaching days. To be done effectively, team teaching requires as much, if not more, work than teaching a course by oneself, but the rewards are much greater—for both students and faculty members. Developing teaching partnerships with others has helped faculty members to see new applications and how the ideas of others overlapped their own ideas.

Collaborative learning strategies make different demands on the institution and its members. The success of collaborative learning strategies depends heavily on how well students interact with each other and help each other learn. The person who teaches the class is less of an authority figure and instead takes on the role of a facilitator or coach:

> Many of us are implementing collaborative learning strategies. This comes out of another pedagogical tradition, but it is consistent with continuous improvement. This strategy shifts the teacher's position at the center of the classroom to the edge of it.

One faculty member explained how he changed the way he taught a history course and the result of that change:

> I wanted to keep students from expecting that the instructor would summarize the reading assignment for them. Instead, I told my students what they would have to master from the reading assignment, then broke them into small groups in which they needed to discuss the material that they had read. As a result, grades on midterms went up. I polled the students and they said this was the most interesting history course they had ever taken.

As seen in this example, when students take responsibility for their own learning, they often learn more than if the instructor keeps that responsibility.

The easiest approach to improving teaching is to ask for feedback from the students in the classes. Most of the faculty members we interviewed were already having students complete end-of-the-course evaluations. In addition, midcourse evaluations are also conducted by some faculty members. Asking for feedback only at the end of the course or only two or three times during a course does little for improving teaching over the length of the course. A much more successful assessment technique for quick feedback is a minute paper. After every class meeting, the instructor passes out index cards or papers with questions on how well students are understanding the material that is being presented and with space for them to suggest ways the class can be improved. The dean of the business school in one of the institutions in our study made the following comments about minute papers:

> Over half the faculty in our school pass out index cards at the end of each class asking for input. I look at mine pretty carefully. I ask were the objectives for the session clear and did I reach them, how they feel about the presentation and order of issues. You get pretty direct comments from students.

Another faculty member commented:

> I have had really good results with minute papers. Mine are not anonymous. I set it up so that we both have a responsibility. The students' responsibility is to tell me the truth, and my responsibility is to address student concerns at the beginning of each class. The responses get more detailed as the term goes on. Trust is essential to make this process work.

A team-based approach to improving teaching and classroom problem solving, LEARN, is used in two of the institutions we studied. (See pp. 112–114 for a more detailed description of this model.) A team consisting of several members of a class (only one team per class) meets once each week for approximately 30 minutes. The team discusses what is going on in the class, and then based on these discussions, conducts surveys, analyzes the data, and presents possible solutions to any problems that might arise. One faculty member who has used this approach commented:

> It really works. It is great to know in the second week whether what you are using is getting through. . . . We get feedback immediately. . . . The students really buy into it. They know the rewards are great, and they are learning about participating in teams.

As a result of these new teaching methods and feedback activities being implemented by faculty members, the amount of student learning taking place has increased, faculty members' pride in teaching has increased, and students have begun to take responsibility for their learning.

Improved Services to Faculty and Students

A second pattern of improved stakeholder satisfaction focuses on services to students and faculty members. Areas in which services have been improved include admissions, physical plant, food service, information systems, housing, and purchasing. Improved stakeholder satisfaction is a result of improved services.

At one institution, the food service for the students has been improved:

> We asked students if we put in a food court, what franchises would they like. We did several hundred thousand dollars of remodeling in the student center, and we now have a food court with five franchise vendors, and the students love it.

At another institution, an effort was made to track down part-time students who were not currently enrolled but were within one or two courses of graduation. They were contacted and informed of this fact. What resulted was that approximately 600 students completed their degrees who might have fallen through the cracks in a poor system. Another example of improved service was credited to the library staff at one of the institutions:

> The library has moved to the point now where I can e-mail them and ask for a book and they'll deliver it to my office the same day. They'll do that for an administrator or any faculty member. They'll also do a search, they'll Xerox an article and deliver it to you. The morale up there has gone up tremendously. If you go over there you'll see flowcharts around the wall of processes they're continuing to work on.

Another improvement in services took place in student records. Previously, if a student didn't go home at the end of the term and wanted to find out his or her grades, the student needed to go to student records. An administrator described the process the student needed to go through and how that process has been improved:

> There was a wall that separated records from the hall, and there was a glass window with a little round hole in it. The student had to stand there and yell, "What grades did I make?" So we asked what we could do to make this less intimidating. Now when you go into that section of the building, there is no hall, there is no wall, instead there is an open office and all the people sitting at desks are people in student records. It's so much better.

Improvements do not need to be large or costly to produce great benefits. In some cases, small changes lead to significant improvements, large savings of time, and greater stakeholder satisfaction. We learned that there may be some simple solutions to problems that really irritate stakeholders. The institutions we studied learned to look for processes that need to be improved. They shifted from thinking that they need to throw money at every problem to thinking creatively about how to improve with little or no money. For example, an inexpensive solution to a customer service problem was discovered at one institution:

> I heard a student in line with five other students at the payment window say, "Well, you can either pay your phone bill or you can eat." All she wanted to do was drop off a payment. The person at the head of the line was taking all the time because they had to call financial aid. I went back and said to the staff, "Why don't we put a drop box in the student center?"

At another institution, teams spent over a year coming up with an innovative way to serve their students that they called "one-stop shopping." They provided students with a central location at which students could pay all of their bills, get information about university deadlines, add and drop classes, get information on financial aid, apply for graduation, and take care of many other needs. Four employees, one each from financial aid, student records, admissions, and student accounts, were brought together to staff this office. They were cross-trained so that each of them could answer questions that might arise. They also stayed in close contact with their home departments so that these offices could help answer more difficult questions if any arose. The four employees who work together adopted the following motto showing that they believe that service to the students is their primary goal, "We won't put aside our work to help students. Helping students is our work." Feedback that they have received indicates that customer satisfaction is extremely high. Since it is a relatively new office on campus, many students still have not heard about it. From the initial success of the venture, though, it appears that this office will become more popular with students in the future.

Another benefit of quality improvement is the reduction in the amount of time necessary to complete tasks. Time is reduced because processes are streamlined, and unnecessary steps are removed from the process. At one of the institutions in the study, the admissions department reduced the time to respond to prospective students from 30 days to 3 days. At another institution, class schedules that had taken six months to complete now take five weeks. At a third institution, emergency student loans that had taken, on average, four hours to be granted, now require two hours. Another process that was changed dealt with setting up interviews between prospective students and alumni of an institution. The time needed to set up these interviews has decreased from three to four weeks, on average, to one week; this improvement allowed the institution to increase the number of interviews from about 900 to 2,200 per year. These and many more examples that were recounted in our interviews repeatedly illustrated that services have been improved by implementing quality initiatives. Because of the awareness that all processes can be improved, institutions are finding endless ways to improve stakeholder satisfaction, which lead to higher retention rates and ultimately to the recruitment of more and better students.

Improved Academic Programs

Customer service also means creating new programs and improving existing programs so that students are helped academically. One institution attributed some of its growth to innovative programming:

> One new program is in the business school, a concentration in music business. It's a B.B.A.; it includes recording, publishing, marketing, and management in the industry. We use a great many adjuncts. We also have a corollary in the music school, a major in commercial music. We also added a master of science in nursing this year; we thought we'd have a class of 10 or 15; we have 48.

At another institution, a self-contained program exists separate from the rest of the campus. Students and faculty members live in the residence halls, and classes are conducted there as well. This arrangement results in a better retention rate, more studying by the students, and more involvement and discussion in their classes. Another new program that was initiated in response to customer requests:

> We started a program for fifth-year students, students with a B.A., who wanted to come back and get a teaching certificate. We received a lot of support for that.

At still another institution, a new program was started to keep track of first-year students:

> We are now tracking students from the time they enter until the beginning of the sophomore year. Some will be tracked longer than that. We will be tracking undeclared majors to determine if there's a greater propensity for undeclared majors to drop out. We want to track freshmen who are not coming to class or are having other problems. I want to get in touch with them. Also we set up a mentoring system with 50 faculty members. My dream is an advising center on the second floor of the university center. Very often students don't know where to go for advice.

In the institutions we studied, representatives of faculty, staff, and administration continuously review existing programs and services to improve them and to think of innovative solutions to current problems such as retaining students, improving learning, and recruiting students. The quality improvement mind-set encourages members of the institution to be concerned about student needs. The quality culture empowers them to try new ideas and to share those new ideas with their colleagues. The end product is an improved organization, not only for the students, but also for all the other members.

Overall, the institutions in our study experienced improved stakeholder satisfaction as an outcome of implementing continuous improvement. We found increased satisfaction among both students and faculty members because both learning and teaching improved. Improving teaching is a goal for many faculty members, and it is beginning to be rewarded in our institutions. Increasing the amount of learning that is taking place in courses has been more difficult, but teachers and students are working together in this area. We also found that services to students and faculty members improved markedly. Members who have the authority to do so listen to suggestions and act on them. As a result, many processes have been overhauled and process times have been reduced considerably. Finally, we discovered that academic programs also improved. New programs are being initiated, and programs that have been in place for quite some time are being redesigned. The result of these actions is increased pride in the institution, more and better academic choices for students, and increased enrollment and retention of students.

CULTURE BASED ON CONTINUOUS IMPROVEMENT

Quality principles and practices are a culture change for higher education. Under this new culture, institutions must measure the outcomes of their processes to determine if improvement has taken place. Assessing higher education practices and measuring the value added are only recent priorities for many institutions. Now educational institutions must be able to demonstrate their value to individuals and to society as a whole. To determine what society values, institutions must listen to stakeholders and make changes that are consistent with stakeholder expectations. How well institutions meet challenges depends upon how well they clarify their purpose and how well members work together to provide and improve programs and services that stakeholders find valuable. Organizations change when individuals change, so personal transformation to a mind-set of continuous improvement is a crucial part of this culture change.

Changing an existing culture is difficult because higher education institutions have a long history of traditions and tend to prefer the status quo. Organizations typically do not change unless there is a clear survival-based reason for change. At this time, many institutions of higher education have yet to perceive the crisis. As a result, many do not see the advantages of changing their behavior patterns. Changing the culture usually produces conflict because old cultures, habits, ideas, and practices rarely change without some irritation. These conflicts should be perceived positively because they indicate that the organization is changing, but they often are perceived quite differently. Members' resistance to change can be reduced if they understand how changes will increase the effectiveness of the organization and how the changes will lead to greater job security and more meaningful work.

It took years of quality leadership to build the trust that is necessary for quality principles and practices to take root in the institutions we studied. The change required an intensive commitment on the part of the leaders of the organization. A long-term plan formulated in understandable language can help participants understand the time-consuming nature of the undertaking. We found that as people became more familiar with continuous improvement and more comfortable with the quality ideas, the principles and practices became part of their institutions' cultures.

Eventually, the ideas of quality improvement become invisible or transparent to the members who begin to automatically apply the ideas without being aware they are doing something different from what they had done under the old culture. They begin to take quality principles and practices for granted. Several administrators and presidents we interviewed pointed out that their institutions are at this stage in their quality journeys:

> The quality improvement process is becoming transparent; we can't see it because people are using it.
>
> Quality is becoming a way of life.

When continuous improvement becomes a way of life for an institution, it is very difficult for the members to go back to the prequality ideas and traditions. It is at this time that continuous improvement becomes the new culture of the institution:

> We take for granted the progress, but we do things differently.
>
> We are forever significantly changed. At least the people that are here will never be able to do what they do without being affected by this.

Quality leaders expressed the concern that the improvements they are seeing are temporary, that they will last only as long as the current leaders are at the institutions to oversee the implementation. They realize that if the underlying culture of the institution is not truly altered, the new philosophy will not be a permanent change for the institution. For the philosophy to be firmly rooted in the institution, the culture change needs to involve all levels of the institution. Several of the administrators we interviewed understand that it is only after the culture has been changed that quality principles can withstand a change in leadership. As the provost at one of our institutions opined:

> There is a possibility of a top leadership change here. I'm near retirement, the president is very marketable. So the question is, would this emphasis survive our departure? And the answer is, it would not survive as an emphasis unless the next person emphasized it. It would not survive as a

methodology unless the next person learned it. But it would survive as a culture if it had become truly normed and truly responsive and truly instinctive as the way we do things.

We were told that when continuous improvement is first introduced in an institution, people often complain about additional work. In the most extreme case, members are upset because they do their work twice, once as they always had and then a second time using quality improvement methods. We found, however, that as people become more accustomed to the new ideas, less and less extra work is done, and continuous improvement becomes the way of life for the institution. When the quality initiatives are just getting off the ground, much attention is paid to small successes; this changes as institutions become more comfortable with the ideas, as was expressed by both administration and faculty:

> As you can see, we continue to evolve in our quality quest. The use of quality tools and philosophy is pervasive throughout the college. There is not as much hype and fanfare as there was in the early days; now it is simply the way we do business.

> We try to make it a force in people's hearts. We try to make it the way we do business.

> I bought into continuous improvement by example. People are living what they preach.

Quality improvement has changed the culture so that these institutions now have a culture of change; people within the institutions are no longer satisfied with the current state of affairs. They are interested in improving continuously. Individuals from the institutions we studied equate this culture of change with continuous improvement:

> Quality is making change happen.

> CQI reinforced community culture—what we are doing well. Our institution has a culture that embraces change.

The institutions realize that every product, every process, and every program can be improved. The new quality culture supports an environment of never-ending improvement. The following comments show how much the institutions' new cultures differ from the traditional higher educational culture:

> We almost have overkill in trying to improve things. I've never run into it anywhere else, and I have been at six different colleges.

> You always see what you can do better. When people get away from the institution (to go to conferences), they come back and realize that the culture here really is different.

> I'd like to think we've made progress, but we definitely have a long way to go.

In the continuous improvement mind-set, individuals within the institutions must be willing to think creatively, to make suggestions, and to take risks. Members cannot be afraid to make mistakes or to have others critique their ideas; they have to support other suggestions if their ideas are not chosen as the best. They also understand that improvement is a continuous process. Two administrators expressed these thoughts:

> There's more of a piloting mentality. Let's try this and work out the kinks. It's OK to take a risk.

> People are not defensive about suggestions. They acknowledge that there is room for improvement. There is a willingness to think about continuous improvement.

Traditional education institutions are out of step with this quality environment. In the traditional culture, leaders change only when they are convinced that no other choice is available. In contrast, the members we interviewed embrace change; they are not threatened by feedback; they welcome it. Their institutions have made it easy for people to complain. Given this attitude, it's not surprising that change happens more quickly in these institutions. The continuous collection of data and the continuous monitoring of stakeholder expectations ensure that changes will continue to occur at a rapid pace. An administrator likened the activity at his institution to the act of "rebuilding a ship while going full-steam ahead." Another administrator described the speed of change at his institution by saying, "We are moving quickly so that if you don't hang on, you will fall off." A faculty member summarized, "Quality is a moving target and you need to keep moving."

With the implementation of quality principles and practices, the institutions we studied developed an awareness of systems and processes that operated within the institutions:

> There is a greater awareness of processes; in the past everything we did was disjointed, now a structure is evolving.

> The value is in the process. Everything is relational.

The institutions that have a quality culture realize problems in any organization can usually be attributed to institutional processes and are not the fault of people within the institution. This mind-set allows individuals to discuss problems rationally without accusing one another of causing the problems. Several faculty members, staff, and administrators agreed on this:

> We do operate differently now. We look at problems in terms of processes rather than blame a person. There used to be a lot of finger pointing.

> I think one of the best contributions of quality improvement is that when something goes wrong it's probably a process problem, not a people

problem. You can solve so many problems if you just communicate with each other.

Because culture is the institutional environment that acts as a framework for how an institution operates, it is significant that people believed quality principles and practices positively changed the culture. Given the challenges of an external environment in which financial resources are tight and enrollments are competitive, being a member of an institution that has a culture in which people can grow and thrive is considered to be a strong intrinsic reward.

SUMMARY OF OUTCOMES

Our qualitative in-depth interviews confirmed that quality principles work, that they are reflected in different practices, and that they do make a difference. Even though it is often difficult to arrive at specific measurements or indicators of some outcomes, our interviewees said that people feel that processes and systems have been improved. For institutions that recently have begun their journey or are contemplating beginning the quality journey, the specific outcomes we discovered show that quality principles and practices make valuable contributions to institutions.

Specifically, we found that as a result of implementing quality principles and practices the leadership of the institution is more collegial, coordination among members has improved, decisions are made based upon data, communication systems are improved to allow two-way dialogue, team members work together to develop better solutions to problems, involvement of members leads to better decision making, satisfaction among various stakeholders has increased, and the culture of the institution has changed to one based on continuous improvement. To arrive at these outcomes, the institutions in our study *asked different questions* from those asked by most higher education institutions. In the process of attempting to answer these questions, they have changed their cultures and have been able to enjoy positive outcomes that differentiate them from other institutions in *these different times*. Continuing to *ask different questions* will allow them to take advantage of opportunities in the future.

Even though we have identified positive outcomes in this section, the institutions learned a great deal from their negative experiences as well. As learning organizations, they use this knowledge to improve their problem-solving skills throughout their institutions. In an attempt to help other organizations learn from the experiences of these institutions, the next section describes the major lessons, both positive and negative, that institutions learned from practicing quality principles. Consistent with the quality principle of benchmarking, the lessons learned can be used to shorten the journey of other institutions and to help them avoid obstacles, enhance their experiences, and remove barriers. The lessons learned by the institutions we studied continue to drive quality initiatives by reminding them of what needs to be improved.

CHAPTER 6

What Lessons Have Been Learned?

*Some of the ideas don't work, but even in developing ideas
that don't work, you learn.*

One theme that arose frequently in our interviews and that emerged
more clearly when we analyzed our data is that the institutions in this
study constantly are learning from their successes and mistakes.
They have put structures and processes into place which are designed to
promote learning, and they support the process of learning within their
organizations. Members are encouraged to think differently about their jobs,
about their institutions, and about interrelationships among members within
their institutions. They are continually urged to learn new ideas, to interact
with others, to state their opinions on issues that are important for the
improvement of the institution, and to pass their knowledge on to others
within and outside their institutions. Although institutions varied on the
degree to which these activities were pursued, we concluded that in most of
the institutions we studied systems were in place for continuous improvement
ideas to continue to grow.

Because continuous learning is so important in these institutions, this last
section outlines what has been learned as a result of this research. We
summarize what we learned about continuous improvement in higher education by assessing how well the institutions' practices reflect quality concepts
and then by describing the lessons we learned about the implementation of
continuous quality improvement from these institutions' experiences.

DO QUALITY PRACTICES REFLECT QUALITY PRINCIPLES?

The overriding questions that drove our study are whether the practices of institutions that are implementing the ideas of quality improvement reflect quality principles and whether quality principles are an effective approach for addressing challenges that face higher education institutions. In chapter 1 we restated quality principles in terms of the following nine questions:

- What is your aim?
- How do the parts fit together?
- Who leads the creation of a new culture?
- How do you update your knowledge?
- How do you make decisions?
- Who makes decisions?
- How do you improve?
- How do you prepare for the future?
- How are the changes supported?

Here we answer those questions based on our findings.

What Is Your Aim?

Are the aims or goals of an institution clearly stated in vision and mission statements that have been created by taking into account the expectations of stakeholders? All but one of our institutions have a mission statement that states the goals of the institutions. The institution that does not have a mission statement is in the process of creating one. Institutional mission statements usually are written by combining the efforts of many members of the institution so that the statements take into account the expectations of all internal stakeholders. In addition, some of the institutions include input from their boards, thereby adding information on the expectations of external stakeholders.

Few institutions have vision statements. Even in the institutions with vision statements, interviewees were not very familiar with these statements. We were told that the vision statements are not frequently consulted in the daily operation of the institutions and in the solving of problems that are addressed in the context of continuous improvement. (See appendix C for the institutions' mission statements.)

How Do the Parts Fit Together?

Does the institution exhibit systems thinking? Members we interviewed appear to have a good understanding of processes and systems. They realize that they are dependent on other members of their own institution and are willing to interact frequently with them. Because they understand that problems within their institutions are usually the fault of the system rather than the fault of individuals, members have a much higher opinion of their co-workers than before the implementation of continuous improvement.

Who Leads the Creation of a New Culture?

Is there strong leadership within the institution to guide the implementation of quality improvement? In most of the institutions studied, the president is a strong proponent of continuous improvement. With the help of top-level administrators, the president leads the continuous improvement effort. Leaders are trying to bring all groups together so that all goals are in alignment with the mission of the institution. Most leaders also recognize that they are role models for their constituents and try very hard to live up to their expectations.

How Do You Update Your Knowledge?

Are members being developed so that they are constantly learning how to improve the organization? Most of the institutions studied have systems in place for professionally developing their members. These systems allow the members to learn new skills, to help them make improvements, and to make it possible for them to learn from their mistakes. This principle is considered so important that members are allowed to attend professional development sessions on institutional time. As a result, the morale of the members is increasing because they understand that they are valued by the organization.

How Do You Make Decisions?

Are decisions based on data or on anecdote or intuition? All of the institutions in the study understand how important the gathering and the use of data are for making informed decisions. Although the process of data collection and analysis often takes additional time, interviewees believe that the resulting decisions are different and better than the decisions that would have been made without data.

Who Makes Decisions?

Are members of the institution allowed to take part in decision making? The institutions are struggling with this principle. Most leaders are able to delegate decision making to the members who are closest to the problems that need to be solved, but some administrators are unable to give up control to those who are beneath them in rank. In those institutions that involve members in making decisions, leaders recognize that better decisions are being made.

How Do You Improve?

Do members work together to solve system problems? All of the institutions in the study recognize that people collaborating solve problems better than individuals working by themselves. Area work teams, as well as cross-functional teams, produce better solutions to problems because they are able to use the knowledge of many versus the knowledge of one. Once a consensus is reached by a team, all the team members own that decision and can take pride in their combined efforts.

How Do You Prepare for the Future?

Are the changing expectations of stakeholders taken into account when plans are made for the future? The institutions we studied recognize that their stakeholders should be consulted when changes are to be made in processes and programs. They also realize that external stakeholders should have input on the mission and vision statements of the institution. Even though people within the institutions understand the importance of this principle, they are just beginning to make extended use of both internal and external stakeholder feedback to help improve the institution.

How Are the Changes Supported?

Are there systems in place to support the quality improvement initiatives? Of all of the principles, this is the one that leaders find to be the most difficult to implement. In some of the institutions, support and reward systems are in place to give positive reinforcement to teams that have improved processes, to those members who have improved at their jobs, and to those members who have gone out of their way to improve the institution. Because little money is allocated to this purpose in most institutions, these incentives often are not monetary awards but instead are token awards. Most institutions find that members value being recognized and that the monetary worth of the award is not important. The award and reward systems remain problematic, however, and are under review at most of the institutions in the study.

In conclusion, it appears that the practices of the institution we studied do reflect quality principles. Some institutions are further along their quality journeys and have developed systems that deal with many of the concepts; others are struggling with some principles and recognize that they need more time to feel comfortable with continuous improvement. Regardless, members of all of these institutions realize that they are working toward improving their institutions and that improvement is a continuous process. The institutions recognize that times have changed and that there will be new challenges for them to meet in the future. They have responded to these challenges by *asking different questions for different times*. Their answers indicate to us that they are practicing the concepts that are articulated in quality principles.

WHAT LESSONS DID WE LEARN?

Once an institution is serious about its quality improvement efforts, it continuously learns from its successes and from its mistakes. In our interviews we wanted to determine what institutions learned in the implementation process. While the replies varied from institution to institution and from person to person within the institutions, when we analyzed the data several themes emerged. These themes are presented as 12 important lessons we learned, lessons that should be kept in mind by any institution implementing quality principles or contemplating doing so. The following is a list of these lessons:

- Lesson 1: Systems Thinking Is Imperative
- Lesson 2: Institutional Culture Must Change
- Lesson 3: Quality Culture Leadership Is Critical
- Lesson 4: An Effective Communication System Is Necessary
- Lesson 5: Professional Development Is Essential
- Lesson 6: Build Partnerships with Stakeholders
- Lesson 7: Implementation Is Time-Consuming
- Lesson 8: Keep Quality Improvement Efforts Visible
- Lesson 9: Skeptics Are Valuable
- Lesson 10: Don't Leave Anyone Out
- Lesson 11: Language Affects Communication
- Lesson 12: Just Get Started

Lesson 1: Systems Thinking Is Imperative

Institutions further along on their quality journey demonstrate a more in-depth understanding of systems thinking. They are concerned about how the numerous parts of an institution are interrelated and why this is an essential component for successfully practicing quality concepts. Until members and groups within an institution understand that the decisions they make affect the entire organization, they are not very likely to take others' interests into account. Separate identities for departments or divisions do not allow the institution to be the best that it can be because they encourage independence rather than interdependence and functioning as a holistic system. Systems thinking requires a change in mind-set that allows people to deal with situations from a different perspective. The institutions that have the greatest understanding of this concept are rewarded with the greatest improvements.

Lesson 2: Institutional Culture Must Change

The implementation of continuous improvement is a change in the culture of an institution. Examples of this culture change include changing from a product focus to a market focus, from managers who direct employees to leaders who involve them, from a belief that knowledge is power to a belief that open and honest communication based on trust is the basis of a continuous improvement organization, and from individuals who only "talk the talk" to leaders who "walk the talk." If the culture does not change, the institution is not truly dedicated to continuous improvement. Adherence to continuous quality improvement ideas by members at all levels of the institution is especially important because of turnover in the top leadership positions. If the culture hasn't changed, it is very likely that all improvement efforts will fail when quality leaders leave.

To accomplish the culture change, leaders in institutions must impress members with the importance of the quality initiative. Consistently demonstrating continuous improvement behaviors is the key to convincing people of the sincerity of those who promote the change. When leaders practice what they espouse, others watch and follow their examples. Establishing recognition systems to cement the culture change, nurturing a prochange constituency within the faculty and staff, and cultivating a climate of trust are several ways to promote the culture change. Members must be urged to work diligently to make their organization better than it was before, to *ask different questions* to stimulate continuous improvement efforts, and to come up with answers to the questions being asked.

Lesson 3: Quality Culture Leadership Is Critical

The leadership on campus is critical to the success of the continuous improvement process. Leadership is needed throughout the implementation of continuous improvement; early on leaders drive the process, later they support the efforts of others. In an institution that was about to undergo a change in leadership, the quality improvement efforts were effectively put on hold. It was observed that unless continuous improvement ideas are solidly grounded in the culture of the organization and a high priority with the leaders, the future of quality improvement is uncertain.

Senior leadership must be involved for continuous quality improvement ideas to be taken seriously by the other members of the institution. Without this dedication, the implementation may stall or even fail. After senior leaders are educated about quality improvement concepts, they are able to work as a team and to demonstrate quality leadership through their daily behaviors. The most successful quality initiatives have senior leaders who prepare their organizations for change. As a result of following quality principles, they have a style of leadership that is more collegial and less autocratic. These individuals believe in continuous improvement and are willing to become examples for the entire institution. They have undergone a personal transformation that enables them to empower, to involve, and to recognize the efforts of members. Their role in creating and sustaining a culture of quality improvement is vital.

Lesson 4: An Effective Communication System Is Necessary

Direct and open communication among members of an institution educates individuals in quality principles and also is an effective way to minimize rumors. It is imperative that employees are kept informed on quality improvement plans; effective means for doing this include newsletters, campuswide quality meetings, formal and informal gatherings, and e-mail.

Communication needs to be carried out at all levels. No one must feel left out. Everyone should be involved in the implementation of quality improvement. The ideas of continuous improvement not only need to be explained and discussed, but the results of the implementation also have to be shared with all persons at the institution in ways that catch their attention.

Effective communication is based on two-way communication. One of the best ways to keep the lines of communication open is for the leaders to ask for honest feedback. Once employees are empowered, they are not afraid to give feedback. However, if too many decisions are made without feedback or if feedback is ignored, people within the organization begin to doubt the leaders' commitment to quality initiatives. An effective manner of collecting feedback is through surveys and focus groups conducted with various constituencies in order to improve processes and systems.

Lesson 5: Professional Development Is Essential

Three decisions need to be made about developing employees at an institution: who should be developed, when the development should take place, and who should lead the development effort. Quality improvement efforts are most successful when all members (administration, faculty, and staff) receive education in quality principles and practices. If any group within an institution is left out of the educational process, barriers are created or strengthened among groups, and hard feelings result. The participation of everyone is necessary for the success of continuous improvement on campus.

All institutional members need to receive overall education on the philosophy of continuous quality improvement. Additional education on tools and techniques is best provided in a just-in-time manner so that members can immediately apply what they learn to their jobs. Just-in-time education appears to be the most cost-effective approach as well. If all the education takes place at one time, too much time may elapse between the education and the use of the information with the result that people may need to be reeducated. Repeating sessions adds significantly to the time and money spent on quality improvement efforts. Wasting these scarce resources is unacceptable to members who repeat sessions, to their colleagues who cover additional jobs while the members are attending sessions, and to administrators who absorb the cost of additional professional development sessions.

Having consultants introduce quality principles and practices to top-level administrators at the institutions at the beginning of the implementation process can be very valuable, but after this initial stage, the responsibility for providing education should be shifted to members of the institution. Consultants provide interesting scenarios and consistent education because of their experience, but internal educators have better knowledge of the institution and its culture. Internal educators are also available to maintain momentum and to answer questions when they arise. If top-level administrators conduct some of the development sessions, these individuals convey how important they feel the quality improvement approach is for their institution. Another advantage to using internal educators to develop members is that faculty members tend to respond better to fellow faculty members as educators.

Lesson 6: Build Partnerships with Stakeholders

Partnering with a business, another institution, or the community strengthens an institution's continuous improvement efforts. It allows both the institution and the partner to learn from each other. Partnerships provide students and employees with opportunities to see how quality principles are implemented in other areas. Individual students or student teams can work in conjunction with these partners on improvement endeavors. Partnering also saves money because it allows institutions to pool their resources and to share costs and benefits with other organizations. Because business and industry help to drive institutions' continuous improvement efforts with their expectations of the graduates, they are willing to partner with higher education institutions.

Partnerships usually pair institutions with local businesses; however, other types of partnerships should also be considered. For example, partnering with elementary and high schools in an institution's area may improve the quality of the students entering the institution and may teach continuous improvement concepts to young students. Partnering with communities that are very active in continuous quality improvement can raise the visibility of continuous improvement on campus and can help encourage change at the institutions. Overall, partnering with an outside organization allows for the exchange of ideas at little or no cost.

Lesson 7: Implementation Is Time-Consuming

Implementation takes time at all levels of the institution. It may take leaders several months to a year or more just to educate themselves on quality principles. This time is usually spent reading books on continuous improvement; studying all the continuous improvement materials that can be found, many of which relate specifically to higher education; and visiting businesses and other higher education institutions that are implementing continuous improvement concepts. Once the decision is made to implement quality principles, the education of members is also time-consuming.

Initially, applying continuous quality improvement ideas in work areas takes a great deal of patience and effort. Some people may drag their heels because they are comfortable with the status quo and do not want to have to learn entirely new ways of operating. Others want to see results from quality improvement efforts immediately. At the outset, professional development is a time commitment for all and serving on teams means added work for institutional members. However, as people become more familiar with quality improvement concepts, less time is consumed in the application of the ideas. When decisions are based on data rather than arrived at arbitrarily, less time is spent on projects because less rework is necessary. Implementation cannot be rushed; the best results are associated with institutions that truly understand the commitment they have made and that take the time to ensure that all members are involved in the process.

Lesson 8: Keep Quality Improvement Efforts Visible

Institutions are using a variety of ways to keep their improvement efforts alive. The key is to keep the efforts visible to members at all levels. Leaders need to look for opportunities to convince others of the value of continuous improvement. It is imperative to work with people who are eager to be involved in the process and to choose projects that are easy and inexpensive early in the implementation process. To lessen problems associated with implementation, inexperienced members should not be assigned to teams that are trying to simplify large and complex processes, nor should they be assigned to too many teams at one time. It is also vital to present all teams with time and budget constraints at the time they are formed so that they do not return with suggestions that are far too expensive to be implemented.

In addition to selecting easy processes and giving teams all the needed information, it is important to talk about the successes, to give examples whenever and wherever possible. Three of the many ways institutions can communicate their successes are by writing about them for campus newsletters, talking about them at campuswide quality meetings, and presenting them at quality improvement fairs. All three of these methods keep continuous improvement efforts visible to participants.

Institutions that have members with a good understanding of continuous improvement have continuous improvement programs with high visibility. These same institutions have a large percentage of their members who support quality improvement concepts and who are involved and interested in improving their institutions.

Lesson 9: Skeptics Are Valuable

It is natural that there will be people who oppose change of any kind. Although skeptics are expected, they still may be difficult to handle especially during the beginning phases of implementation. It is important to involve these individuals in the process as soon as possible rather than to argue with them about the rationality of the approach of continuous quality improvement. Some of these same individuals become zealous converts once they see the principles in action and witness some successes. Whether they become involved or not, skeptics and cynics *ask difficult and different questions* about continuous improvement. Members of institutions with vocal skeptics have a better understanding of quality improvement because they have to answer the probing questions being asked. People in opposition force leaders to continually articulate quality principles and practices and the value of these principles to the institution.

Lesson 10: Don't Leave Anyone Out

All members of an institution must be educated in the philosophy of continuous quality improvement at the outset of the implementation efforts, although specialized education on using quality tools should wait until there is an opportunity to use the tools—just-in-time learning. A blanket invitation for all to participate may not be taken seriously by some individuals or groups on campus, and some members may not take part in the educational opportunities provided. We concluded that the most serious flaw in the continuous improvement implementation process at any higher education institution is to leave people out of the process, particularly the faculty. When faculty members are not involved in quality improvement efforts from the beginning, it is difficult to get them interested later. As a result, faculty members may oppose or resist changes and concepts that they do not understand.

Most faculty members are interested in learning new ideas. When they find new ideas stimulating, they generally help promote them. Because faculty members are constantly interested in gaining knowledge and developing professionally, they must be approached differently from some of the other constituencies on campus. To make new ideas more palatable, faculty members should be used to teach and educate other faculty members. Regardless of the methods used for professionally developing the faculty and other members of the institution, though, it is essential to include everyone in the process.

Lesson 11: Language Affects Communication

One of the biggest challenges higher education institutions face is resistance to the quality improvement language. This lesson may be unique to higher education because the profession revolves around imparting knowledge and information to others. For the transfer of information to take place, words are critical, and people in academia are educated to critique words, thoughts, ideas, and theories. Staff members are generally not upset by language that is commonly used in business, i.e., customer, total quality management, but faculty members often are. Interviewees stressed that they spent far too much time making decisions on language. Several of our institutions even concluded that they would have been better off to avoid the continuous improvement language altogether.

Institutions further along in their quality journeys have turned to emphasizing continuous improvement concepts without even using the word "quality." They are focused on *asking different questions* from questions asked in the past. These new questions focus on the aims of the institution, interrelationships among the parts of the organization, leadership, information updates, decision-making processes, improvements, and preparations for the future of the institution. By asking these types of questions, institutions can move beyond the language barriers and deal directly with what needs to be improved.

Lesson 12: Just Get Started

There are many reasons why institutions may drag their heels and not engage in the quality journey. Because of the allocation of time, money, and personnel, leaders may decide now is not the best time for implementation to begin at their institutions. The problem, however, is that the best time may never come. Implementation should begin as soon as a core group within the institution is engaged in the quality improvement initiative. Once the decision to begin implementation is made, additional difficult decisions need to be made. The implementation process is one of trial-and-error; mistakes are expected and are part of the learning process. The biggest mistake that can be made is not starting at all.

It is easy to let the challenges paralyze institutions. It is hard to know where and when to start. When trying to balance budgets, institutions typically try unsuccessfully to raise more money or, according to Levine (1992), "randomize mediocrity" by cutting people or deferring maintenance, all or which have negative long-term consequences. Continuous quality improvement is a systematic approach that improves the financial position in a rational way.

Although interviewees warned not to try to do too much too fast for fear that continuous improvement efforts will backfire, they also said to just get started! Institutions that embark on the quality journey are better able to meet the crises that they confront head-on and are able, as a result, to be better positioned to survive future problems.

CONTINUOUS IMPROVEMENT AS A WAY OF LIFE

As one administrator stated, "We eat change for breakfast. We love to make improvements." The institutions we studied, for the most part, have shifted their thinking. This in turn has changed their behaviors. They understand systems thinking, have developed new systems, and have improved existing systems using this new viewpoint. Institutions are consciously aware of the interconnections and interdependency of systems and people within the system. They recognize that people cannot be functional in dysfunctional systems. People understand that they need to agree on a common purpose for everyone to move in the same direction. Teamwork is the foundation upon which the other principles are built. New thinking and new behaviors are reflected in working together. People feel more involved and empowered, which contributes to their feeling that they have more ownership in the institution.

The institutions in our study have developed systems that encourage openness. We often heard interviewees talk about reflecting on their work, asking themselves what could be improved and what changes should be made. They indicated a strong desire to learn from their mistakes. They understood that "good enough" was no longer acceptable, that everything could be improved in some way, and that suggested changes were not threats. Because they have implemented systems to regularly collect feedback, they are incorporating the opinions of others into their decisions. They are using cross-functional teams to make sure that multiple voices are heard in the problem-solving and decision-making processes. This involvement encourages ongoing participation, which reinforces two-way communication. Across institutions, new systems and processes have been developed and implemented so that continuous learning takes place. This process of learning to learn is what differentiates a learning organization from most organizations.

The institutions we studied have institutionalized structures and processes that promote learning. In fact, at one institution, it is common to ask the following questions of one another after lunch, "How could that experience have been improved? What should we have done differently?" For the most part, continuous improvement is a way of life at these schools. People have a personal commitment to improve every day. According to one respondent: "We have people practicing continuous improvement, and they do not even know it." That is the goal. Don't just talk about it, do it!

APPENDIX A

TQM On Campus Questionnaire

1. Institution name: _____

   _____

2. Name, address, and telephone number (and/or e-mail) of person(s) filling out this questionnaire: _____

   _____

   _____

   _____

3. What year did your institution begin implementing TQM? Please give an example of this implementation. _____

   _____

4. Indicate the primary driving force(s) behind the implementation. Circle both if appropriate.

   1 external force(s) (Please specify)

   _____

   2 internal force(s) (Please specify)

   _____

   _____

   _____

5. Was there a change of leadership within six months before or after the time TQM was implemented?

   1 yes
   2 no

If yes, which position(s) experienced change? Circle as many as apply.
1 President
2 Provost–vice president for academic affairs
3 Academic dean
4 Other (Please specify)

6. What level initiated the leadership for TQM?
1 Central academic administration
2 Central business administration
3 Noncentral business administration
4 College or departments
5 Other (Please specify) _____
6 Other (Please specify) _____
_____

7. What is the **title** of the person responsible for overseeing the implementation of TQM? _____

What is the time commitment devoted to this responsibility?

1 full-time
2 part-time (Please check) _____ 25% _____ 50% _____ 75%
3 consultant

8. Are you following a specific implementation plan?

1 yes
2 no
If yes, was this plan:

1 internally developed
2 adapted from an outside source
3 a combination

9. How are you generally educating your campus? Circle as many as apply.

1 Newsletters
2 Special mailings
3 Brochures
4 Newspaper articles
5 Training sessions
6 Discussion groups
7 Pilot projects
8 Readings
9 Other (Please specify) _____
10 Other (Please specify) _____

10. Who is receiving the training? Circle as many as apply.

 1 Faculty
 2 Administration
 3 Support staff
 4 Other (Please specify) _____
 5 Other (Please specify) _____
 6 Other (Please specify) _____

11. Who is providing the training?

 1 Institutional staff
 2 Institutional faculty
 3 Consultants
 4 Combination of staff and consultants
 5 Other (Please specify) _____

12. Are you measuring the effectiveness of your training?

 1 yes
 2 no
 If yes, please explain how you are measuring the effectiveness of your training. _____
 _____

13. Does your institution have a formal statement on quality?

 1 yes
 2 no

 If yes, please include a copy of your quality statement.

14. What administrative and academic areas of your institution are using TQM? Circle as many as apply.

Administrative	Academic
1 Top-level administration	8 Business administration
2 Information technology	9 Engineering
3 Accounting	10 Arts and sciences
4 Registration	11 Other colleges (Please specify)
5 Physical plant	_____
6 Admissions	12 Departments (Please specify)
7 Other (Please specify)	_____
_____	13 Classroom instruction
_____	_____
_____	14 Other (Please specify) _____
	_____

15. What TQM tools are used most frequently? Rank the top three tools. (1 = first, 2 = second, 3 = third)

_____ Affinity diagram	_____ Operational definition
_____ Cause-and-effect diagram	_____ Pareto diagram
(Fishbones, Ishikawa diagram)	_____ Relations diagram
_____ Control charts	_____ Run chart
_____ Flow charts	_____ Scatter diagram
_____ Force field analysis	_____ Scenario builder
_____ Histogram	_____ Systematic diagram
_____ Nominal group process	_____ Other (Please specify)
	_____

16. Circle the number that best indicates the management style in the institution as a whole **before** TQM was implemented.

1   2   3   4   5   6   7

Autocratic   Collegial
Traditional Directive Leadership   Participative Management

17. Circle the number that best indicates the management style **at this stage** of TQM implementation.

1   2   3   4   5   6   7

Autocratic   Collegial
Traditional Directive Leadership   Participative Management

18. What are the key benefits of TQM to date? Circle as many as apply.

1 Decreased costs	8 Improved customer satisfaction
2 Increased morale	(Please circle which customers/
3 Improved communication	constituents)
4 Improved teaching	a Staff
5 More coordination among units	b Faculty
6 Less "re-work"	c Students
7 Changed culture	d Administration
	e Alumni
	f Community
	9 Other (Please specify)

_____

10 Other (Please specify)

_____

19. What are the major frustrations or problems you have experienced with TQM? Circle as many as apply.

    1 Impatience

    2 Time consuming

    3 Perception that it is a fad

    4 Not the right approach for higher education

    5 No extended commitment from the top

    6 Measuring "success" only in quantitative ways (time, money)

    7 Perception that no value is added

    8 Experienced political/turf problem

    9 Other (Please specify)

    _____

    10 Other (Please specify)

    _____

20. Identify two examples of how TQM is being utilized at your institution.

    _____
    _____
    _____
    _____
    _____

21. Explain specific measurable benefits identified through the use of TQM.

    _____
    _____
    _____
    _____
    _____

22. Would your institution be willing to cooperate with us in a more in-depth study of the implementation of TQM in higher education?

    1 yes
    2 no

    If yes, would your institution be willing to let us speak to persons who resist the implementation of TQM as well as to persons who are in favor of TQM?

    1 yes
    2 no

23. Do you have a business school or engineering school in which the principles of TQM are being **taught**?

    1 yes   Name of school(s) _____
    2 no _____

24. Do you have a business school or engineering school in which the principles of TQM are being **implemented (practiced)**?

   1 yes   Name of school(s) _____

   2 no _____

25. Please state the names and telephone numbers of other contact people at your institution who would provide more insights about the implementation of TQM on your campus. _____

   _____

   _____

   _____

   _____

26. Please send us any statements on quality, brochures, reports, implementation plans, organizational charts **before** and **after** implementing TQM, and other publications that your institution has produced that would help us to understand your experiences during your efforts to implement TQM.

   1 Yes, this information will be forwarded to you.

   2 No, it is not possible to send this information.

   3 Other (Please specify) _____

   _____

   _____

APPENDIX B

Results of TQM On Campus National Survey

Representatives of 168 institutions completed the entire questionnaire (appendix A), or a majority of it, and reported that their institutions were actively implementing quality improvement. These 168 institutions are a mixture of four-year public, four-year independent, and two-year community colleges or technical schools. (See table 2.)

TABLE 2		
WHAT INSTITUTIONAL TYPES RESPONDED TO THE QUESTIONNAIRE?		
Institutional Type	Number of Interviewees	Percent
4-Year Public	87	52
4-Year Independent	46	27
2-Year Community College and Technical Schools	35	21
Total	168	100

The data that were analyzed came solely from the 168 completed or mostly-completed questionnaires. Frequencies and percentages were calculated both for the 168 institutions and for the three institutional types mentioned above; however, information for the type of institution is reported only when there were substantial differences among the types. Because the interviewees could not be considered to be a random sample from the population of higher education institutions that have implemented the quality principles, no statistical tests were performed on the results.

The questionnaire had four main sections. First, background on the institution was requested, including when implementation began, what the driving forces were, who the initial leader was, who currently oversees implementation, and how much time was committed to that activity. The questions in the second section asked about education on quality improvement: who is educated, who provides the education, and what methods are used in the process. The third set of questions was designed to determine which administrative and academic areas were using continuous improvement and what tools were being used. The last section of questions asked about changes in management style due to the implementation of quality improvement and what benefits and frustrations had been noted. (See appendix A for a copy of the questionnaire.)

A large proportion of the responding institutions stated that they adopted quality principles in 1991 or later. (See table 3.) Higher percentages of four-year independent institutions (15 of 45 or 33 percent) and two-year community colleges and technical schools (11 of 35 or 31 percent) began implementation earlier than four-year public institutions (15 of 85 or 18 percent). Most of the institutions have efforts guided by an individual whose time commitment to quality efforts is 25 percent or less. (See table 4.) Although a relatively large percentage of institutions had full-time employees in charge of quality efforts, some institutions still relied entirely upon outside consultants and some had no one in charge.

TABLE 3

WHEN DID IMPLEMENTATION BEGIN?

Year Implementation Began	Frequency		Percent	
Before 1991	41		25	
4-Year Public		15		9
4-Year Independent		15		9
2-Year Colleges		11		7
1991 - Early 1994	124		75	
4-Year Public		70		42
4-Year Independent		30		18
2-Year Colleges		24		15
Total	165		100	

TABLE 4		
WHO IS IN CHARGE OF THE QUALITY EFFORTS?		
Person in Charge	*Frequency*	*Percent*
Employee — full time commitment	28	18
Employee — more than 25% time commitment	26	17
Employee — 25% or less time commitment	72	47
Consultant or consultant plus employee with part-time commitment	14	9
No one	14	9
Total	154	100

The support staffs and the administrators are being educated on continuous quality improvement in greater numbers than are faculty members. (See table 5.) Staff, faculty, consultants, and combinations of these three groups provide education in most of the institutions. (See table 6.)

TABLE 5		
WHO IS BEING EDUCATED ABOUT QUALITY?		
Groups Educated	*Frequency*	*Percent*
Support staff	149	89
Administration	143	85
Faculty	112	67

TABLE 6		
WHO IS PROVIDING THE DEVELOPMENT?		
Trainers	*Frequency*	*Percent*
Staff	36	22
Faculty	25	15
Consultant	12	7
Combinations	88	53
Others	5	3
Total	166	100

Top-level administration, registration, admissions, and physical plant are the administrative groups most likely to practice continuous improvement. (See table 7.) On the academic side, classroom instruction and business administration are the areas most frequently cited as implementing quality principles and practices. The top five tools used in quality processes, in order of importance to the interviewees, are flow charts, cause-and-effect diagrams, nominal group process, affinity diagrams, and Pareto diagrams.

TABLE 7		
WHAT AREAS ARE PRACTICING QUALITY IMPROVEMENT?		
Areas	Frequency	Percent
Administrative		
Top-level	76	45
Registration	75	45
Admissions	74	44
Physical plant	72	43
Accounting	61	36
Information technology	50	30
Academic		
Classroom instruction	64	38
Business Administration	62	37
Engineering	51	30
Departments	27	16
Arts and Sciences	20	12

Sixty-three percent of the institutions responded that the current management style is more collegial than before the implementation of quality principles, only 2 percent responded that the management style has become more autocratic. Improved communication and customer satisfaction are the two key benefits identified by the interviewees, and the two major frustrations identified are the perception that continuous improvement is a fad and the amount of time needed to implement quality principles. (See table 8.)

TABLE 8		
WHAT ARE THE BENEFITS AND FRUSTRATIONS?		
	Frequency	Percent
Benefits		
Improved communication	111	66
Improved customer satisfaction	104	62
More coordination	91	54
Increased morale	79	47
Less re-work	54	32
Changed culture	48	29
Decreased costs	40	24
Improved teaching	38	23

TABLE 8 (continued)

WHAT ARE THE BENEFITS AND FRUSTRATIONS?

	Frequency	Percent
Frustrations		
Perceived as fad	105	63
Time consuming	104	62
Impatience	79	47
Political/turf problems	78	46
Not enough commitment from top	64	38
Inappropriate for higher education	61	36
No value added	37	22
Too quantitative	21	12

APPENDIX C

Profiles of the 10 Institutions Studied

T he 10 institutions in this study were chosen deliberately so that a wide variety of schools that had implemented quality principles were included. All of the institutions had at least one person who was interested in continuous improvement and who convinced others that implementation of quality principles would improve the institution itself. Except for the University of Chicago Graduate School of Business, all of the institutions had been or are currently members of the AAHE Academic Quality Consortium. A short introductory section is provided on each school, and copies of their mission statements have been included to highlight each institution's quality improvement philosophy.

RICHLAND COLLEGE

Richland College, located in Dallas, Texas, opened in 1972 and is the largest of the seven community colleges in the Dallas County Community College District. It enrolls more than 13,500 college credit students and 10,000 noncredit continuing education students each semester. Continuous quality improvement began throughout the Dallas County Community College District in 1991. At that time the chancellor's cabinet (made up of the chancellor, the seven college presidents, one provost, and three vice chancellors) began to explore principles of continuous improvement. The vice chancellor for business services sent some of the business services personnel for training, after which the continuous improvement process was implemented in their areas. Since 1991 the district has provided the training in quality improvement.

The president of Richland, Steve Mittelstet, was interested in continuous improvement and encouraged the use of quality tools for the Southern Association of Colleges and Schools (SACS) reaccreditation process. He is involved in the Continuous Quality Improvement Network for Community Colleges, which meets several times per year and is made up of CEOs of community colleges that are implementing quality principles.

In 1993 Burt Peachy was hired to lead Richland in its quality improvement efforts. That year Richland College began serious training of all administrators, some professional support staff, and some faculty members. Since that time, numerous work groups and cross-functional CQI teams have improved processes both in the classroom and in support systems throughout the college including redesigning a multifaceted ESL program; streamlining registration, financial aid, and student referral systems; designing a fast-track associate's degree program; and redesigning a program to increase the number of A.A.S. degree graduates by 100 percent.

Mission Statement: The purpose of Richland College/DCCCD is to equip students for successful living and responsible citizenship in a rapidly changing local, national and world community. We do this by providing accessible, accredited, affordable, cost-effective quality educational opportunities for development of intellectual skills, job skills, personal growth, and/or transfer to a baccalaureate program. In fulfilling our purpose, we further cultural, economic, and workforce development in the communities we serve. In all our efforts, Richland strives to meet the needs and exceed the expectations of those the college serves.

RIO SALADO COMMUNITY COLLEGE

Rio Salado Community College, located in Phoenix, Arizona, is a member of the Maricopa Community College District. Rio Salado does not have a traditional campus, but instead it uses classroom sites throughout Maricopa County. It annually serves 28,000 credit students and 10,000 noncredit students. Linda Thor, the current president, came to the institution in 1990 and has championed quality implementation. In 1991, after six months on the job, she went to each of the constituent groups individually and asked them if they would be interested in pursuing quality improvement. There was a consensus that they would like to know more about it. A consultant was brought in to introduce the concepts to the groups. The initiative was collegewide from the beginning, and the first teams that were formed were cross-functional. A quality coordinator was appointed to oversee the day-to-day management of the initiative. In October 1993, Rio Salado was awarded the Arizona Governor's Award for Quality.

Mission Statement: Rio Salado Community College creates convenient, high-quality learning opportunities for diverse populations. We specialize in customized, unique programs and accelerated and distance delivery formats. In all that we do, we pursue continuous improvement and innovation, and we challenge the limits of tradition.

BELMONT UNIVERSITY

Belmont University, located in Nashville, Tennessee, is a comprehensive, independent institution affiliated with the Tennessee Baptist Convention that has more than 3,000 students. Interest in quality improvement began in 1988 with President William Troutt. A friend of his gave him a copy of *The Deming Management Method* by Mary Walton, and he realized that the management method described therein was a tangible expression of his core values. He then brought people within the university together to read and discuss the ideas in Walton's book.

In 1989, Susan Hillenmeyer was invited to research the implementation of quality improvement at Belmont. In 1990, she was hired as the vice president for quality and professional development and formed the Center for Quality and Professional Development. During this time, all deans and vice presidents attended a Deming four-day seminar, and discussions were held on how Deming's system could work at Belmont.

Since that time, the Center for Quality and Professional Development has become Belmont's internal training source. Training has been offered to all employees of the university—members of the faculty, staff, and administration. Many faculty members use the LEARN model (developed by Belmont administrator Kathryn Baugher) to help them improve classroom teaching. (See pp. 112–14 for a detailed description of the LEARN model.)

Mission Statement: Belmont University is a student-centered institution dedicated to providing students from diverse backgrounds an academically challenging education in a Christian community.

ST. JOHN FISHER COLLEGE

St. John Fisher College, located in Rochester, New York, is an independent liberal arts institution in the Catholic tradition with an enrollment of 2,700 full- and part-time students in its undergraduate and graduate programs. Quality improvement efforts began with President William Pickett in 1987. He was introduced to the idea by two members of the college's board of trustees who had been involved with similar processes at their places of employment.

Approximately two years after implementation began, the assistant to the president for quality leadership and five staff/faculty members who had exhibited leadership in quality formed the Quality Council. Originally, consultants were hired to train the senior staff. After senior staff training was completed, training was turned over to the Quality Council. After a series of attempts to lead the movement were not overwhelmingly successful, the Quality Council was dissolved. Responsibility for directing the college's quality initiatives now rests with the president and the senior staff of the college. Early successes within administrative departments and in cross-functional teams led the entire administrative side of the campus to realize the value of quality. Faculty were purposely excluded from the training until 1992, but have been involved since that time.

Mission Statement: St. John Fisher College is an independent, liberal arts institution in the Catholic tradition of American higher education. Guided since its inception by the educational philosophy of the Congregation of St. Basil, the College emphasizes liberal learning both for students in traditional academic disciplines and for those in more directly career-oriented fields. In keeping with the openness that is characteristic of its Basilian heritage, Fisher welcomes qualified students, faculty, and staff regardless of religious or cultural background.

In addition to its baccalaureate degrees, Fisher offers a Master of Business Administration, a Master of Science in Nursing, and a wide range of continuing education opportunities. Through these, the College serves part-time undergraduate, graduate, and professional/personal development students from the greater Rochester area. Our commitment to individuals from varied backgrounds and with differing educational needs reflects both our emphasis on life-long learning and our direct involvement in the community of which we are a part.

As an institution of higher learning, we engage our students in the quest for knowledge and truth, believing that such engagement will equip them to make sound judgments as individuals, family members, and citizens. We provide individual guidance to students as they strive for academic excellence and develop values that will guide them in meaningful and productive lives. Our dual emphasis on intellectual and personal growth derives from our belief that learning is valuable for its own sake, for the sake of those who learn, and for the sake of society as a whole.

SAMFORD UNIVERSITY

Samford University, located in Birmingham, Alabama, is an independent Southern Baptist-affiliated comprehensive university with approximately 3,100 full-time undergraduate students, 1,000 full-time graduate students, and 400 part-time professionals. President Thomas Corts became interested in the quality initiative because of his interest in marketing. John Harris, associate provost for Quality Assessment, was hired in 1989 to help the university implement an assessment plan, but he urged that the university go beyond assessment to implement continuous improvement. In November 1989, Samford's leadership made a commitment to quality management across the university. This commitment was followed in 1990 with the appointment of a lead quality team and with learning activities and readings. The implementation of quality principles began in September 1990.

Training was first conducted by a consultant, after which people within the university did the developing. Development began with deans or their associates and middle managers. It has been the practice to wait until people ask for training before it is provided to them. In 1994, a part-time person was hired for training of all kinds. A number of faculty use the LEARN model to improve classroom teaching. This model was developed by Kathryn Baugher while she was employed at Samford. In 1991 a Mission, Customers, Process, Values, Vision (MCPVV) document was written for the university as a whole. That same year, each of the 90 budget units within the university was asked to come up with its own MCPVV. All units are to communicate their MCPVVs to their customers and are to ask to be evaluated by these customers. Initially, instructional units were to concentrate on documenting student achievement, and noninstructional units were to concentrate on the improvement of a process that they chose. Quality efforts have made significant inroads in admissions, the schools of education and pharmacy, the library, and a variety of administrative and physical plant functions.

Mission Statement: The mission of Samford University is to nurture persons, offering learning experiences and relationships in a Christian community, so that each participant may develop personal empowerment, academic and career competency, social and civic responsibility, and ethical and spiritual strength, and continuously to improve the effectiveness of the community. (Motto: We nurture persons—for God, for learning, forever.)

WINONA STATE UNIVERSITY

Winona State University, located in Winona, Minnesota, is a mid-size comprehensive institution with an annual enrollment of approximately 6,200 full-time students. The quality initiative was brought to the institution primarily by President Darrell Krueger, who had been very involved in assessment at Northeast Missouri State University before he came to Winona. In the summer of 1989 he met with the higher administration, deans, and the faculty and presented quality ideas to them. Together they read and discussed books on quality. Aside from the president, the university was also influenced by the community of Winona and businesses there that had implemented quality initiatives, by IBM Rochester, and by the Steven Covey Leadership Center. The campus has no office of quality, but many people are involved with its implementation. When IBM Rochester won the Baldrige Award, the university used their training program. More recently, the training has been done by qualified individuals within the university, including the president, members of the faculty, and staff. All employees within the university have been invited for training, and many have responded. Several faculty members have been involved in the quality initiative from the beginning, and several courses on quality improvement are taught by the faculty. These courses are available to anyone on campus and in the community. In addition, the faculty have been providing Covey's 7 Habits training to individuals in low-income housing within the community.

Mission Statement: Winona State University (WSU) provides well prepared students with high-quality educational programs and student services in an all-inclusive learning community. Students should expect rigorous programs and instructional excellence in an environment that respects diversity and fosters intellectual maturity.

Winona State University baccalaureate graduates will have the foundations necessary for meeting the challenges of society and formulating a viable philosophy of life, through: mastery of basic skills, expertise in chosen disciplines, ability to think critically, understanding of cultural differences, positive regard for self and others, respect for different value systems, ability to work together collaboratively, appreciation of aesthetic values, and commitment to life-long learning.

WSU's graduate programs provide students the opportunity to build upon undergraduate foundations by achieving mastery in a chosen discipline.

The WSU Rochester Center specifically offers professional upper-division and graduate programs and is a center for professional growth.

UNIVERSITY OF MINNESOTA—DULUTH

The University of Minnesota—Duluth (UMD) is a comprehensive regional university. It is the second largest campus of the University of Minnesota with an enrollment of 7,600 full-time students and 2,500 continuing education students. A vice chancellor, Bruce Gildseth, heard about the quality ideas from a good friend and thought the quality initiative might work at UMD. In 1990 he hired consultants to present information on the quality principles to the senior administrative team, which included the chancellor, vice chancellors, and deans. The chancellor was interested, and the team decided to begin quality implementation in the Division of Academic Support and Student Life. A consultant was hired to train the staff within this division and to do follow-up training as needed. At the beginning, the faculty were not directly involved, but subsequently some faculty have been interested and have been trained. The deans wanted to be confident about what they were doing before they took the program to the faculty.

UMD became the University of Minnesota pilot for a quality initiative in the state. The other three institutions within the system became interested in continuous improvement, and the quality coordinators of the four institutions decided that each institution should pick two of the Baldrige Award criteria and try to do a self-assessment. UMD was paired with IBM Rochester in this exercise and looked at all seven of the criteria. UMD chose an internal team to do the assessment and in 1993 sent the self-assessment to the Minnesota Council on Quality for feedback. Based on the feedback, UMD picked out several areas to improve and then did another self-assessment. They now use this process as an annual assessment for the university.

Mission Statement: The University of Minnesota, Duluth (UMD), serves northern Minnesota, the state, and the nation as a medium-sized comprehensive university dedicated to excellence in all its programs and operations. As a university community in which knowledge is sought as well as taught, its faculty recognize the importance of scholarship and service, the intrinsic value of research, and the significance of primary commitment to quality instruction.

At UMD, a firm liberal arts foundation anchors a variety of traditional undergraduate degree programs, outreach offerings, and selected professional and graduate fields. Active learning through internships, honors programs, research, and community service promotes the development of skills, critical thinking, and maturity sought by society. Demanding standards of performance for students, faculty, and staff make UMD attractive to students with strong academic potential.

The campus contributes to meeting the cultural needs of the region and serves as a central resource for the economic development of the region through community outreach and through an emphasis on the sea-grant and land-grant components of its program.

UMD significantly contributes to enhancing the national stature of the University of Minnesota by emphasizing quality programs central to the mission of the University of Minnesota and the distinctive mission of UMD within the university system.

UNIVERSITY OF WISCONSIN—MADISON

The University of Wisconsin, located in Madison, Wisconsin, is a public research land-grant university that annually enrolls approximately 40,000 students, including more than 9,700 graduate students. A special assistant to the chancellor had been a mayoral aide for the city of Madison and had been instrumental in Madison's efforts to implement quality. He began building interest in the quality initiative throughout campus. In 1989 the Office of Quality Improvement was created. This office reported to the special assistant and was to be a catalyst for and a resource to the university as it began to integrate quality concepts. The provost assumed a leadership role in the quality effort in 1990 and used an informal team of campus leaders to guide the effort. The provost is now the chancellor but continues to lead campus planning and improvement efforts by supporting the Office of Quality Improvement. Pilot implementation areas were the graduate school and student academic services (admissions, registrar, financial services), followed by housing, office of the dean of students, purchasing, and facilities planning and management. Several academic departments, including history, zoology, chemistry, pathology, English, engineering, and business, have volunteered to use quality approaches to address some of their issues; they were selected based on criteria including management's (department chairs') willingness to take an active role in learning about quality improvement and in leading the effort to implement it. Maury Cotter is the current director of quality. She and her staff provide consulting and training to departments and individuals on an as-needed basis, or just-in-time.

Mission Statement: To create, integrate, transfer, and apply knowledge. (This statement is widely used across the campus as a condensed, working version of its mission.)

UNIVERSITY OF MICHIGAN—ANN ARBOR

The University of Michigan, located in Ann Arbor, Michigan, is a public research university. The Ann Arbor campus is the largest of the University of Michigan system, with over 36,000 students, including approximately 22,000 undergraduate students and 14,000 graduate students. In response to accreditation demands, the university hospital started looking into the continuous quality improvement around 1987, but at that time there was not widespread interest on other parts of the campus. In 1990, the information technology division became interested, followed soon by the business school and the college of engineering.

In 1989, the president of the university created a task force to study the costs of education at Michigan. One of the task force's key recommendations in their 1990 report was that a new perspective was needed that would simultaneously focus on quality improvement and cost containment. The task force stated, "Quality must be transformed from meaning more and better of everything to searching relentlessly for means of improvement that reduce costs, are cost neutral or low cost, while maintaining or enhancing quality."

As one response to the task force report, the university formed a quality council in 1991 consisting of executive officers, some deans, and others. The quality council developed drafts of the university mission and vision statements. This step was important because the council had to ensure that the quality approach would be consistent with the university's mission and would be a vehicle to help move toward the university's vision. The quality council also established a design team that spent the 1991-92 academic year developing a specific implementation plan that was approved by the quality council in 1992. This plan focused the university's quality efforts on business and administrative processes.

An outside contractor provided training in 1992 and 1993, but since then the training has been done internally. Thus far, most of the training has centered on staff, although a small number of faculty have also received training.

Mission Statement: The mission of the University of Michigan is to serve the people of Michigan and the world through preeminence in creating, communicating, preserving, and applying knowledge, art, and academic values, and in developing leaders and citizens who will challenge the present and enrich the future.

UNIVERSITY OF CHICAGO GRADUATE SCHOOL OF BUSINESS

The University of Chicago Graduate School of Business currently operates both M.B.A. and Ph.D. programs for approximately 2,500 full-time equivalent students. Quality management at the school began in the 1980s. Several faculty members in statistics and operations management began bringing quality management concepts into their classes. Within a year or two, more faculty had begun to focus on quality, and several quality-specific courses were developed. In the late 1980s, a quality management M.B.A. major was approved as part of the curriculum.

The administration recognized the power of quality management tools and decided that the school should begin practicing what it was teaching. By 1989, the school had established a formal suggestion system and had organized a student committee to focus on quality issues of concern to students. In mid-1990, the school appointed an administrator to investigate the use of quality management within higher education and to develop a plan to implement quality within the school. In late-1990, the school appointed a Quality Executive Council to oversee quality improvement efforts and began to offer quality training programs to all the staff. Several teaching improvement programs were also offered to faculty.

During the early 1990s, a wide variety of improvement projects were undertaken throughout the school, and nearly all staff were trained in quality tools and ideas. Student suggestion programs and regular customer surveys were instituted to understand needs and expectations. The school also embarked on an effort to bring quality concepts to the university as a whole. Several administrators and faculty of the school presented quality management "overviews" to key university administrators, and the school developed a new quality training program that they offered to staff throughout the university.

As a result of new priorities and shifting responsibilities confronted by a new administration in 1993, time and attention paid to formal quality programs has been reduced. Many of the lessons and tools are still used, but formal training programs and centralized administration of improvement projects have been put on hold.

There is some indication that there is a growing interest in refocusing on quality improvement issues. The school's administration has recently developed a new plan for improving customer service, which will include a new training program and focused efforts on process improvement. The university is in the second year of a major cost-reduction and reengineering effort. Many of the engaged departments are applying quality ideas and tools, which they learned in the school's staff training program.

Mission Statement: The school does not have a formal mission statement, but operates on a philosophy that "holds that it is wasteful and inefficient for a university to try to provide a pale substitute for business experience. What the university can do well is develop the student's critical, analytical, problem-solving, and decision-making capabilities. . . ." It is currently involved in a planning effort that will help define the school's core values and goals for the future.

APPENDIX D

Site Visit Questions

SITE VISIT QUESTIONS FOR INTERVIEWS WITH INDIVIDUALS

A. Overview of Quality Efforts

1. Where did the interest in quality improvement begin on your campus?
2. Why did your institution embrace quality improvement? (external and internal forces)
3. When did your institution begin implementing quality improvement?
4. Who was involved in that implementation?
5. What are your overall impressions of your quality efforts?

B. Philosophy

6. How did senior leaders first begin formally learning about and being trained for quality?
7. What are the core quality principles to which your institution now most subscribes?
8. Is your quality philosophy based primarily on any of (or a combination of) the so-called quality gurus, Deming, Juran, and/or Crosby? Aside from those three, what other persons or organizations have helped to shape your quality philosophy?
9. At what level is the institution committed to the principles of quality, i.e., campuswide?
10. What evidence supports that commitment? Provide examples.
11. Does the campus have a formal statement on quality? If so, what is it?

C. Mission

12. What is your mission statement? When was it written?
13. To what extent do faculty and staff know about the mission statement? To what extent do they agree with it? To what extent were they involved in developing it?
14. Has the mission changed since embracing quality improvement? If so, how has it changed, and what process was used to develop the new mission statement?
15. How closely linked is the mission statement to your quality efforts?

D. Leadership and Management

16. Was there a change of leadership within one year before or after the time quality was implemented? If so, when?
17. Which positions experienced change? President? Provost? Academic dean? Other?
18. Was the change in leadership related to quality implementation?
19. On a Likert scale from 1 to 7 (1 = autocratic, 7 = collegial), how would you rate the management style in the institution as a whole before quality was implemented? After quality was implemented?
20. To what extent are the top leaders committed to the quality efforts? Are they committed enough?
21. To what extent has the top leadership commitment and activity been important to implementation? If high, what difference would it have made to the overall success if the commitment had not been there? If low, what difference would it have made to the overall success if the commitment had been there?
22. Has the institution implemented other campuswide management practices before? If so, how has this been different?
23. How has the culture of the institution changed? How has this been done? If not, give some examples that indicate that a supportive climate has not been created.
24. Are top managers more effective leaders since the adoption of quality improvement? If so, how have they improved? If not, why do you think they have not improved?
25. Have employees been given the authority to make quality a priority (empowerment)? How are employees participating in the quality efforts?
26. What incentives have been used to encourage the adoption of quality? Do you think they have worked?

E. Implementation

27. How did implementation start on your campus? How were the initial projects and teams chosen? By whom?

28. What person(s) or group(s) is(are) in charge of implementation? How are those responsibilities divided?

F. Training, Teams, and Tools

29. How did your quality training begin? Was it focused on projects and teams or on more general audiences?

30. What person(s) and/or group(s) began quality training for the campus? Are those person(s) and/or group(s) still conducting the training?

31. What kind of training do teams receive? Tools? Philosophy? Team skills? Other? Has the training changed over time?

32. Who has primary responsibility for each team and/or project? Do teams have sponsors? Team leaders? Process facilitators? Has this framework changed as your quality efforts have matured?

33. How has the approach to training changed over time, if at all?

34. How has the approach for selecting projects and teams changed over time, if at all?

35. Which quality tools have been the most useful?

SPC	Cornesky	Memory Jogger Plus +
Cause and effect diagram	Affinity diagram	Affinity diagram
Control chart	Force field analysis	Interrelationship digraph
Flow chart	Nominal group process	Tree diagram
Histogram	Operational definition	Prioritization matrices
Pareto chart	Relations diagram	Matrix diagram
Run chart	Scenario builder	Process decision chart
Scatter diagram	Systematic diagram	Activity network diagram
Others?		

36. How would you evaluate the effectiveness of the training? Why?

37. Did the institution identify other institutions to study or use as examples to follow? If so, which institutions or organizations were used? For what purpose?

38. Often people get "hung up" on the language of quality. What language are you using? How did you overcome the obstacle of terminology?

39. What are you calling your program? What kind of discussion took place concerning what to call it?

G. Successes, Obstacles, Results

40. What were the initial obstacles to implementation? Are there obstacles now? If so, what are they?

41. What have been your major successes thus far?

42. How do you measure the success of a quality effort? Do you do cost/benefit analyses of projects? How?

43. In hindsight, what would you have done differently with regard to implementation?

H. CQI and Teaching (also to be used with the faculty focus group)

44. To what extent are the quality principles used to improve teaching and learning?

45. What formal mechanisms exist to encourage the use of quality improvement in the classroom?

46. What evidence has been collected to support that the principles in the classroom are effective?

47. What are some examples of the use of quality improvement in the classroom?

48. Are courses being taught on the quality principles? If yes, where?

49. To what extent have administrators on the academic side "bought in" to the quality principles?

50. What strategies have been used to engage faculty in a "conversation" about quality improvement and its relevance to their work?

51. In what areas on the academic side, aside from the classroom, have the quality principles and tools been used or attempted? How successfully?

52. What prospects do you see for quality principles having a major impact on the academic side?

I. Future Steps

53. What are the plans for the future in terms of quality implementation?

54. Is there anything else I should have asked about the adoption of quality improvement on your campus?

SITE VISIT QUESTIONS FOR FOCUS GROUP INTERVIEWS

1. What seems to be working with your quality efforts on campus? Why?

2. Where has CQI made the greatest impact on the organization? Why is that?

3. From where is the most resistance coming? Why do you think this?

4. What were your hopes when you began implementing CQI?

5. What is the difference between your hopes and the reality of the situation?

6. If I called 20 people on your campus, what would they say about the quality efforts on campus? Why would they say this?
7. What could be done to improve the quality movement on campus?
8. Why is the institution involved in total quality?

QUESTIONS FOR FOLLOW-UP INTERVIEWS

1. What changes have taken place in the quality movement on your campus since our site visit with respect to the following?
Leadership
Training, Teams, and Tools
Culture
Successes, Obstacles, Results
2. Where has continuous improvement made the greatest impact and why?
3. From where is the most resistance coming and why?
4. Is there anything else I should know about your quality efforts?

APPENDIX E

Data Analysis Procedure

One of the investigators unitized the data, that is, identified the smallest pieces of information that could be understood in the context of the study. The interview transcriptions were divided into these units of information and mounted onto 5" x 8" cards. Each card was coded by institution and by the general grouping of the interviewee (president, administration, faculty, and staff). Approximately 2,500 cards represented the data units for this study.

The cards were categorized through a process that allowed patterns in the data to emerge. The process began with the selection of one card that was a product of the unitizing process. The information on the card was studied and the card was placed in the first pile of a category to be named later. The second card was then studied and a decision was made as to whether its contents were similar to the first card's contents; if similar, the second card was placed in the same category with the first card; if different, the second card was placed in a new category. Every successive card was treated similarly; if a card fit into no existing category, it was placed in a miscellaneous category.

A large number of categories had emerged after studying several hundred of these cards; at that time, each group of cards was labeled with a short phrase that captured the overall topic that appeared on those cards. After all the cards had been studied, the cards in the miscellaneous category were studied again to determine whether any of these cards fit into the categories that had emerged. Most of the miscellaneous cards were placed into existing categories at this time, although a few remained that could not be classified.

The first pass on this categorization process was done by the investigator who had not participated in the unitization of the information. The cards were then passed to the other investigator who then checked the categorization, reclassified cards that may have been misclassified, made up new categories, and then divided the major categories into subcategories. Each investigator made one more pass through the cards to check if there were any obvious discrepancies in the classifications and to determine if there were any patterns that had been missed. At the end of this process, there were approximately 25 major categories identified, many of which had several subcategories. At this point, the categories were viewed as being relatively independent of one another. To bring order to these results, we searched for interrelationships among the categories. The result was the model that is presented in figure 1.

REFERENCE LIST

Ackoff, Russell L. 1993. *Ackoff's Fables*. New York: John Wiley and Sons.

————. 1995. "The Challenges of Change and the Need for Systems Thinking." AAHE Conference on Assessment and Quality, June 11-14. Boston, MA.

American Association for Higher Education. 1994. *25 Snapshots of a Movement: Profiles of Campuses Implementing CQI*. Washington, DC: American Association for Higher Education.

Angelo, Thomas A. and Cross, K. Patricia. 1993. *Classroom Assessment Techniques: A Handbook for College Teachers*. San Francisco: Jossey-Bass.

Baker, Wayne E. 1994. "The Paradox of Empowerment." *Chief Executive*, April, 62-65.

Barker, Joel Arthur. 1992. *Paradigms: The Business of Discovering the Future*. New York: Harper Business.

Baugher, Kathryn H. 1992. *LEARN: The Student Quality Team Process for Improving Teaching and Learning*. Birmingham, AL: Sanford University.

Bennett, Joan K. and O'Brien, Michael J. 1994. "The Building Blocks of the Learning Organization." *Training*, June, 41-49.

Brassard, Michael. 1989. *The Memory Jogger Plus+: Featuring the Seven Management and Planning Tools*. Methuen, MA: GOAL/QPC.

Chaffee, Ellen Earle and Sherr, Lawrence A. 1992. *Quality Transforming Postsecondary Education*. ASHE-ERIC Higher Education No. 3. Washington, DC: Association for the Study of Higher Education.

Chickering, Arthur W. and Gamson, Zelda F. 1987. "Seven Principles for Good Practice in Undergraduate Education." *The Wingspread Journal*: 1-4.

Coate, L. Edwin. 1991. "Implementing Total Quality Management in a University Setting." In L. A. Sherr and D. J. Teeter (eds.) *Total Quality Management in Higher Education*. New Directions for Institutional Research no. 71, 27-38. San Francisco: Jossey-Bass.

Cornesky, Robert, et al. 1991. *Implementing Total Quality Management in Higher Education*. Madison, WI: Magna Publications, Inc.

Covey, Stephen R. 1989. *The 7 Habits of Highly Effective People*. New York: Simon and Schuster.

Crosby, Philip B. 1979. *Quality is Free*. New York: McGraw-Hill.

———. 1992. *Completeness: Quality for the 21st Century*. New York: Penguin Books.

DeCosmo, Richard D., Parker, Jerome S., and Heverly, Mary Ann. 1991. "Total Quality Management Goes to Community College." In L. A. Sherr and D. J. Teeter (eds.) *Total Quality Management in Higher Education*. New Directions for Institutional Research no. 71, 13-25. San Francisco: Jossey-Bass.

Deming, W. Edwards. 1986. *Out of the Crisis*. Cambridge, MA: MIT Center for Advanced Engineering Study.

Dertouzos, Michael L., Lester, Richard K., and Solow, Robert M. 1989. *Made in America*. Cambridge, MA.: MIT Press.

Doyle, Michael and Straus, David. 1976. *How To Make Meetings Work*. New York: Jove Books.

Dumaine, Brian. 1994. "Mr. Learning Organization." *Fortune*, October 17, 147-57.

Evans, John P. November 1992. *A Report of the Total Quality Leadership Steering Committee and Working Councils*. The Procter & Gamble Company. Cincinnati, Ohio: The John K. Howe Company.

Ewell, Peter T. 1993. "Total Quality and Academic Practice: The Idea We've Been Waiting For?" *Change* 25(3), 49-55.

———. 1996. "Indicators of Good Practice: An Assessment 'Middle Ground.' " The 11th AAHE Conference on Assessment and Quality, June 9-12. Washington, DC.

Fairweather, James. 1993. *Teaching, Research, and Faculty Rewards: A Summary of the Research Findings of the Faculty Profile Project*. University Park, PA: National Center on Postsecondary Teaching, Learning, and Assessment.

Freed, Jann E. 1996. "Employee Involvement and TQM: Clarifying the Mixed Messages." *Organization Development Journal*, 14(2), 19-29.

Freed, Jann E. and Klugman, Marie. 1996. "Lessons Learned from Campus Visits: The Quality Principles and Practices in Higher Education." Poster session at the AAHE Conference on Assessment and Quality, Washington, DC.

Freed, Jann E., Klugman, Marie, and Fife, Jonathan D. 1994. "Total Quality Management on Campus: Implementation, Experiences, and Observations." Paper presented at the Annual Meeting of the Association for the Study of Higher Education. 24 pgs. ED375734 MF-01; PC-01.

Freed, Jann E., Klugman, Marie, and Fife, Jonathan D. 1997. *A Culture for Academic Excellence: Implementing the Quality Principles in Higher Education*. ASHE-ERIC Higher Education Report No. 1. Washington, DC: Association for the Study of Higher Education.

Glaser, B. G. and Strauss, A. L. 1967. *The Discovery of Grounded Theory: Strategies for Qualitative Research*. Chicago: Aldine.

GOAL/QPC. 1988. *The Memory Jogger: A Pocket Guide of Tools for Continuous Improvement*. Methuen, MA: GOAL/QPC.

Juran, Joseph M. 1988. *Juran on Planning for Quality*. New York: The Free Press.

———. 1989. *Juran on Leadership for Quality*. New York: The Free Press.

————. 1995. *A History of Managing for Quality*. Milwaukee: ASQC Quality Press.

Kerr, Steven. 1995. "On the Folly of Reward A, While Hoping for B." *Academy of Management Executive*, 9(1), 7-14.

Kofman, Fred and Senge, Peter M. 1993. "Communities of Commitment: The Heart of Learning Organizations." *American Management Association*, 5-23.

Kuh, George D. and Whitt, Elizabeth J. 1988. *The Invisible Tapestry: Culture in America's Colleges and Universities*. ASHE-ERIC Higher Education Report No. 1. Washington, DC: Association for the Study of Higher Education.

Levine, Arthur. 1992. "Why Colleges Are Continuing to Lose the Public Trust." *Change*, July/August, 4.

Lincoln, Y. S. and Guba, E. G. 1985. *Naturalistic Inquiry*. Beverly Hills, CA: Sage.

Marchese, T. 1991. "TQM Reaches the Academy." *AAHE Bulletin*, 3-9.

Morgan, Gareth. 1986. *Images of Organization*. Newbury Park, CA: Sage.

Morganthau, Tom and Nayyar, Seema. 1996. "Those Scary College Costs." *Newsweek*, April, 52-68.

Neave, Henry R. 1990. *The Deming Dimension*. Knoxville: SPC Press.

Nevis, Edwin C., DiBella, Anthony J., and Gould, Janet M. 1996. "Understanding Organizations as Learning Systems." [Online] Available: http://learning.mit.edu/res/wp/learning_sys.html. [June 1, 1997].

Robbins, Anthony. 1991. *Awaken the Giant Within*. New York: Simon and Schuster.

Ryan, Kathleen D. and Oestreich, Daniel K. 1991. *Driving Fear Out of the Workplace*. San Francisco: Jossey-Bass.

Schmidt, Warren H. and Finnigan, Jerome P. 1992. *The Race without a Finish Line*. San Francisco: Jossey-Bass.

Senge, Peter M. 1990. *The Fifth Discipline: The Art and Practice of the Learning Organization*. New York: Doubleday/Currency.

————. 1996. "Leading Learning Organizations: The Bold, the Powerful, and the Invisible." In F. Hesselbein, M. Goldsmith, and R. Beckhard (eds.), *The Leader of the Future: New Visions, Strategies, and Practices for the Next Era*, 41-57. San Francisco: Jossey-Bass.

Seymour, Daniel T. November 1991. "TQM on Campus: What the Pioneers Are Finding." AAHE Bulletin. Washington DC: American Association for Higher Education. HE 025063 4pp MF-01; PC-01.

————. 1992. *On Q: Causing Quality in Higher Education*. Phoenix, AZ: American Council on Education and The Oryx Press.

————. 1993. "TQM: Focus on Performance, Not Resources." *Educational Record* 74(2): 6-14.

————. 1995. *Once Upon A Campus*. Phoenix, AZ: American Council on Education and The Oryx Press.

Seymour, Daniel T. and Collett, Casey. 1991. *Total Quality Management in Higher Education: A Critical Assessment*. Methuen, MA: GOAL/QPC.

Sherr, Lawrence A. and Teeter, Deborah J. 1991. *Total Quality Management in Higher Education*. New Directions for Higher Education No. 71. San Francisco: Jossey-Bass.

Siebert, Mark. 1996. "Obtaining a Degree Is Getting Harder." *The Des Moines Register*, page 4M, July 11, 1996.

U.S. Department of Education, National Center for Education Statistics. 1995. *The Condition of Education*. Washington, DC.

Walton, Mary. 1986. *The Deming Management Method*. New York: Perigee Books.

Wheatley, Margaret and Kellner-Rogers, Myron. 1996. *A Simpler Way*. San Francisco: Berrett- Koehler.

Wingspread Group on Higher Education. 1993. *An American Imperative: Higher Expectations for Higher Education*. Racine, WI: Johnson Foundation.

Winter, Roberts. 1991. "Overcoming Barriers to Total Quality Management in Colleges and Universities." In L. A. Sherr and D. J. Teeter (eds.) *Total Quality Management in Higher Education*. New Directions for Institutional Research no. 71 53-62. San Francisco: Jossey-Bass.

Wishart, Nicole A., Elam, Joyce J., and Robey, Daniel. 1996. "Redrawing the Portrait of a Learning Organization: Inside, Knight-Ridder, Inc." *Academy of Management Executive* 10(1), 7-20.

INDEX

by James Minkin